ADVANCE PRAISE FOR
GRIT TO GLORY

"A raw and highly worthy book, *Grit to Glory* takes you straight to the front lines in Northeast Baghdad in a complicated era when death surrounded Special Forces troops day and night. Green Beret Darrell Utt is a quiet sledgehammer of a military leader. His story is filled with humanity, action, intensity, and grit. I found myself humbled and awed, filled with gratitude, while reading about his overseas accounts."

—Marcus Brotherton, *New York Times* bestselling author of *We Who Are Alive and Remain* and *The Long March Home*

"A humbling look at what grit really means, *Grit to Glory* is the fascinating journey of a boy from small-town West Virginia to the streets of Baghdad as an elite US Army Green Beret. It's a wild ride of extraordinary stories filled with invaluable lessons for any reader. I am grateful to call Darrell a friend, proud to call him a fellow American, and honored to call him a brother in arms."

—Kyle Carpenter, US Marine, author of *You Are Worth It: Building a Life Worth Fighting For*, speaker, Medal of Honor recipient

"Darrell Utt's and ODA 043's journey through the height of the Iraq conflict adds a powerful chapter to the annals of war history, and his Grit Code a valuable tool applicable to any life or profession."

—Dan Schilling, *New York Times* bestselling author and thirty-year Special Operations Forces veteran

"*Grit to Glory* is an incredible firsthand account of reality. Darrell has always been, and remains, the real deal, there on the ground leading when it mattered. In his first book, he captures the reality, rawness, and exceptional impact of life on a Special Forces A Team in combat. Insightful and gripping, his accurate perspective is what you'd have seen on the X if you were there jocked up and locked and loaded with him and his amazing men. His service and his story contribute to what makes our nation so great."

—Lieutenant General Fran Beaudette (Ret.), US Army

"Darrell Utt has run the miles as a Green Beret and has now converted those miles and lived experiences into this beautiful book you are holding in your hands. His love of country and our warrior community shows up in every page!"

—Scott Mann, *New York Times* bestselling author of *Operation Pineapple Express*

"A powerful and page-turning look at Green Berets at war. One of the finest Special Forces soldiers I served with, MSG Darrell Utt (Ret.) provides an insider's view of a Special Forces team navigating the complexities of urban combat in the most dangerous place in Iraq—Camp Apache in Baghdad—as the war transformed from a 'straightforward' counterinsurgency into a sectarian civil war. More than just a war story, *Grit to Glory* provides the blueprint for what makes Green Berets so successful—lessons that hold true for anyone in any endeavor."

—Lieutenant General Ken Tovo (Ret.), US Army

"Darrell Utt unflinchingly takes the reader by the hand (and, at times, by the throat) into the complex and brutal arena of frontline combat as only a legendary Green Beret can. His remarkable (and even humorous) journey from humble beginnings to the elite levels of Special Forces operators is a masterclass in grit, humility, commitment, sacrifice, and exceptional leadership. The lessons in this book—literally tested by fire and proven by heroic valor—represent a powerful guide we can all follow in our battles of life to become our best selves."

—Dr. Kevin Basik, PhD, USAF Lt. Col. (Ret.),
president of Basik Insight, LLC

"Darrell Utt's *Grit to Glory* showcases the transformative power of adversity, illustrating how Special Forces warriors are molded by life's toughest challenges long before they set foot on the battlefield. Readers looking for a boost of confidence and a measure of hope will find inspiration and empowerment in Utt's compelling story and steadfast leadership code."

—Eric Blehm, *New York Times* bestselling
author of *Fearless, Legend,* and *The Darkest White*

"*Grit to Glory* is an inspiring journey through the crucible of adversity and triumph, a testament to the resilience of the human spirit. This book is a compelling reminder that with unwavering determination, anyone can overcome the toughest of obstacles to achieve greatness."

—Chris Cassidy, former NASA astronaut, former Navy SEAL, president and CEO of the National Medal of Honor Museum Foundation

"*Grit to Glory* is far more than a real account of life as a Green Beret in combat. It's a description of the human and personal elements of being a brother in arms, father, leader, role model, mentor, and confidant as well as what it takes to succeed in some of life's toughest moments, from West Virginia to Baghdad to DC. The sacrifices, challenges, dilemmas, and hilarity that are only possible in combat come to life in this recounting of a life led at the tip of the spear."

—Ryan Fugit, host of *Combat Story,*
former Apache pilot and CIA officer

"Darrell Utt's *Grit to Glory* is a candid and revealing look at what it's like to be 'boots on the ground' and operating in some of the toughest places in the world. Darrell chronicles his journey through multiple overseas deployments and frontline combat that puts you in the middle of the action with immense detail and charm. A gripping and inspiring read."

—Amy Forsythe, US Marine veteran, author of *Heroes Live Here*

"*Grit to Glory* is an instant classic and a must-read for those wanting to understand today's people's war and what it takes to win. Darrell Utt is one of the rarest of authors, a small unit leader at the bleeding edge of combat who can write about it. A master storyteller who led men in combat for months on end, he has given us a rare and authentic glimpse inside of his Special Forces team. Consider yourself privileged. Sit back with a beer and a Fat Nasty and enjoy the read. I can't wait for the movie."

—Lieutenant General Charles "Charlie" Cleveland (Ret.), US Army

"*Grit to Glory* is a high-adrenaline recounting of a combat deployment that underscores the power of resilience, the value in being able to forge alliances in trust-depleted environments, and the importance of making the most of what you have in the moment by one of our nation's elites. Green Berets get it done, but it takes so much blood to make those few words a reality in death's lair. Darrell Utt colors in every traumatic and triumphant detail in this chronicle of a life in service. Generals today would do well to learn the lessons held in these pages—lessons that carry through into everyday life and light the path for the rest of us. With its practical punch list for the rest of us to put these skills into practice to achieve excellence in all we do, *Grit to Glory* is a MUST-read for anyone who wants to live a life that matters."

—Ben and Jessica Owen, founders of We Fight Monsters and Flanders Fields

"Compelling—a must-read with combat-proven leadership lessons we can all use in life and business. Darrell Utt is that rare storyteller with humanity, humility, and humor."

—Anthony Brock, US Navy Commander (Ret.),
executive leadership coach and executive director
at the National Medal of Honor Griffin Institute

"Darrell Utt and I served in similar 'war zones,' conflicts in which we were required to follow established 'rules of war' under the watchful eye of a less-than-friendly media while fighting against frequently brutal adversaries operating without any sort of rules with psychopathic and Aztec-like brutality against both civilians and soldiers unfortunate to be captured alive. The grit so well described by Darrell accumulated in layers, beginning with experiences in his native West Virginia where people faced hard tasks on a near-daily basis. The grit, integrity—note the 'grit' root of this word—courage, and accumulated wisdom in Darrell Utt, along with loyalty to his teams that kept him in service, resulted in the development of a key Special Forces soldier, the team sergeant responsible for holding it all together. His life and leadership lessons in his book are invaluable reading for everyone."

—David L. "Doc" Phillips, Special Forces and CIA,
member of Team Jawbreaker, 2001 (Afghanistan)

"Darrell has captured the origin story of a Special Forces soldier. He has also captured the complexities of the Global War on Terrorism in a story that puts you in the seat next to him, no doubt inspiring future soldiers to start the long path into 'the Regiment.'"

—Earl Plumlee, Marine Force Reconnaissance,
US Army Special Forces, Medal of Honor recipient

"I served with MSG Darrell Utt (Ret.) on my first Army Special Forces team in two war zones. Darrell had a massive impact on my formative years as a young Green Beret officer. Darrell's hard-earned wisdom, fierce integrity, and innate courage to visualize and seize high-value opportunities served as a priceless guidepost throughout my career as an SOF soldier and national security professional. From distant post-9/11 war zones to dark alleys in foreign cities to the White House, I've repeatedly drawn from the familiar leadership lessons found in Darrell's book. For all seeking to take their leadership, business, parenting, or performance to the next level, my dear friend's book is a must-read."

—Tripp McCullar, former director for intelligence programs, White House National Security Council (NSC)

"Authentic and irresistible, *Grit to Glory* takes readers on a white-knuckle ride from West Virginia to Baghdad, Iraq, where the rubber hit the road as US Army Green Berets fought through bullet-strewn houses and alleys for each other and in service to their country. Destined to be a classic."

—Edward G. Lengel, PhD,
author of *Never in Finer Company: The Men of the Great War's Lost Battalion*

"High-octane adventure; men you will instantly connect with; pure storytelling; and keen insights. Such are the qualities of books we need now, and Darrell Utt delivers on all fronts. Put this one high on your reading list."

—Susan Katz Keating, publisher,
Soldier of Fortune magazine

"*Grit to Glory* is an American dream page-turner I didn't want to put down. Darrell's vulnerability and humility in discussing his leadership experience under harsh combat conditions take you inside this warrior's thought process. You can feel the pressure and humor on each page. I'm proud of Darrell for writing this book, but I'm even prouder to call this man my friend."

—Herb Thompson, Special Forces Team Sergeant (Ret.)

"*Grit to Glory* provides a well-honed template for success as a soldier/operator in battle and in life. Darrell Utt shares his incredible Special Forces journey shaped by his key mentors, along with a sound application of his core principles continuously improved to achieve all facets of excellence. His body of work and operational experiences should be shared extensively in our Special Operations community."

—CSM Charles (Chuck) Sekelsky (Ret.)

"Darrell Utt's mentorship has been priceless to me and many others who have had the good fortune to get it in person. He's been kind enough to offer it up in detail and in writing to anyone. If you want to level up your life by taking on some hard-won lessons about putting in the work to do hard and important things, you can't do better than *Grit to Glory*."

—Colonel Jordan Becker, PhD, Special Forces, academy professor at United States Military Academy, West Point, NY

"Darrell's book takes readers on a thrilling journey, shifting from sledgehammers to heavy combat operations to psychic mind readers. Despite the abundance of insights from Darrell's experiences, the narrative never feels preachy or didactic. This seamless blend of action and wisdom makes it a compelling read."

—Lisa Jaster, PMP, Lt. Col. (Res.), executive coach, first female reserve Ranger School grad, author of *Delete the Adjective: A Soldier's Adventures in Ranger School*

"In *Grit to Glory*, Darrell Utt brings out the raw impact of modern combat—dirt, sweat, and fear—conquered by an inner calmness of what a true combat leader is meant to be. Special Forces operators are not born; they are honed and sharpened by months of intense, repetitive training. This process takes time, and the result is handsome, sharp, deadly weapons of the American Special Forces. As Darrell describes, on the constant quest of learning, one learns as much from success as from failure. Further, in the Grit Code that he presents are the pearls of wisdom that should be taught in every high school graduating class and in all universities. These are the building blocks of inner growth with exterior results. Those of you who read his book will be richer both in mind and spirit."

—Eugene "Gene" H. Pugh, Military Assistance Command, Vietnam – Studies and Observation Group (MACV-SOG) – RT Asp 68-69, author of *Surrender Not an Option*

"A brilliantly told combat story that offers lessons to people in any profession."

—Special Forces Colonel Liam Collins (Ret.), author of *Understanding Urban Warfare* and *Leadership and Innovation During Crisis: Lessons from the Iraq War*

GRIT TO GLORY

A Green Beret's Journey from West Virginia to the Streets of Baghdad

DARRELL UTT
WITH LAUREN UNGELDI

Ballast Books, LLC
www.ballastbooks.com

Copyright © 2024 by Darrell Utt

All rights reserved. No part of this book may be reproduced in any form or by any electronic or mechanical means, including information storage and retrieval systems, without permission in writing from the publisher, except by reviewers, who may quote brief passages in a review.

The views expressed in this publication are those of the author and do not necessarily reflect the official policy or position of the Department of Defense or the US government. The public release clearance of this publication by the Department of Defense does not imply Department of Defense endorsement or factual accuracy of the material.

ISBN: 978-1-964934-85-3

Cover graphic by Clandestine Media Group,
Luke Peelgrane and Matt Lingo
Cover design by Mirko Pohle

Printed in the United States of America

Published by Ballast Books
www.ballastbooks.com

For more information, bulk orders, appearances, or speaking requests, please email: info@ballastbooks.com

AUTHOR'S NOTE

The authors have taken measures to protect the identities of the individuals mentioned in this book. As a result, certain names and characteristics of US soldiers and Iraqi citizens have been changed. Some events and conversations may have been condensed or reconstructed.

"'The green beret' is again becoming a symbol of excellence, a badge of courage, a mark of distinction in the fight for freedom."

—John F. Kennedy

TABLE OF CONTENTS

Prologue i

Introduction v

Chapter 1: From West Virginia to Green Beret 1

Chapter 2: An Unforgiving Business 23

Chapter 3: Camp Apache 33

Chapter 4: Honey Trappin' 39

Chapter 5: The Carnage of War 53

Chapter 6: Psychic Intelligence 69

Chapter 7: Alive Day 97

Chapter 8: Ski Mask Terrorists 123

Chapter 9: Grand Theft Auto 141

Chapter 10: DUSTWUN 155

Chapter 11: Kidnapped 167

Chapter 12: Rattlesnakes and Assassins 181

Chapter 13: Honor and Humility 191

Chapter 14: The Grit Code 203

Closing 255

PART 2: Sneak Peek 257

Acknowledgments 259

In Memoriam 261

Pay It Forward 263

About the Authors 265

PROLOGUE

The air was filled with the deafening sound of AK-47 fire and PKM machine gun rounds. The explosive impact of rocket-propelled grenades (RPGs) at close range rang in my ears as we entered Adhamiyah, Baghdad, from the east and began the drive to Antar Square. An inexperienced soldier can't distinguish between these sounds; he'll duck in fear of an explosive miles away. Hell, I did once too. But it doesn't take long before you become attuned to that song of war and learn to differentiate one instrument of destruction from the other and gauge the distance and viability of a threat just from the sound.

Damn.

I didn't like the tune of this one.

We pulled into the area with two gun trucks—*MacGyver* Special Edition—proudly touting steel I-beams as front bumpers. I peered out the side window and got my first look at the local Iraqi Army caught in a heavy crossfire. Their eyes were wide with fear. They'd been in a sustained firefight against a well-equipped enemy for hours, and things weren't going in their favor. The weather was bad, and the low ceiling had emboldened the insurgents who damn well knew that our air support was grounded for the day. It was clear they intended to take full advantage of that fact.

I watched the expressions of the soldiers go from terror to surprise to relief at the sight of us. We were the salvation they'd been praying for, and the weight of responsibility sat squarely on our shoulders. We didn't look anything like the 101st guys they were accustomed to seeing. We sported full beards, chest rigs, and unique helmets. It would be their first time witnessing our team of Green Berets in action during daylight hours.

After identifying what appeared to be a hastily established Iraqi Army command post inside a small building, I directed the drivers to position themselves outside the line of direct fire. I needed to establish contact with the command post to understand what kind of situation we had on our hands and how we could help turn things around. I also needed to know the exact location of the Iraqi Army members and the 101st guys who were pinned down to avoid a "blue on blue" incident, better known as "friendly fire." The tough thing about urban warfare is that you can't tell shit about where the enemy is positioned just by looking.

But there was one problem. The distance between where my ass sat in the front seat of the gun truck and the Iraqi command post was approximately 100 to 150 meters. Not so far under normal circumstances, but a mile-long death march when you're under heavy fire from an unseen enemy. Given the complex, urban environment, it was challenging to pinpoint the exact source of the incoming rounds as gunfire and explosions reverberated from all directions. I stared at the open space between me and the command post for a second before opening the truck door.

Now I had a choice to make. I could run the distance and attempt to minimize the danger. Seemed like the obvious thing to do. But at the first sight of me doing a Tom Cruise sprint to the command post, everyone watching would switch to full panic mode, and that's never a good thing. I couldn't afford to have a bunch of panicked men on my hands not thinking clearly. Panicked people do strange things, and strange things get people killed.

That left option number two: I could walk quickly but calmly to the command post. No sprinting, just a nice, smooth pace as if I were headed into Gino's Pizza on Fifth Avenue back in West Virginia before the college crowd hit after a football game.

Prologue

Stepping out of the gun truck, I made my decision. I needed everyone to stay clearheaded and calm. Experience taught me that if a leader was strong-minded enough to stand up and display courage, others would follow suit. And as the team sergeant, it seemed that leader was me. I might have looked more confident than I felt, but feelings don't matter much in the heat of combat—just action. Head held high, I dismounted the truck and took my first step. Joe Joe, my faithful interpreter, fell in lockstep beside me.

Ten feet tall and bulletproof, D. You're ten feet tall and bulletproof.

It was the smell that hit me first. The air was thick with the acrid odor of gunpowder and burning tires from vehicles set ablaze. Nothing good ever happens when that smell is in the air.

Another step. Another loud crack of gunfire sounded in the air like thunder, and the roar of gunfire echoed through the concrete canyons, assaulting my ears and reverberating through my bones. Unfortunately, I *was* well attuned to the songs of war. I *could* differentiate one instrument of destruction from the other and gauge the distance and viability of a threat just from the sound.

Fuck, that one was close.

INTRODUCTION

"What is a Green Beret, Dad?"

My son was eleven years old when he asked the question. He was holding a photo—a picture of a younger version of me dressed in uniform with the iconic Green Beret atop my head, standing tall and proud. I looked at the photo, and the younger me stared back. As I stood there, I saw more than a photo in his hands. I saw years of hard work and sacrifice. I saw a warrior. I saw a small-town boy from West Virginia who everyone said wouldn't amount to much.

Suddenly, I felt an overwhelming surge of feelings that left me searching for the right way to express the thoughts in my mind to my son. Silence followed his question, and the weight of unspoken words hung in the air. There was no explanation that I could give him that would capture the full magnitude of what that photo meant to me. I didn't answer for several moments. I wanted to share the depths of my experiences with him. I wanted him to see the world through my eyes, to understand what had built the layers of the man in the photo and the one standing in front of him.

"Green Berets are soldiers with unique skills who are trained to handle tough missions anywhere in the world," I began, trying to find the right words. "They belong to a group of elite soldiers that we call the United States Army Special Forces."

My son looked from the photo to me and then back to the photo again. "And what makes them special, Dad?"

That's when I felt a smile playing at the corners of my lips. At eleven years old, he'd just asked the million-dollar question, the one everyone wants to know—the one that I once asked myself.

"Green Berets aren't born different from everyone else. Nope, not at all. They are different because they are willing to do the things that everyone else isn't. They aren't born special; they're *made* that way. Layer after layer of courage, sacrifice, hard work, determination, and pure grit."

My son nodded his head that day without a word, but I saw a spark light up in his eyes. I left it at that, knowing that my words couldn't possibly carry the weight of my experiences. I knew they couldn't convey the depth of my feelings that clung to each syllable as I spoke. He wasn't ready yet to see the world through my eyes, to understand what made the layers of the man in the photo or the one standing in front of him. I promised myself to find a way to tell him *someday*.

This book has been years in the making. The stories within these pages might take you a few days or weeks to read. For me, they represent a collection of experiences that I accumulated over a lifetime. Books are designed to share the extraordinary—the parts of our lives that are noteworthy, exciting, heart-pounding, and transformative. They are designed to inspire, teach, entertain, expand, and instruct.

As a young man, I had a handful of books that inspired me and gave me heroes to look up to.

There was *The Three Wars of Roy Benavidez* by Roy P. Benavidez and Oscar Griffin, which detailed Roy's incredible story as a Special Forces Medal of Honor recipient in Vietnam. There was also *Five Years to Freedom: The True Story of a Vietnam POW* by James N. Rowe, which chronicled the extraordinary resilience and survival of Green Beret Lieutenant James N. Rowe, who was captured in Vietnam and spent five years as a prisoner of war.

I was also deeply inspired and impacted by the actions of MSG Gary Gordon and SFC Randy Shughart, both Medal of Honor recipients, for their heroic actions in Somalia in October 1993. Their courage and sacrifice were portrayed in the book and movie *Black Hawk Down: A Story of Modern War*.

These stories shaped me. They allowed me to learn from the victories and mistakes of those who have gone before. They gave me the courage to chase bold dreams and to stand up and say, "If he did it, then I can too." Courage is contagious.

Twelve years after my son held that photo, he left home to join the military. It's his turn now to forge his path, to build his own experiences layer by layer, just like I did. And now I realize that there is a whole generation of young men and women, like my son, who are looking for stories that they can hold on to, something that gives them the courage to believe *they can*. There is also a whole generation of veterans like me who are looking for something to guide them in translating the lessons they learned on the battlefield into civilian life after the battle is over. This profound realization, above all else, ignited a fire within me to share my experiences in the book you now hold in your hand, spotlighting a pivotal chapter of my twenty-six-year military career: an eight-month rotation in Baghdad, Iraq, that took place in 2006.

If sharing my life experiences and the lessons I learned as a result can inspire others, it's my duty to do so. This book is full of wild, hilarious, and heartbreaking stories as well as hard-earned life lessons that will smack you in the face just like they did me as I lived them. But it's also a little different than most military memoirs, and I'll tell you why.

All too often, when we watch movies or read books, we only see the highlight reel, the mountaintop moments, the glory stories. This makes it seem as though some people come into this world as experienced professionals, successful leaders, and elite warriors. We like to zoom the camera in when our hero reaches the top of the mountain, not when he's knee-deep in a muddy trench on the way up. We don't focus on the work, dedication, time investment, or sheer determination it takes to achieve greatness. We focus on the glory, not the grit. As a result, many people assume that heroes are different from the rest, that they are just born special. I'm here to tell you that's bullshit.

Everything I've ever achieved in my life is a result of hard work, not natural talent. I have never been the most physically fit, articulate, skilled, or sociable. Far too often, people have underestimated the depth of my capabilities because I don't fit the stereotype that most expect from a warrior. But you know what life has taught me over and over again?

Work hard. Be humble. Don't quit.

I'm a living testament that if you are crystal clear about what you want to accomplish, if you are willing to go to extreme measures to work for it, and if you refuse to surrender, you can accomplish just about anything. You just gotta have the grit to do it.

Grit, when broken down, has two primary definitions. The first definition is "courage and determination despite difficulty."[1] These values are not just words in a dictionary to me; they form the very code by which I live my life. Grit is all about having the courage to take risks, the resolve to persevere through challenges, and the strength of character to stay true to yourself even when things get tough. Grit propels you forward when everything else falters. Grit gives you an inner reservoir of hidden power that pushes you to keep going when everything around you screams for you to give up. Grit is a fire within that refuses to back down, dares to defy the odds, and ultimately leads to triumph against all odds.

The second meaning of grit is "rough, hard particles of sand, stone, etc."[2] This hits home for me in a special way. As a kid, I spent hours in the woods, playing in the creeks and catching crawdads. I came from a town of down-to-earth people and a family that was dirt-poor. Our community was made up of a tight-knit group of hardworking people—the kind with a little dirt under their nails and a heritage of honest work to take pride in. The real backbone of America.

---

[1] *Cambridge Dictionary*, s.v. "grit (*n*.)," accessed July 1, 2024, https://dictionary.cambridge.org/us/dictionary/english/grit.
[2] *Webster's New World College Dictionary*, 4th ed. (2010), s.v. "grit."

Introduction

And you know what? Those gritty, tough-as-nails bits and particles from my upbringing are still embedded deep within me today, fueling my fire, driving my ambitions, and shaping my story. That grit inside of me is a badge of honor that represents resilience, tenacity, and a never-back-down attitude.

And for that, I'm damn proud.

So, before I dive into my story as a team sergeant and Special Forces operator in Baghdad, before I tell the wild, hilarious, action-packed stories that took place over the course of my eight-month deployment in 2006, I'd like to first introduce you to a small-town boy from West Virginia.

CHAPTER 1

FROM WEST VIRGINIA TO GREEN BERET

Growing up, the only silver spoons in my family were the ones used to hit me. I was born in Huntington, West Virginia, to two hardworking, blue-collar Americans who earned every dollar they had. The town of Huntington might not have been noteworthy at all if it hadn't been for a tragic airplane crash that occurred in the 1970s. A DC-7 chartered jet, carrying most of the Marshall University Thundering Herd football team, crashed into a hillside just two miles from the Tri-State Airport in Huntington, killing all seventy-five passengers on board. This incident happened just a year before I was born and had a profound impact on the entire community of Huntington. We were all just one friend, cousin, or acquaintance away from somebody who had lost a loved one in the crash. The tragedy affected all of us in some way or another.

I like to say I came from humble beginnings, but that's just a nice way to say that our family was dirt-poor. Burger King was considered fine dining, and we always bought shoes just a half-size too big to make sure we got a full year of wear out of them before it was time to buy another pair. Neither of my parents graduated high school. They dove headfirst into adulthood instead, juggling the responsibilities of work and family life when they were barely more than kids themselves. My dad worked for Owens-Illinois, a glass factory in Huntington, while my mom worked at a mental health facility called Twentieth Street Hospital.

Like most kids of my generation, I grew up getting hit with spatulas, wooden spoons, and anything else my mom could get her hands on. But in my family, things went a little further than a switch on the backside. My mom often came home from work with a busted lip or a black eye from altercations with mental health patients. My father's battle with alcoholism exacerbated the strain on their already-rocky relationship. The toxic cycle of their arguments often spiraled into violence, leaving my mother to bear the brunt of the pain. Far too often, my mom would get one black eye from work and another to match it when my dad got his hands on her at home. Maybe that's why mom got physical with us kids: me, my brother, and my sister. My poor sister always took the brunt of Mom's violent outbursts. Years later, she would thank me for saving her life one day when I ran inside from mowing the lawn to help pull Mom off of her. I don't remember it exactly like that, but I take her word for it. Mom was one tough lady; I'll give her credit for that. She sure made us tough as well. Being the youngest of three siblings put me through my fair share of scrapes, bruises, and black eyes to match my mom's more times than I could count.

I played sports year-round as a kid: baseball, basketball, and football. My dad was a hotshot basketball player in his younger years and naturally assumed that I would follow in his footsteps. But basketball was never my sport. I was too slow to catch up with the speedy players and too aggressive for my own good. Besides, it seemed that fate had it out for me during the shirts versus skins showdowns. No matter what, I always found myself on the skins team, and I didn't like it at all. I was a chunky kid and saw no need to advertise that fact. What's more, I hated running suicides up and down the same court that the other guys had puked on that morning.

I liked baseball well enough, but football was my true passion. I still wasn't a fan of all the running involved in football, but I got to hit people, so it felt like a fair trade-off. Playing as a fullback and defensive end, I was an above-average player, but the league's age and weight setup pushed me to starve myself to meet the requirements. On more than one occasion, I deprived myself of food for days on end and wore a garbage bag to lose water weight for the weigh-ins. Our team didn't win often, but I did gain valuable lessons on toughness, hard work, positivity, resilience, and overcoming adversity through the experience.

When I wasn't doing sports or coasting through school with a solid 2.0 GPA, I'd tag along with my dad on his fishing, hunting, and trapping adventures. We'd usually hit up the lakes that were known for their fishing competitions. We'd cough up a small fee that made us eligible to win prizes for the biggest fish of the hour or the day, throw our pole in the water, and hope for the best. Sometimes it was a cash prize on the line; other times it was a new rod and reel or tacklebox. It was the poor man's lottery. As such, we were all about that catfishing. Those whiskery rascals come in all shapes and sizes, from tiny guys to beasts over twenty pounds if you're really lucky.

I also went hunting with my dad—mainly for squirrels, but sometimes for deer or turkeys. I never seemed to have any luck with turkeys, a fact that haunted me for years. Time after time, I sounded that mating call, then waited, watched, and sprang into action at what I believed to be just the right time. And time after time, the smart, feathered bastard eluded me.

Dad always worried that we'd be mistaken for a deer or turkey and get shot by another hunter with an itchy trigger finger. That made squirrel hunting his preferred choice, which minimized the risk. I loved it. It was a thrill to wake up while it was still dark outside and head out to the woods with my dad. The peacefulness of nature, the sounds of birds, and the sweet silence were a welcomed contrast to the chaos of our home life for both me and my dad, who had recently recovered from alcoholism. When we did manage to kill a few squirrels, we would take them home, skin them, and cook them for a delicious meal. Grandma made the best biscuits and squirrel gravy.

Aside from hunting, my dad often took me muskrat trapping. Muskrats are aquatic rodents that live in the wetlands with short, dark brown fur and long tails covered in scales. They tend to live in family groups and build nests in banks with underwater entrances to protect themselves and their young. In the late 1970s and early '80s, muskrat pelts could earn you a crisp $5 bill—$10 if you were lucky. So, during the months when the budget was extra tight, we'd take to the creeks with our traps to see what we could bring home. We used conibear traps (body traps) with metal squares that snapped together in a scissor motion as a kill trap. They were designed to kill the muskrat swiftly and effectively by crushing its body or neck without causing damage to the fur and were powered by one or two springs that compressed when the trap was set. The trick was luring the muskrats in. We would start by digging a little hole in the bank. Then we'd slice up an apple, position it just right, and place the trap over the bait to catch them when they came in for a bite. The irresistible scent and sight of the apple would entice the muskrat to swim toward the trap, and *snap*. Once trapped, we'd skin them and hang their pelts to dry.

By today's standards, it might seem barbaric to hunt the little fellows for money. But this was the '80s; we didn't think of it that way. As a young teenager, I was proud to stand next to my father and help provide for our family. Selling muskrat pelts always ensured we had a few decent Christmas presents under the tree each year.

In the fall of 1986, as I entered Vinson High School, I met Coach Carl T. Thornburg, a tough and respected football coach who was a Green Beret and a sergeant major in the Nineteenth Special Forces Group. Coach Thornburg ran our football team with the same discipline and teamwork as a Special Forces team sergeant. Under his guidance, I learned important life lessons, such as discipline, resilience, and the value of hard work.

During my senior year, Coach Thornburg took me and a few teammates to Camp Dawson, West Virginia, for a taste of military life. We served as practice subjects for National Guard drill instructors, honing their skills before going to active duty bases for basic training. Yep, it was as bad as it sounds. They hit us with all the classics—five-mile runs, fitness tests, and early morning wake-up calls using metal trash cans and lids. We underwent physical fitness tests, learned drill and ceremony, and were pushed to our limits. It served as great preparation for what was to come next: basic training.

In 1990, after graduating high school, I joined the military as a light infantryman (11B). I trained at Fort Benning, Georgia, and was stationed at Fort Ord, California, as a member of the Seventh Infantry Division "Lightfighters." Though I missed out on Operation Desert Shield and Desert Storm, I had deployments with Joint Task Force Six to support law enforcement in countering drug flow along the New Mexico–Mexico border. We didn't confiscate or see any illegal drugs, but we did run into a few rattlesnakes and roasted our ass in the sun. We also trained in Germany and Panama and spent a significant amount of time in Fort Hunter Liggett, California.

I achieved several personal accomplishments during that time, from completing Air Assault School, to earning the Expert Infantry Badge, to being promoted to sergeant. I attribute these accomplishments to influential leaders like First Sergeant Tim Rego and Staff Sergeant Lopez, who taught me valuable lessons in leadership during that period of my career. First Sergeant Rego once told me, "If you plan on being a good leader, you need to have the ability to look your mom right in the eyes and say, 'Mom, I love you, but you're fuckin' fired!'" First Sergeant Rego clearly didn't know my mom, but I never forgot that lesson. A good leader has to be willing to have hard conversations and make tough decisions for the sake of their team.

After being stationed at Fort Lewis, Washington, and Fort Campbell, Kentucky, I deployed to Sinai, Egypt, as part of the Multinational Force and Observers from July 1995 to January 1996. During my time in Sinai, a new dream began to form in my mind. At first, it seemed crazy, too lofty and unreachable for a West Virginia boy. But that dream began to solidify into a plan—one that I would successfully execute or die trying. I was going to become a Green Beret.

The Green Berets' enigmatic reputation and legendary capabilities had appealed to me for a long time. They were not just soldiers; they were masters of strategic warfare. They were an elite brotherhood that excelled in unconventional missions. Their commitment to mastering languages, understanding cultures, and honing their training skills set them apart as the standard of excellence. I wanted to see if I had what it took to stand shoulder-to-shoulder with such an elite class of warriors.

In Sinai, I began training rigorously for Special Forces Assessment and Selection (SFAS). Unfortunately, I broke my left fibula right before redeploying. Once my cast was removed and I was able to start training again, I got after it. I had never been a physical training (PT) stud, but I could run and ruck all day long. I was twenty-four years old; my body could take a lot of punishment and keep going. I decided that they would have to drag my lifeless body out of SFAS; there was no way I would quit. *No surrender.* That's what got me through. And it worked. I attended SFAS in 1996 and was fortunate to get selected and receive a slot at the Special Forces Qualification Course (SFQC), known as the Q course.

On March 6, 1998, I proudly earned the coveted green beret and the privilege to wear the Special Forces tab. I was assigned to the Tenth Special Forces Group (Airborne). It was an honor beyond words. I'd worked hard to join that elite group of operators. It seemed that all the hunting, fishing, and trapping in my younger years had paid off. My childhood experiences had made me a better marksman. I was intimately familiar with firearms and had a heightened awareness in the woods, which served me well during my training and beyond (thanks, Dad). Besides that, I wasn't afraid of a little pain (thanks, Mom). The small-town boy from West Virginia had made it to the big leagues.

I relocated to the First Battalion in Stuttgart, Germany, where our focus was the European Theater. During my time in Alpha Company, First Battalion, Tenth Special Forces Group, I learned what it *truly* meant to be a Green Beret. Most of all, I learned the importance of consistent training and preparedness.

Participating in numerous missions and operations in Bosnia and Kosovo, I met with the first realities of combat. One particularly eventful helicopter flight during the Kosovo War in 1999 almost ended in disaster when our team, providing combat search and rescue support, came under fire from an SA-6 Gainful ground-to-air missile. That one was a wake-up call. Despite the challenges, we were the first Special Forces company to cross into Kosovo from Skopje, Macedonia, after the aerial bombing. We successfully established the infrastructure for subsequent teams. This experience, along with conducting special reconnaissance missions on the Kosovo-Macedonia border, tested my physical and mental limits but made me a much stronger operator as a result.

Among the significant missions I participated in, there was a sensitive operation in Sarajevo, Bosnia and Herzegovina, as well as two high-profile missions involving the protection of the US president. In 1999, we safeguarded President Bill Clinton in Sarajevo, positioned on the infamous Sniper Alley. Later, in 2001, we played a critical role in the security detail for President Bush in Kosovo. As a member of the counter sniper security team during both missions, the responsibility and stakes couldn't have been higher.

Throughout these experiences, I pushed myself to continue to expand my skills and abilities. I graduated from Ranger School, the Special Operations Target Interdiction Course (SOTIC), and the Special Forces Advanced Non-Commissioned Officer Course (ANCOC). This resulted in my promotion to sergeant first class (E-7).

My time in Alpha Company, First Battalion, Tenth Special Forces Group exposed me to a variety of intense missions and taught me the importance of continuous training and adaptability. It also forged in me a deep camaraderie within the Special Forces community. One person who played a pivotal role in my development was my mentor, Company Sergeant Major Michael (Scott) Breasseale. As a former Ranger Regiment soldier who had served in Grenada and later in Panama as a member of the Special Forces, Scott earned my respect instantly. Scott also knew and worked with a handful of my heroes and shared stories of their courage and sacrifice. He told me about Medal of Honor recipients Master Sergeant Gary Gordon and Sergeant First Class Randy Shughart, who were both killed in Mogadishu, Somalia, in 1993. Throughout my time knowing and working for Scott, he proudly displayed a picture of Gary and Randy in his office, and I often looked up at that image, drawing strength and courage from all that it represented. I can still recount the lessons Scott taught me:

1. Always make the difficult *right* call instead of an easy *wrong* call.
2. The actions you take when nobody is around will define your character.
3. Integrity is paramount. Never compromise, even with your commander.
4. If something goes wrong, communicate. No one can read your mind, and silence implies that everything is fine.
5. Never substitute actual combat loads during training. Train with ammunition, full gear, and weapons.
6. Incorporate live ammunition into training sessions as frequently as possible.
7. Start every week by imagining that you are deploying on Friday. Consider what adjustments you would make to your training schedule. Identify and eliminate any unnecessary activities accordingly.

After four years in First Battalion, I was assigned to Second Battalion, Tenth Special Forces Group.

Unfortunately, we had a weak team leader and an infamous team sergeant who had been involved in a fatal bar fight during his time in the Ranger Regiment. If we weren't the worst team in the battalion, we were pretty close. All of Tenth Group was supposed to be gearing up for the invasion of Iraq, and we weren't looking good.

Fortunately, before we deployed, our team sergeant was fired and a man by the name of Matt Girard took over. Matt, a native of Mount Clemens, Michigan, quickly became one of my closest friends. His sharp wit and dark sense of humor never failed to keep us entertained, but beyond that, he proved himself to be a remarkable leader and a hell of a warrior. He started in the Ranger Regiment, surviving a combat parachute jump into Panama during Operation Just Cause in 1989 before transitioning to the Special Forces. I couldn't have been happier to see him take control of the team.

For our first mission, the plan was to fly into Turkey, rendezvous with our gear, and then drive into northern Iraq. There, we would meet up with a group of Kurdish Peshmerga soldiers, a military force made up of Kurdish fighters from Iraq, Syria, Turkey, and Iran. They were our in-country contacts, ready to assist us in establishing a presence in northern Iraq. Our mission after that was simple enough, at least in concept: hold the Iraqi army up north so they wouldn't be able to come down and reinforce Baghdad.

But things didn't go as planned. At the last minute, Turkey denied us permission to enter their airspace. So, we found ourselves in Constanta, Romania, in a deserted hotel in the dead of winter—the best option for holding all members of the regiment until we figured out our next move. The hotel was located on the Black Sea in a ghost town of a city. There were no signs of life or civilization for miles. It was empty and positively *frigid*. The dimly lit rooms looked like they hadn't seen a guest in years, and the cold air was musty with the smell of neglect.

"This place is like a fucking prison," Matt had muttered under his breath. "No heat, no food, nothin'." I nodded but didn't answer.

Inside the rooms, there was nothing but two single beds covered in a blanket barely thicker than a sheet. The walls were paper thin and poorly insulated—no match for winter outside. For five days we stayed in that godforsaken hotel while the command worked out a new plan for us to make our entry into Iraq. More than once, they called us into formation in preparation for flying out, only to send us back to our cold rooms after hitting a snag. Finally, on day five, it looked like it was finally going to happen.

First, we'd made a brief stop in Jordan and then began the trip to northern Iraq. Because we were flying directly into a very dangerous part of enemy territory, the flight path was anything but simple. We'd be flying NOE, or nap-of-the-earth, a type of low-level technique used by military aircraft to fly close to the ground and avoid detection. In NOE flying, the aircraft flies at very low altitudes (typically below five hundred feet above ground level) and follows the contours of the terrain, hidden from radar and other detection systems. The pilots spent hours planning a route that would offer the best chances of avoiding heavy fire. After they were done, one of them took a look at the flight plan outline and said, "Looks like an ugly baby."

No one knew then just how important those words would be. We loaded up onto six birds, all MC-130s. I was in bird number three. The entire inside of the aircraft had been stripped down to the bare minimum. No benches or seats—just cold, hard steel. The only gear and resources we had were the ones strapped to our backs. Each soldier was responsible for carrying more than 150 pounds. We each took turns sitting down, strapping on the damn thing, and then grabbing the outstretched hands of two men on either side to pull us up to a standing position. The first few steps seemed like a joke until reality set in. *One foot in front of the other.*

The first hour of the flight was uneventful and uncomfortable. We sat on bare, cold steel with our gear in almost total darkness. It was nighttime and all the windows were covered in Armor Express ballistic blankets. Several of the guys used snap links to secure themselves to the floor. About an hour and a half into the flight, long enough for at least one ass cheek to go completely numb, we heard the sound of an explosion in the distance. No one was thinking about a numb backside now.

Another explosion sounded, and then another. Suddenly, the plane dove and then took a straight upward turn.

"Holy shit!" someone shouted from the back.

The force was enough to make my stomach clench. We dove, twisted, and turned. I tried desperately not to vomit—nobody likes the vomit guy. Two things became clear to me in a matter of about seven seconds. First, these *Top Gun*-style maneuvers were sexier in the movies without a half-digested dinner trying to make its way up your throat. Secondly, we were under heavy fire and things were probably not going to end well.

What a way to go out.

One of the guys popped his head up and opened the cover of the window portal, trying to catch a glimpse of what was happening outside. All we could see were flashes of light. I made eye contact with the guy closest to me. We didn't say a word, but we were both thinking the same thing: *Should we take our armor off our chests and put it underneath us?* Nothing but a pair of pants was protecting our vulnerable lower half from the underbelly of the plane, which could come under fire at any time. It's instinctual, you know, wanting something more than the aircraft floor and a piece of fabric between your balls and a heavy round of antiaircraft artillery.

But neither I nor the soldier in front of me moved an inch. We'd both run through the scenario and come to the same conclusion. If they hit us, we'd be fucked anyway. And no piece of armor under our ass would help.

Control what you can control.

It was a phrase that I had adopted as a mantra of sorts. When all hell breaks loose, when the chaos comes, when you're up against the impossible, just focus on controlling what you can control. And at that point, that was not much of anything. It was all up to the pilots. For an hour and a half, all six birds remained under heavy fire. One plane was badly hit and made an emergency landing in Turkey. The other planes were hit but not damaged enough to warrant an emergency landing. The pilots did maneuvers that made our stomachs clench and throats ache with the taste of vomit. At times, we were flying one hundred feet off the desert. But we made it.

There was no time to feel relief when the plane finally landed. We were given orders to run off the ramp and immediately secure the perimeter. I'd seen the intel and knew that the chances of us running into trouble on the ground were next to none, but I wasn't about to argue with our leadership team. The whole lot of us charged down that ramp with weapons drawn like we were shooting a Hollywood movie, only to find a little group of scrawny Kurdish soldiers waiting with trays of tea for us. Later, we received reports about the amount of damage the aircraft had taken. That's when the reality of what we had just survived really set in. Those pilots were our heroes. Little did we know at the time, we had just participated in the longest low-level combat air infiltration by US Special Operations aircraft since the Second World War, which ended up with the name Operation Ugly Baby. I'm still angry at whoever decided on that dumbass name, but it was a hell of a way to kick off our deployment.

But while our entrance into the country might have been dramatic, what followed was just one anticlimactic event after another. While all the other teams were fighting and calling in airstrikes on the Green Line, we were playing slap-ass with the Red Cross at an Enemy Prisoner of War (EPW) camp. Intelligence had indicated and expected a mass capitulation of senior Ba'ath Party members and senior Iraqi Army officers, and we were the team tasked with building and initially running it. After the mass capitulation failed to occur, largely due to the intimidation and murder of initial deserters by the paramilitary group Fedayeen Saddam, our team found ourselves waiting with no actual mission at the desolate EPW camp.

Eventually, we were called forward by S3 Major Francis "Fran" Beaudette to liberate Altun Kupri, an infamous Iraqi town known for a massacre in 1991. Surprisingly, we encountered no resistance and were greeted warmly by the locals. Following this success, we became part of the first American Special Forces to enter and secure Mosul, facing minor skirmishes but never being decisively engaged. Our tasks included presence patrols, engaging with locals reporting weapons of mass destruction, and the responsible disposal of unexploded ordnance in and around Mosul.

We were eventually replaced by the 101st Airborne Division and redeployed to Fort Carson, Colorado. Subsequently, my team was deployed to Kosovo in 2003, where we were tasked with tracking down and capturing personnel indicted for war crimes. After returning from another Iraq rotation in 2004–2005, the moment I had been waiting for finally came. I was promoted to master sergeant (E-8) and appointed as the operations sergeant, also known as the team sergeant, of Operational Detachment Alpha (ODA) 043. As the senior non-commissioned officer and the most experienced Green Beret on the team, I was finally reaching the pinnacle of my career. That moment was fifteen years in the making.

It was an extraordinary privilege to have the opportunity to lead a team of my own into a combat zone, and it was one that I didn't take lightly. Tensions in the Middle East were escalating quickly, and we were about to be in one of the world's most dangerous cities: Baghdad, Iraq.

We were headed to Camp Apache in Adhamiyah, a Sunni suburb of Baghdad, from January to August. Our mission at Camp Apache was to conduct sensitive special operations and work alongside our local Iraqi partners and surrogates. While these operations were expected to yield valuable intelligence, it's important to note that our primary objective was to create a significant impact through these missions, not just gather intelligence. Our mission statement intentionally remained vague to provide us with a wide range of operational freedom and the ability to achieve tangible results. But ODA 043 needed a complete rebuild, and time was ticking. January 2006 was fast approaching, and I needed to recruit members for the team. I set to work building out the team.

A typical Special Forces team consists of the following individuals:

Detachment commander/team leader (18A): The detachment commander is a captain and has full command authority and responsibility for the detachment.

Assistant detachment commander (180A): The assistant detachment commander is the ODA's second-in-command. They are responsible for long-range planning, intel-operations fusion, and evasion planning. A warrant officer from the Special Forces community's enlisted ranks is selected to fill this position.

Operations sergeant/team sergeant (18Z): The team sergeant is the ODA's senior non-commissioned officer and typically the most experienced Green Beret on the detachment. In Special Forces, the team sergeant operates the team's day-to-day activities.

Assistant operations and intelligence sergeant (18F): The assistant operations and intelligence sergeant is usually a sergeant first class who is trained in advanced special operations techniques, including target analysis and intelligence collection and processing.

Two weapons sergeants (18Bs): Weapons sergeants are experts in the employment of US and foreign weapons systems, including small arms, mortars, air defense systems, and antitank weapons. Weapons sergeants also employ conventional and unconventional tactics and techniques as tactical mission leaders. They assist the team sergeant in the preparation of training and operational plans.

Two engineer sergeants (18Cs): Engineer sergeants plan, supervise, and perform all aspects of combat engineering and light construction. Their knowledge of construction techniques includes expertise in creating buildings and field fortifications. They are also highly skilled in all areas of demolitions, including land mine warfare and constructing and using improvised munitions.

Two medical sergeants (18Ds): Medical sergeants are well-versed in many different areas of human and animal physiology. They specialize in trauma management, infectious diseases, cardiac life support, and surgical procedures. They can also perform basic veterinary medicine. Medical sergeants provide emergency, routine, and long-term medical care for their teams, allied members, and host nation personnel. They train, advise, and direct the detachment's routine, emergency, and preventive medical care. They can also establish field medical facilities to support detachment operations.

Two communications sergeants (18Es): Communications sergeants are the ODA's link to the rest of the world. They are experts in sending and receiving critical communications to the ODA's command and control elements. Communications sergeants are familiar with cryptographic systems, burst outstation systems, antenna theory, radio wave propagation, and common radios found throughout the army. Communications sergeants install, operate, and maintain FM, AM, HF, VHR, UHF, and SHF communications in voice and burst radio networks. They advise the detachment commander on all communications matters.

After much begging, borrowing, and stealing, ODA 043 took shape as follows:

Captain Mark Douglas, the detachment commander/team leader (18A): Mark was a seasoned veteran, having previously served as our company executive officer in Baqubah, Iraq from 2004 to 2005. His calm demeanor and easygoing attitude made him widely liked and respected among the team. Mark possessed a unique ability to seamlessly balance the responsibilities of an officer while still maintaining a strong camaraderie with his teammates. His intelligence and sharp wit served as an undeniable reminder that there was more to him than met the eye. Mark's understanding of team dynamics and his comfortable reliance on me to handle the day-to-day training and operations made us a strong duo.

Warrant Officer Randy Brighton, the assistant detachment commander (180A): With an extensive background as an 18D and a wealth of Special Forces and combat experience, Randy brought invaluable expertise to our team. His meticulous nature and exceptional organizational skills were evident in his advanced special operations reporting, which was second to none. I knew that Randy's attention to detail and ability to maintain a structured approach to our missions would make him an indispensable asset to our team.

Sergeant First Class Travis Dupoint, the assistant operations and intelligence sergeant (18F): Travis was a highly experienced operator, possessing both recent combat experience and strong leadership skills. His level of expertise made him one of the most experienced operators on the team aside from myself. Notably, Travis was a graduate of Ranger School and had successfully completed various advanced Special Forces training courses. We had previously served together on ODA 041 in Iraq from 2004–2005, fostering a sense of trust and understanding between us as we prepared for the 2006 rotation.

Staff Sergeants Luke Roberts, Aaron Gallagher, and Dave Roten, the weapons sergeants (18Bs): We had a unique team structure with three weapons sergeants, which I knew would enhance our team's capabilities. Luke brought a wealth of experience to the team. I had the pleasure of serving with Luke on ODA 041 in Iraq from 2004 to 2005, where his young, sharp, and capable nature was evident. He was an obvious choice for our team.

Aaron boasted an impressive background serving in the Eighty-Second Airborne before transitioning to Special Forces. Despite his sunny California origins, Aaron embodied a striking balance between California cool and a gritty warrior spirit. Aaron had a quick wit and sharp intelligence. What's more, he was a smooth talker, a charm that made him a hit with the ladies. I had the honor of serving with Aaron on ODA 041 in Iraq as well, and his battle-tested nature earned him the respect of our entire team. His valorous actions in a direct-fire engagement with an al-Qaeda training camp in Diyala province earned him the Bronze Star Medal with valor. The operation resulted in significant casualties among the enemy forces, but unfortunately, our partner force from the 278th Regimental Combat Team suffered two killed in action (KIA) casualties of its own. Aaron's solid reputation and respected status within our community was well-deserved. I was happy to have him by my side.

Dave Roten was another weapons sergeant who possessed striking confidence and was incredibly naturally talented, which made up for the fact that he didn't have any combat experience. Together, Luke, Aaron, and Dave shaped up to be a strong trio of weapons sergeants who were equipped to handle any challenges that came our way.

Sergeant First Class Rick Townsen and Staff Sergeant Ryan Land, the engineer sergeants (18Cs): I knew that Rick's extensive Special Forces experience, coupled with his service in the Balkans, would make him an invaluable asset to our team. Despite being the oldest member due to a break in service, he served as a remarkable role model for the younger guys on the team. I knew his guidance and expertise would prove highly valuable in the dangerous environment we were stepping into.

Ryan, although a new addition to the team, carried himself with the confidence and wisdom of a seasoned veteran. Hailing from Texas, he embodied strong physical fitness, intelligence, and talent across the spectrum of Special Forces tasks. Ryan's capabilities were evident to me when we attended a pre-deployment driver's training course in Melbourne, Florida, where he showcased his exceptional skills behind the wheel. His unflappable nature under pressure, proficiency with a pistol and rifle, and overall persona made him an instant favorite among the team. Recognizing the importance of having a skilled driver for our impending combat deployment in and around Baghdad, I made the decision that Ryan would serve as my primary driver.

Sergeant First Class Brian Rainwater and Staff Sergeant Daniel "Diablo" Allen, the medical sergeants (18Ds): Brian, also hailing from Texas, was the epitome of a redheaded country boy. With a soft-spoken Texan accent and an unassuming demeanor, Brian had a knack for luring people into underestimating him. Anyone who made that mistake quickly discovered just how wrong they were. Brian was exceptionally competent, stemming from a solid background in the regular army before joining the Special Forces. Despite his lean physical stature, weighing in at 125 pounds soaking wet, Brian was a force to be reckoned with, especially while manning the .50-caliber machine gun.

Staff Sergeant Daniel "Diablo" Allen was born in a small West Texas town and had an unconventional path to the military—he took a nice detour as a professional bull rider before joining the regular army and Special Forces. In addition to his impeccable skillset as an operator, Diablo had a particular affinity for high-quality cigars and .45-caliber pistols. He proved his worth during our pre-deployment driver's training and at the shooting course in Arizona. Diablo's reliability was quickly evident, and I knew from the start that I could count on him without hesitation.

As our medical sergeants, Brian and Diablo brought their distinct personalities and expertise to the team. Their combined skill sets and reliable nature were invaluable not only in providing medical support but also in fostering a sense of trust and camaraderie within the unit.

Sergeant First Class Bobby David and Staff Sergeant Russell "Russ" Hiatt, the communications sergeants (18Es): Although new to the Special Forces, Bobby brought with him several years of valuable experience, including combat experience, from his time in the regular army. His graduation from Ranger School showcased his dedication and mastery of small unit tactics. Bobby was also proficient with all the various communication systems that our team would be utilizing. I knew that Bobby would be a reliable asset when it came to maintaining effective communication channels within our unit.

Russ, hailing from Nyssa, Oregon, served several years in the regular army before joining the Special Forces. Despite being new to the Special Forces, Russ displayed an eagerness to learn, a strong work ethic, and an overall positive attitude. That made him a rock star in my book. His ability to connect and get along with everyone on the team was remarkable, and I, too, immediately found myself taking a liking to Russ.

All in all, I had a solid team . . . on paper. But it was up to me to get the guys ready to perform on the dangerous and violent streets of Baghdad, where every decision could potentially be a matter of life and death. To reach the level of unity and competency we'd need to execute well, I knew we were going to have to work our asses off and embrace the grind. My team was young and inexperienced, but what we lacked in age and experience, we were ready to make up for in relentless execution and an extreme work ethic. We were hungry and ready to go the extra mile to excel.

In addition to the driver's training and shooting school that we all attended, I continuously trained the guys on a variety of contingencies that could potentially arise. The only ways to create a cohesive team were consistent practice, communication, and training. No way to cut corners, no way to save time—you just had to put in the work.

To spark a sense of unity and test our level of mental preparedness, I arranged a team exercise that consisted of a single task: climbing Pikes Peak, the highest summit in the southern Front Range of the Rocky Mountains, coming in at 14,115 feet. It was a grueling hike, but I could feel a spark of camaraderie in the team as we headed back to base that night. We had a long way to go, but it was a good start.

My vision for the team in Baghdad was to D-O-M-I-N-A-T-E. I wanted us to go on the offensive and take the fight to the enemy rather than sit back, play defense, and react. We spent many afternoons training while the other teams in the company and battalion took the afternoon off. I wanted the guys to be proficient in tactical operations, cultural awareness, and technical competency, as well as adaptable to Baghdad's dynamic and unforgiving environment. I knew this would enhance our ability to effectively accomplish highly complex and dangerous missions while minimizing risk. If I could lead the guys to accomplish this mission and get them back home safely to see their families again, I would count it as a success.

In the fall of 2005, as I geared up for our departure, I arranged a special trip to New York City with my two kids, Britney and Darrell

"D" Utt II (or "Lil D"). I spared no expense. We secured the best seats at all the hit Broadway shows, visited all the major sites, and savored all the culinary delights New York had to offer. While they were young and simply thrilled to experience the Big Apple, I cherished every moment we shared before my departure. The truth is, I wanted them to remember our time together as happy, safe, and connected in case I didn't have the chance to hug them again. It was a hard reality to face, but there was no way around the truth that I might not have the chance to watch them grow up. I didn't admit to anyone the reason behind my big, lavish trip, but inside, I knew. Watching their joy-filled, innocent faces parade through the streets of New York made me wish the trip would never end.

When I hugged them goodbye, my heart ached. I took a deep breath and shut out all the thoughts and feelings rising inside of me. As the team sergeant, I had a profound sense of responsibility and obligation towards the Special Forces regiment, my men, and their wives and families. I recognized the weight of this burden from the very beginning, and I never took it lightly. It was my responsibility to ensure that my men were thoroughly trained and fully prepared for the challenges of combat so that we could successfully execute our mission. I was determined to provide them with every advantage and opportunity to succeed. If I had to look a young wife in the eyes and explain why and how her husband was KIA, it damn sure wasn't going to be because he wasn't trained, prepared, or ready for the fight.

By the end of December 2005, the ODA 043 rebuild was complete. When January 2006 rolled around, I knew in my heart of hearts that I was ready for Baghdad. I'd been preparing for that moment for fifteen years. Even more important, I knew that ODA 043 was ready for Baghdad.

As it turns out, Baghdad was ready for us too.

CHAPTER 2

AN UNFORGIVING BUSINESS

January 2006

It was the second time the young private in front of me had wiped his forehead. There was no visible sweat on his face, at least not that I could see from my seat just a few feet away. His face was clean, almost shiny, and round with youth. Hair buzzed to the scalp, uniform immaculate. The kid shifted his feet across the blue airport carpet. He was anxious. Although the expression on his face was calm enough, the signs were there . . . the fidgeting, the hand on the forehead, the bright eyes. That calm expression he wore, the game face that probably got him through basic training with a reputation as being a tough guy, was rehearsed.

First timer.

There was a flicker of recognition in his eyes when he looked at me. *Yep, we're playing for the same team.* We'd both be on an international flight soon enough. Both headed to fight the same war. He stared for a second and then promptly turned away.

"Special Forces?" Curiosity had gotten the better of him in a matter of sixty seconds. The question was loud enough for everyone in the airport waiting area to hear.

"Yup," I nodded.

He waited expectantly for me to continue, but I didn't. I could see the pictures playing behind his eyes, images created by the movies he'd seen about my particular line of work.

"What's it like?" he asked. He was hungry for a good story, food for his imagination, for some proof that it did exist—the action that we had all trained for.

"Honestly? Just a lot of paperwork."

He laughed and didn't ask any more questions. We both knew there was much more to say and no time to say it.

"Good luck," I said, nodding at the kid as I headed to catch my flight. But the kid's boyish face lingered in my mind as I walked away. There was something about that look of hunger, excitement, and innocence in the eyes of young soldiers that always gave me mixed feelings. They were so curious, so *eager*.

Be careful what you wish for, Young Gun.

I knew all too well that war was not what the kid imagined it to be. It is an unforgiving business, one that offers no second chances, no buffer for the cold, hard realities of life, and no mercy for the young and innocent. He would find out soon enough.

Less than eighteen hours later, I found myself strapped down beside the rest of the team, preparing for a corkscrew landing in Baghdad after the international commercial flight was over. At eighteen thousand feet, still safely beyond the range of weapons, the pilot banked sharply and began our descent toward the runway in a slow, tight circle. I wondered if the kid would manage to keep his lunch down when it was his turn.

Once on the ground in Baghdad, we were immediately transported to the Radwaniyah Presidential Complex (RPC), a palace that had functioned as a presidential resort for the late Iraqi president Saddam Hussein before it was taken over by coalition forces during the 2003 invasion. The sun was setting as we arrived at the palace, casting a golden glow over the light-colored stone. I grinned at the sight of American boots scuffing across the same floors that used to glisten in honor of King Hussein. *One down and a lot more to go.*

Inside the RPC, the feeling was electric. A hum of voices echoed through the halls, interrupted by bouts of raucous laughter. Dirty jokes seemed to be the nervous soldiers' favorite way to blow off a little steam. I didn't engage. I wasn't interested in listening to them swap combat stories from previous deployments, the *whose-dick-is-bigger* contest, which never seemed to end. We lived for these stories. We *needed* these stories. We needed the reminder that all the years of training and preparation that we'd put ourselves through had real-life applications.

In the past, I might have been right in the middle of the circle, telling a few stories of my own. The young guys who'd never seen real combat would lean in a little closer, their eyes bright with hunger. They liked hanging around guys like me who had been to *the other side*. Guys who'd been in the game long enough to see behind the curtain. They clawed into those stories like fresh meat and devoured them.

But I wasn't interested in storytelling that night. I had lived on the sustenance of my stories for long enough. I'd told them a thousand times; I'd chewed them to the bone. And it no longer satisfied me. I'd spent years systematically and painstakingly preparing the mission ahead, and I was ready for some action. *I was hungry.*

My first rotation had started with a bang, with bullets flying in that dramatic entrance we called Operation Ugly Baby. But the deployment that followed was just one anticlimactic event after another. I finally had the opportunity I'd waited and trained for as well as an all-star cast of team members ready to dominate. While I'd served with many experienced and highly skilled teams in the past, this one was different. There was a brotherhood bond that formed between us instantly, a sense of unity that cannot be forced or manufactured. Anyone who's had the great fortune of experiencing this kind of connection with comrades in arms knows exactly what I'm talking about and should consider themselves lucky. I was one of the lucky few.

We were scheduled to have a few days of in-processing before linking up with the outgoing team from the Fifth Special Forces Group (Airborne) (also known as the Fifth Group) and settling into Camp

Apache, our new home for the next eight months. Those days should have gone by in a flash, should have been the forgettable timeline in stories I would collect and later tell—the part you skip to get to the good stuff. But not in my case.

Within twenty-four hours of being on the ground, I caught wind of several nasty rumors sweeping through the ranks of the Special Forces teams. It seemed that my team, ODA 043, was at the center of that gossip storm. News had circulated that ODA 043 was a "party team"—one that was only interested in booze and partying. The tales spread like wildfire, and the rumor mill churned with the intensity of a high school drama. *Mean Girls* doesn't hold a candle to Special Forces Guys. Even the toughest soldiers can't seem to resist a juicy rumor. I was angry. And that's putting it mildly.

If there had been even a *little* bit of merit to these stories, I would have held my head high and worn the reputation like a badge of honor. But there wasn't a shred of truth to it. Our team was straight. We were well-trained, focused, and ready to execute. I knew all too well that if we lost the respect of leadership, it would be a major setback and potentially jeopardize the success of our mission.

Suddenly, the combat rotation we had all anticipated was morphing into a battle of perception and truth. If this rumor continued to spread, we would have a long uphill battle ahead of us. No one likes the party boys when you're supposed to be fighting a war. If the rumor continued, we might even be in danger of getting benched. This gossip was a threat that had to be eliminated or else we might not be able to do what we came to do. As the team sergeant, it was my responsibility to protect my team, and that meant hunting down exactly where these nasty rumors had gotten started. But for the life of me, I couldn't understand where and how such rumors had come from when we hadn't even been in-country for more than a day. But it didn't take long for me to put the pieces together.

A few months before our team deployed, I decided to send Travis, one of our senior and experienced operators, ahead of us to do the pre-deployment site survey (PDSS). PDSS is invaluable for information collecting and gathering atmospherics on a location before deployment. Travis seemed like the perfect choice at the time. Not only was he one of the more experienced, senior operators on the team, but he was also going through a nasty divorce. The military lifestyle wasn't always conducive to long, thriving relationships, and we all felt bad for the ones among us who were weathering bad breakups or divorces. I felt sorry for the guy, and I saw an opportunity to help a brother out while he was down. By sending Travis ahead of us to conduct the PDSS, he would get two months of hostile fire pay and combat zone tax exclusion. Not bad when you're getting cleaned out financially by a rough divorce. But instead of putting his head down and getting the job done, he had entertained himself by telling stories about our team—giving us a reputation that preceded our arrival in the worst way. He had made quite an impression on the Fifth Group team. *What a jackass.*

Stupid me for trusting Travis. *Stupid me* for trying to take care of the guy with a little extra pay and time away from his rocky divorce. The consequences of the rumor for my team weighed heavily on me. I wasn't about to risk getting benched due to his careless actions. Travis was single-handedly sinking our team's reputation before we even arrived at Camp Apache and started combat operations. It was time to confront the situation head-on.

Every time I heard whispers or caught side-eye glances from other teams, I hit it head-on. I reassured everyone that we were a serious team, that we were hungry and ready for this mission. I spoke up for my team and set the record straight. But it wasn't enough. Within a few days, the Fifth Group team picked us up from RPC to take us to our new home: Camp Apache, located in an area called Adhamiyah.

Immediately, the insinuations and sideways glances started up again. They thought we were a joke. I was livid. That's when I went into full damage control mode. It was clear to me that we had a lot to prove before we were going to be taken seriously. "Show 'em exactly what we're made of and don't take shit from anyone," I told my guys.

But the proof was irrefutable: Travis was a cancer. His thoughtless short-sightedness had already cost him my loyalty and the loyalty of everyone on the team. We were warriors, and we took the job very seriously. Our reputation was everything. A man like him could not be trusted—not anymore, at least.

I called our team leader, company commander, and the company sergeant major to discuss the situation. They both confirmed my gut feeling about what I had to do next.

I made my plan. I would pull Travis aside the first chance I got and tell him that he was out and would not be allowed to step foot in Camp Apache. He would be assigned to the battalion in an administrative role, and our team would survive just fine without him.

I shared my plan with the team sergeant from the outgoing Fifth Group team. Word spread fast. Suddenly, we weren't known as the party boys. We were ruthless, serious, and ready to mow down anything in our sights. The fact that someone was getting fired over the misinformation that had spread was enough to get everyone's attention. It immediately eliminated any remaining tension between our two teams. Crisis, it seemed, had been averted. I couldn't have been more wrong.

The next morning, we convoyed to RPC with a combined Fifth and Tenth Group team. The plan was to drop off a few members of Fifth Group so they could redeploy back to Fort Campbell, Kentucky, and pick up the incoming members of ODA 043. I'd also have the opportunity to speak with Travis and let him know that he wouldn't be joining us at Camp Apache. But five minutes before arriving at RPC, I received a call from the team sergeant of the Fifth Group team.

"I need to let you know that there is a CYZ-10 that's gone missing. We looked everywhere but couldn't find it. When you get a chance, please check the gun trucks."

"Roger that."

The CYZ-10 is a cutting-edge, portable data transfer device specifically designed for the distribution of cryptographic keys and other crucial data between cryptographic devices and secure communication equipment. In simple terms, it is the secret little black box that holds the key for encrypting all radios. Losing any type of crypto device is unforgivable, but losing the key to it pretty much guarantees that someone is going to lose their job. *Sucks to be Fifth Group,* I thought. *Heads are gonna roll for this shit.*

I promised that our group would be on the lookout for it and then hung up the phone. My mind was still preoccupied with our preparations and rehearsing my "You're fired" speech for Travis, who I would pick up along with the rest of the team in a matter of minutes. I spent a few minutes hastily searching through the vehicles for the missing CYZ-10 but didn't find it. Then my cell phone rang again. This time, it was Bobby, my 18E who had loaded the crypto into our vehicles earlier that morning. His words tumbled out without any sense—something about the CYZ-10. I could hear the stress in his voice as I tried to make sense of what he was saying.

"Dude, calm down," I said. "Losing the CYZ-10 is Fifth Group's problem, not ours."

Pause. Silence. Then the truth.

"D, it's our CYZ-10. Our CYZ-10 is the one that's missing."

Fuck. So *we* were the idiots trying to locate the whereabouts of *our* CYZ-10. Here I was on the verge of firing one of the most highly skilled and experienced operators on our team who had tarnished our reputation, and now our CYZ-10 was missing. The hits just kept coming. I instructed Bobby to continue searching within Camp Apache while I scoured the area surrounding the vehicles. I didn't find a damn thing. *It's gotta turn up somewhere.*

Our four gun trucks arrived at the temporary tents that housed outgoing and incoming Special Forces teams. When our vehicles pulled up, the guys grabbed their gear and began loading it onto the waiting vehicles while I looked for Travis. It didn't take long to find him.

Travis was slowly walking around with a long asp in one hand, smacking the other palm over and over and over again. I called his name and motioned him toward me. He approached and squared his shoulders to mine. We were both fully geared up, armed from head to toe with enough weaponry to do some real damage. We just stood there for a while, eye to eye, without saying a word. He never stopped hitting his hand with that asp.

I wasted no time getting to the point. Without a trace of emotion, I informed Travis that he wouldn't be joining us at Camp Apache but instead staying at RPC and working on the battalion staff in an administrative role. Travis shouted after me as I walked off the moment my rehearsed speech had finished. I knew he was having a tough year, and my decision to take him off the team just made it worse. But at that moment, I didn't care. I wasn't here to make people like me or feel comfortable. I was here to fight a war. He was furious, but I didn't give a damn. First Sergeant Rego's words came back to me: "If you plan on being a good leader, you need to have the ability to look your own mom right in the eyes and say, 'Mom, I love you, but you're fuckin' fired!'" I'd take firing Travis with an asp any day than going toe-to-toe with my mom.

I directed Ryan Land, the junior engineer, to help Travis move all his gear and equipment up the hill to RPC. *Case closed.* The eyes of the younger team members were wide. They were just starting to understand that war is an unforgiving business. *Nobody is safe.*

After Travis and Ryan departed, I clutched my phone and steeled myself. The next phone call was not going to be easy. I needed to inform company leadership that I had not only benched one of my guys but was now dealing with a new issue—a missing CYZ-10. Dread filled me as I waited to dial the number. I would have rather traversed the depths of Hades than endure another moment grappling with the situation. But there was no way around it. Bad news doesn't get better with time, especially in the military.

I dialed the number and took a deep breath.

As the words rolled off my tongue, a sinking realization settled in. The next guy dropped off at RPC to work on the staff in an administrative role was probably going to be me. Having to bench a loudmouth from the team was one thing; losing a precious piece of equipment that was integral to the security of the entire group was another. When I ended the call, fury surged through me. After a few hours, we departed for Camp Apache.

I wasted no time in finding Bobby. "How the fuck could you lose the CYZ-10? You just used the damn thing to load crypto into the radios in the truck!"

Bobby remained silent with his head down and shoulders slumped. It was clear that Bobby didn't need a talk from me. He was already more than a little rattled. We needed solutions, not finger-pointing and ass-chewing. I walked away. With a few minutes to think, I formed two hypotheses.

Hypothesis number 1: Bobby failed to secure the CYZ-10 properly after loading the vehicle radios. He inadvertently left it on top of one of the vehicles (possibly on the bumper) or in some other unnoticed location, and the CYZ-10 eventually fell off outside Camp Apache on the road.

Hypothesis number 2: The local Iraqi guard force that was assigned to our unit saw a target of opportunity to steal the CYZ-10 and sell it for a handsome fee to Shia insurgents.

In any case, immediate action had to be taken. As with any circumstance that involves any type of missing crypto devices, we'd need to "dump" the loaded crypto and get a new fill. That meant that everyone, and I mean *everyone*, would know about my team's mighty fuckup. We showed up with the reputation of party boys and seemed to be proving that theory in action by losing a crucial piece of equipment. I was humiliated as the call went out for reloading the crypto because of a security breach from our team. I could only imagine the other Special Forces teams' reactions, how they must have cursed our team under their breaths.

I'd spent years honing my skills, meticulously preparing, and patiently climbing the ranks to get here. Every painstaking step I had taken since signing up for basic training had been building up to this very moment. This was supposed to be *my time*. My time to show what I was capable of, my time to lead. But it seemed that the opportunity was slipping through my fingers.

First day here and I'm about to get benched.

An unforgiving business indeed.

CHAPTER 3

CAMP APACHE

Camp Apache, our home for the next eight months, was situated in northeastern Baghdad in an area called Adhamiyah, one of the largest Sunni strongholds in the city. It was nestled alongside the Tigris River smack-dab in the middle of the Red Zone—the one place you *shouldn't* go and exactly where we needed to be. The term "camp" should not be confused with the much larger forward operating base (FOB) where many American soldiers spent their Baghdad deployment. The FOB offered modern conveniences like big chain fast-food joints and trendy coffee shops, but Camp Apache most certainly did not. Years later, one of the FOB guys would ask me if I learned how to fly fish during my deployment. It turns out free flyfishing lessons were just one of the many pastimes and entertainment offerings on the FOB. Not in our neck of the woods.

I'd been poring over as much intel as I could get my hands on about our location, but nothing was quite like seeing it for the first time. Sand-colored stone formed an almost palace-like structure, ornate remnants of the royalty that once walked the halls. It wasn't hard to imagine its opulence back in its glory days. Ornate decorations, chairs, and unused tables were still stacked in the corners of several rooms, a haunting reminder of how much had changed in a short period. Heavy concrete walls topped with razor wire, along with a series of layered barriers, encircled the perimeter—a testament to exactly what kind of danger lay beyond the walls. Gunfire, rocket attacks, and explosions had become a dissonant soundtrack echoing through the streets of Adhamiyah around the clock. We didn't say much as we walked. It wasn't fear we felt so much as respect for the nature of our surroundings.

Upon arriving, a man stepped forward and introduced himself as Hussein. He appeared to be in his early thirties, well-built with piercing blue eyes. He would serve as our primary in-country contact available to arrange goods, services, and anything else we might need. He would also serve as a bridge between our team and the local Iraqi family assigned to our camp for the duration of the deployment. They were responsible for cooking, cleaning, supplies, and maintenance around the camp. Both Hussein and the Iraqi family had worked with multiple teams before ours at Camp Apache. He was all smiles and full of polite generosity. Those blue eyes nearly drilled a hole into my soul as he shook my hand for the first time. Despite making an exceptional first impression, intuition and experience told me I could only trust Hussein so much. *Trust, but verify.*

For the first few hours after arrival, we worked on unloading our gear and settling in while assessing the camp's security, vulnerabilities, and weaknesses. From blind spots in the surveillance system to potential breaches in the perimeter, we examined every potential threat meticulously. I also studied both Hussein and the local family who would be living with us for the duration of the deployment. The local family had three daughters and one nephew—a tall, good-looking kid barely in his twenties named Abdul. He was kind and respectful, his eyes betraying a sort of young innocence that I feared would vanish soon. In another life, he might have been thinking about getting to his university classes on time instead of working at a military camp. I liked the entire family immediately but decided to take the same approach with them as I was taking with Hussein. *Trust, but verify.*

I found myself in a delicate situation—trying to strike a balance between our need for protection and provision by the locals while simultaneously acknowledging the potential risks that came with it. A new concern was forming in my mind, one that possessed a greater threat than any surveillance system blind spot—the possibility of an insider threat. The thought brought an unsettling sense of uncertainty. We'd need to keep a close eye on them. Could the Iraqi guards who protected the camp and the Iraqi family responsible for logistics and day-to-day operations be potential security threats?

A weight of responsibility tugged at my conscience. I knew creating allies was necessary to feed us intel and build rapport between the American military and the locals. On the other hand, I was keenly aware of the fact that any one of them could also be a double agent feeding intel about *us* to the highest bidder. It was not uncommon. I had seen it happen with my own two eyes while in Diyala province the previous year. While I recognized the importance of maintaining trust and rapport with the local workforce, the nagging doubt persisted. *Were they loyal, or did they have ulterior motives for working with us? With the right incentive, would they betray us?* There was nothing to do but wait and see. This was the nature of the game. You couldn't let fear paralyze you or you'd never get anything done.

Just as expected, I received word that our group commander, Colonel Ken Tovo, would be visiting Camp Apache that day. My stomach clenched into a knot. I knew exactly why he was coming. He was deciding whether I would be staying at Camp Apache or heading straight for desk duty. There was nothing I could do but hope for the best.

When Colonel Tovo arrived, he asked to speak with me privately. I nodded with a pit in my stomach. There were two ways that the conversation could go. I could point my finger and blame Bobby for his negligence and incompetence, making him the sacrificial lamb, and hope the blame didn't come back on my shoulders. Or I could man up and fucking own it. I could take responsibility for it as the team sergeant and hold myself accountable. I knew that a good leader should take responsibility for mistakes and give credit for successes back to the team. A good leader is in the front in a time of absolute crisis and in the back when a victory celebration occurs. I *wanted* to be that kind of leader. I *agreed* with being that kind of leader. Coach Thornburg taught me that; Scott Breasseale reinforced it. But when it's your career on the line and you're faced with losing something you've worked years for, taking one for the team is a lot easier said than done. This was my test, and it wasn't an easy one. But I knew what I needed to do.

"Sir, I take full responsibility for the lost CYZ-10. There are no excuses. I can assure you that this will never happen again, sir," I asserted.

Colonel Tovo didn't say much. He was a pragmatic leader. He said he understood and talked to several other team members. He was clearly inquisitive and perceptive, observing the team's dynamics and interactions.

The local Iraqi family prepared a large meal that night as the sun set. I only ate a small portion; the spices were too strong for my taste and my appetite was low. A hundred different thoughts passed through my mind, none of them pleasant. Every interaction during Colonel Tovo's short visit was positive, but it was still uncertain what the outcome would be. Just before leaving, he set my mind at ease. He, along with Lieutenant Colonel Sean Swindell, would allow me to remain the team sergeant of ODA 043.

"Thank you, sir. I won't let you down. You will not regret this decision."

After he left, I took a deep breath. I called everyone outside the equipment room as darkness blanketed our first night. It had been a long day. When the team formed a circle around me, I dropped a thick sledgehammer onto the ground in front of my feet. The team was dead silent. I had everyone's attention.

"Tonight, we introduce the Hard Hitter Award. Every week, we'll each nominate a team member for an extraordinary performance and take a vote. Whoever wins will take ownership of this sledgehammer for seven days. During that time, he can do whatever he wants with it—engrave quotes, attach a coin, paint it, or carve it. You can sleep with the goddamn thing; I don't give a fuck. Once our time here is done, I'll tally the votes from all the weeks combined, and we'll have our own private ceremony to acknowledge the winner. The Hard Hitter Award will find a permanent home with one deserving team member. Anyone, except for leadership, can be nominated for positive actions displayed in any capacity, whether it's acts of bravery under enemy fire, commitment to a challenging job, or a winning attitude. And we start now."

Grunts of approval and congratulatory slaps circulated among the team. But I wasn't finished. "We've trained for this, guys. We're built for this. But we can't afford to make another mistake."

I lifted the sledgehammer and slammed it against my palm. Silence fell over the group again. "It's time to show everyone what we're fucking made of."

CHAPTER 4

HONEY TRAPPIN'

February 18, 2006

Once we were comfortably settled into Camp Apache, we started prioritizing our time, resources, and targeting efforts. We also received a gift—at least, that's how we liked to think of it. The gift was a target intelligence packet (TIP) for an individual of interest who lived in Sadr City. A TIP typically includes detailed information about a target, such as their location, description, picture(s), associates, phone number(s), and any other relevant data. It also includes the structural layout of their residence and what security measures they've employed, their acts against the US military, and other information as to why the individual is a target. All the information in the TIP was linked to a man who went by the name of Omar.

The packet was a nice little goodbye present from Fifth Group as they prepared to board their plane back to the United States. They'd spent the entire rotation trying to catch Omar—dead or alive—but hadn't been successful. They were passing the baton to us. Omar was a known mercenary in the area. He had not only orchestrated attacks on the American military but also inflicted egregious violence against countless innocent local people. But bringing him in was not going to be an easy task. First of all, he was a powerful man with eyes and ears all over the city, keeping him one step ahead at all times. The second issue was his location: Sadr City.

Back in the 1980s, the district was known as "Saddam City." Throughout the decade, the area gained notoriety as a hub for communist organizing and for its poverty. Following Saddam Hussein's ousting in April 2003, an unofficial renaming occurred, with the district unofficially adopting the name "Sadr City" in honor of the late Shiite leader Mohammad-Sadiq al-Sadr. His son, Muqtada al-Sadr, created and formed the Mahdi Army in June 2003. The Mahdi Army rose to international prominence in 2004 when it spearheaded the first major armed confrontation against US forces in Iraq from the Shia community. This uprising originated from the ban of al-Sadr's newspaper and his subsequent attempted arrest. The following years were a constant fight between US forces and the heavily armed Mahdi Army. It was a difficult area to operate within unless you had a sizable force. Even then, there was a good chance that you were probably going to find yourself eating multiple improvised explosive devices (IEDs) on the way in and out of Sadr City.

In just a few short weeks since our arrival, we had already seen mangled bodies in the street and received reports about numerous violent incidents just inside Sadr City, not far from Camp Apache. I knew that inside Sadr City, it would be nearly impossible to catch Omar. It was a violent place with complicated streets and alleys like a spiderweb.

We had a target with American blood on his hands. But if we had any hope of catching him, we'd need to lure him out of the city. The question was how. In front of me were a name, phone number, and address for a man with the reputation of having evaded an entire Special Forces team for months. Bringing him in would undoubtedly save countless lives. It would also be just the win we needed to prove ourselves after getting a rough start. For hours after reviewing the TIP, I paced the dining room where we had a whiteboard conveniently placed for strategizing. And then the words began to play in my mind.

Honey trappin' and turkey huntin' . . . Fucking honey trappin' and turkey huntin'!

An idea was forming in my head, and it was just ludicrous enough that it might just be brilliant.

First came the honeypot, a deceptive technique used by law enforcement and intelligence agencies to attract an adversary by luring them into a trap. I remembered a story I once heard back in Washington, DC, about how law enforcement had sent out free Washington Redskins football tickets to a whole roster of wanted criminals. When they showed up for the game thinking it was their lucky day, *snap*—on went the cuffs. It was one of the oldest tricks in the book.

Then came the turkeys. I had accompanied my dad on numerous turkey hunts when I was younger, but I never had any luck nabbing one. Turkeys, by nature, are paranoid as hell, and with those eyes and small heads, they damn near have 360-degree vision and the instincts to match it. Sure, I was close to getting one once or twice, but never bagged it. Maybe that's because turkey hunting is more of a seduction than anything. It goes like this: A male turkey comes walking slowly through the woods, proudly flaunting his array of feathers. He struts confidently, hoping to attract a bit of amorous attention from the fairer fowl. The dude's bringing his A game. But behind a tree waits a hunter, who has stepped onto this romantic scene with a plan to use the ancient art of turkey courtship to his advantage. A mating call reverberates through the forest, and the male turkey suddenly snaps to attention. *The female can't be far,* he thinks. The male turkey follows the sound instinctually. The mating sound continues, a breathy purr that tickles his eardrums and sends shivers down the turkey's spine. But as the spellbound gobbler approaches, ready for a little hanky-panky, the hunter remains hidden behind his camouflage. Under the canopy of nature's embrace, the hunter has now been able to lock his sites on the bewitched turkey. And then, with steady hands and sharp aim, the hunter takes the shot.

BAM.

Hunter: 1

Horny turkey: 0

Honey trappin' and turkey huntin'. Suddenly, I knew exactly how I planned to catch Omar. You can't imagine the look of surprise that registered on my men's faces as I outlined my plan. Even still, they didn't hesitate. They were down. It might just be crazy enough to work.

The mission would take place in broad daylight. Our plan was to lure Omar outside Sadr City so we could catch him. *Honey trappin'.* We planned to do this by arranging a little mating call of our own. *Turkey huntin'.* That's where the challenge came in. We weren't exactly sure what kind of hot and heavy moves they were doing in the Sadr City dating scene, but we formed a plan that we thought might just work. A woman would call Omar by "accident." As soon as he answered his cell phone, she would come on strong with a little sexy dirty talk. Then, just as quickly, she would "realize" that she had called the "wrong person" and apologize profusely to Omar. She would claim that she'd meant to call a different man and just happened to dial the wrong number when Omar answered the phone. Depending on how the apology went and if Omar enjoyed the little XXX-rated call, she'd push it a little further: compliment Omar, massage his ego, build rapport, and establish common ground.

Once the initial hook was set, she would continue building upon their initial connection and eventually arrange a face-to-face meeting. At that meeting, Omar would show up expecting to meet with a beautiful, sexy woman in hopes of a long night full of sexual fantasies. Instead, he'd be greeted by vehicles full of sweaty American and Iraqi freedom fighters kitted up and ready to kick ass. *Surprise, motherfucker.*

It was a great plan. There was only one major problem—we needed a woman who knew how to get down and dirty on the phone. My boys weren't exactly going to do the trick. And there was only one person who could arrange it for us. *Hussein.*

"If you need anything, just ask," he'd told us about a thousand times since we arrived.

"Okay, Hussein. We need a sexy female with a sexy voice. Can you get us one of those for temporary use?"

It turned out that ol' Hussein knew just the person who would be perfect for the job—a friend of a friend (or something like that) who was known and trusted. Hussein connected her with our interpreter so she could hear the rough outline of the plan. She would be perfect for making the phone call to Omar and luring him outside the city with the promise of a romantic rendezvous. And this would allow her to make some cash. She would remain in a safe, off-site location for the entire ordeal and use her best powers of seduction over the phone to get him interested enough to attempt to meet up with her. She'd make more money than her typical day rate with a lot less work. We spared no expense for the operation, and Hussein's choice for a female sex worker reflected that. Photos of her circulated; just one look confirmed that she was the perfect choice. She oozed seduction. I could only hope that her pillow talk skills were as effective as her visual appeal. Time would tell.

The last piece of the puzzle was bringing on the right interpreter as our go-between. For this unorthodox and unconventional mission, we selected a man we affectionately referred to as "Pipe Hitter." Pipe Hitter came from the bustling streets of Rabat, Morocco, and had immigrated to America in the mid-1990s with $400 in his wallet and a dream to give back to his newfound country by serving in the military. At Naval Station Great Lakes, young Pipe Hitter was transformed from a boy into a man as he learned the true meaning of camaraderie, honor, and patriotism while serving alongside several high-level teams. Pipe Hitter served with the US Navy SEALs and the Joint Special Operations Command

(JSOC) due to his rare blend of linguistic prowess in Arabic and his heritage. He was the perfect man for the job.

At approximately 3:00 p.m. the next day, it was time to sound the first mating call. We arranged a phone call between the woman and Omar using the number that we had on file. We all waited nervously. *Just keep him on the phone.* Pipe Hitter would keep us abreast of everything that was going down since none of us understood the native tongue. But our plan worried me a bit. A suspicious phone call from a woman looking for someone else could raise a lot of red flags. But at the end of the day, nothing else had worked on this guy. This was our shot, and we were going to take it. The nuts and bolts of the mission and execution were simple, like a basic infantry raid: approach the objective; isolate the objective area; set conditions for the assault element; assault the objective; and move away from the objective area. This was just like that, but with a little Arabic dirty talk, of course. I'd leave the art of seduction up to her—God knows it was never my strong suit.

"Hello?" A man's voice came on the other line after she dialed the phone. It was him.

"I'm alone now, and I can't stop thinking about you. Your hands sliding down my hips, your body pressed into me, your lips on me. I need you; I need you *right now.*" Her velvety voice slid through the air like butter, like rapid-fire foreplay from a minigun.

"Wait, who is this? Who are you trying to call?" He was confused but intrigued.

"I'm so sorry, isn't this Malik?" she breathed.

"No, it isn't," Omar shot back.

"Oh, I'm so embarrassed. I met a man named Malik the other night and told him I'd call. I must have written down his number wrong. He wanted to see me again, but now I have no other way to contact him. I'm so sorry to bother you."

"Well, I'm not him and you have the wrong number."

She paused for a minute.

"What is your name?" he said.

"My name is Amina. Again, I'm very sorry. You must think I'm shameless, calling like this," she breathed.

There was a brief silence on the other end of the phone. "I like a shameless woman." Omar let out a low chuckle. "I know all about shameless women. Doesn't that make you nervous?"

"First of all, I don't get nervous," her voice changed from coy embarrassment to the low, seductive tone of a sexually experienced woman. "And I know a thing or two about men."

There was no pause this time. "Do you, now?" he asked. "What exactly do you know about men?"

"Mmmm," she said softly, as though she had just seen a warm brownie oozing with chocolate. "I suppose I know enough. What men like, what they think about when no one is around, what pleases them."

Again, the voice on the other end of the line grew silent.

And the male freezes as the mating call is sounded.

It was the moment of truth.

"So, what if instead of meeting this *Malik*, you were to meet, let's say . . . me? What would you say to that?"

It was her turn to pause this time. She couldn't appear overly eager. "I suppose if it were just for coffee or maybe a little shopping in a quiet neighborhood outside the city, I'd say yes. Better to meet in a place where no one knows us, you know. In case we want to spend a little *more* time together. Can I call you tomorrow?"

"Anytime," he said.

"We'll talk tomorrow then, *habibi* [my love]," she said and hung up the phone.

The seduction continued for about a week. Several more erotic phone calls took place over several days, and Omar became increasingly interested in the brave-talking woman on the phone. Finally, a meeting time and location were set at a small clothing shop just outside Sadr City. Omar insisted that the rendezvous take place in the middle of the day.

"There will be a lot of people outside shopping, and American forces will be less active," he told her. We belly laughed when we heard that.

The trap was set, and finally it was time to make our move. We were confident that we'd be able to bring him in—whether or not he'd be alive was another question. He was a significant threat, was armed, and had killed Americans in the past. If he went for a weapon and tried to fight his way out, he would die immediately.

And the male begins to walk in the direction of the mating call.

We assembled the "hunting team" the next morning and divided ourselves between multiple vehicles.

Vehicle #1 carried our snipers, including Dave. We decided on a very low-visibility transportation option that we'd gotten Hussein to arrange for us to use for special missions when we needed to keep a low profile. It consisted of a small box truck with a big AC unit at the top. It had a perfect built-in sniper "platform" that we enhanced with ballistic blankets and plenty of storage for various required items. It was a real redneck specialty, all painted and *Macgyver*ed up to the max. We were proud of it. We painted it a different color every month to keep it from getting burned. It made its debut mission sporting a nice bright white color. The box truck would be driven by members of our local Iraqi scouts and parked across from the target location. The Iraqi drivers were dressed as locals. Both Luke and Dave were wearing desert flight suits in the rear of the box truck. Luke and Dave would be able to provide sniper overwatch through the AC unit at the top of the bread truck. If anything went south on or around the target, we'd have concealed sniper support to lay down precision fire immediately.

Vehicle #2 carried a handful of local Iraqi scouts tasked with reconnaissance and security in a civilian vehicle. They were dressed in typical local clothing, not uniforms. They would park adjacent to the small clothing shop to provide coverage of the rear of the building. They were instructed to put on red hats to ensure their safety as soon

Honey Trappin'

as our gun trucks collapsed on the target location. We didn't want to take any chances with someone getting nervous on target and shooting our Iraqi scouts.

Vehicle #3 carried Ryan, Pipe Hitter, and me. Pipe Hitter would be primarily tasked with relaying what was going on between Omar and Amina, as well as assisting with positive identification. Typically, Ryan would have been the first to jump at the chance to be on the sniper team. But Ryan had a little secret—just days before shipping out for deployment, he broke his collarbone in a freak skiing accident. He knew all too well that he'd be benched the moment he reported it and didn't want to risk it. So, what did he do? Nothing. Not a damn thing. He just decided not to lift his right arm for a few weeks and wait for it to fuse again. We all tried to tell him that it might go back together the wrong way, but he didn't care. He'd rather have a crooked collarbone than miss out on the chance to get out there and fight the war he signed up for. So Ryan would drive, and I would serve as the "actions on the objective" guy. I'd be an orchestrator of sorts, tasked with making sure all the pieces were in place and that we executed a successful mission. Our civilian vehicle had tinted windows, which aided tremendously in reducing our signature and profile. Because the operation would be going down in broad daylight, we couldn't be in uniform. With dark hair and a beard, Ryan could pass for a local his age. With pale skin and reddish hair, I didn't stand a chance. Hussein helped us out by swinging by a local clothing shop to arrange civilian clothes.

Vehicles #4–8 carried the Quick Reaction Force (QRF) team and two gun trucks from our team (led by Mark). Three vehicles were from the 101st Airborne Division, including a truck full of Iraqi scouts that were all pre-staged at a secure Iraqi police compound approximately two minutes away. Once the target was identified and confirmed, the QRF would collapse onto the target, and the Iraqi scouts would enter the small clothing shop and detain Omar. We were all set.

Showtime.

I changed into the civilian clothes that Hussein had arranged and exited the compound in a bright, Celtics green, 1980s-era Adidas jacket and a *keffiyeh* (the traditional square scarf worn by the locals) on my head. Within half an hour, our vehicle made the first pass by the target location. We scanned the area but didn't see anything noteworthy. No positive identification. Nothing. Omar clearly wasn't there yet.

Cue Amina. "Are you on your way?" she asked. "I'm waiting for you and can't wait to see you."

We listened as the call went through, Pipe Hitter giving a blow-by-blow account of everything being said.

"Yes, I am very close by," Omar's voice came through loud and clear. "Tell me, what are you wearing?"

"Oh, you want to know, do you?" she said playfully. She was toying with him.

But while she took her time luring him in, we were in an increasingly compromised position. We had already circled the area twice, and it wouldn't take long until people started getting suspicious. Everyone seemed to know everyone in those small neighborhoods. I was keenly aware of the dangerous area we were in. Bodies had been found just a few blocks away, discarded leftovers from a brutal interrogation between the Sunnis and Shiites. It was clear from the appearance of the bodies that a power drill had been used to conduct the interrogation. Flayed flesh and holes in places where holes should never be served as a grim reminder of the type of people we were dealing with.

"Come on, come on, just come out and meet the girl," I pleaded under my breath. I could only hope that Omar woke up extra horny that day.

"I'm wearing a black hijab," she said smoothly. "But it's not what I'm wearing that you should be thinking about; it's what's underneath."

Eight vehicles full of soldiers and operators ready to pounce waited anxiously. Would Omar take the bait?

"I'd like the chance to see what's underneath," his voice was low and dripping with meaning this time.

"Then come and meet me like we planned," she begged in a silky tone. "And maybe I'll let you see for yourself. Or should I describe exactly what's underneath while you're still on the phone?"

"Please tell me, I'm on my way, I promise." He was hooked, and she didn't hold back, describing her body in enough detail to make Hugh Hefner blush.

The mating call is coming through loud and clear.
The hunters are in position and waiting.
The male is expected to come into the open at any minute.

I checked in with the sniper team, but they had no sign of the target. We waited three blocks from the target, scanning the area and searching for any sign of him, but still saw nothing. Two blocks from the target and nothing. One block from the target—still nothing. Suddenly, from the backseat, Pipe Hitter started pointing and said, "That's him! That's him!"

And there he was. Perpendicular to the small clothing shop and out of view of our sniper team, holding a cell phone to his ear and slowly walking around his vehicle while moving small rocks from his path with his right foot, was none other than Omar. He was in his own little world and oblivious to us, probably halfway to an erection at the sound of Amina's voice. I quickly directed Ryan where to park the vehicle and immediately got on the radio to instruct the QRF to collapse the target and give his location.

We were going to have to quickly change our plan since Omar wasn't inside the clothing shop as planned. As soon as I caught sight of the gun trucks approaching him and knew I had some ass (i.e., firepower) behind me, I decided to take him down myself.

The gun trucks floored into their positions, and I didn't waste any time. I flung open the door and broke into a sprint to close the short distance between me and Omar. I wasn't about to let him get away.

Now imagine that you woke up anticipating a romantic rendezvous with a sexy-sounding woman you just met over the phone. You got up and dressed in your best clothes, sprayed on a little cologne, and let yourself indulge in a few wild fantasies about what that brave-talking woman on the phone will be like in bed. Now you're standing on the street, listening to that feminine, velvety voice describe every inch of her naked body. You are already getting aroused by the idea of your hands sliding across those curves she's describing.

And then, a sweaty, 220-pound, middle-aged, redheaded Darrell Utt in an '80s tracksuit the color of a cheap gas-station lime slushie comes barreling toward you with full force. *Surprise, motherfucker.*

It's safe to say that in about a matter of two seconds, all the blood flow that had gathered in his crotch was immediately diverted to his heart as it began to pound in a full-blown, *oh-shit* moment. The poor bastard didn't even have time to draw his weapon as I tackled him at full force and slammed him to the sidewalk. As I disarmed him and pinned him down, Pipe Hitter exited the vehicle and assisted in zip-tying his hands and securing him. Ryan jumped out as soon as the truck was parked and made sure that the other guys standing on the street didn't try anything stupid.

As we loaded the target into the back of the vehicle, team morale could not have been higher. We'd been able to bring in the target that other teams had spent years trying to catch, and we'd done it in broad daylight. The story spread like wildfire among the other teams. We were still underdogs but now had one of the first high-visibility, successful operations in Baghdad to start the rotation. Omar proved to be incredibly valuable, providing far more intel than we could have ever hoped.

We laughed all night about the ordeal as we gathered in the courtyard back at Camp Apache. Poor Omar thought he was going to get laid and instead got laid the fuck out on the sidewalk.

"Today was a good day," I said as I sat back and watched the sky turn from blue to deep orange, still proudly sporting my green tracksuit.

"Any day is a good day when you're wearing that green Adidas jacket, D. You looked like fucking Green Lantern out there today," one of the guys said. We all laughed.

"We're just getting started, guys," I said, even though they were too busy laughing to hear me. "Just getting started."

CHAPTER 5

THE CARNAGE OF WAR

March 2006

We considered ourselves fortunate to earn a big win within a few weeks of arriving at Camp Apache, and it only intensified the hunger for more. But we knew that it would take time to lay the groundwork for future victories. Operating Camp Apache was no small task. It required substantial resources, both in terms of manpower and finances. One of our most expensive assets was the security guard force, the team of dedicated locals who we hired for extra protection. It was up to me to make sure that those security guards were promptly paid for their services. I never missed a payment. The potential consequences of delayed payments for the security guard force were vivid in everyone's imagination. We were realistic enough to know that the monthly paycheck was more than likely the only bond between us, each dollar buying us enough loyalty to keep us sleeping at night.

The guard force wasn't the only expense. We invested in upgrades and enhancements for our force protection measures, including HESCO barriers, concertina wire, concrete, and more. We also invested in internet access, mechanics, and other essential resources that were not readily available in our small camp with limited resources. Ryan asked Hussein to arrange supplies and tools for the improvements around camp and Hussein delivered. They even repaired the pool from damage done by one of the other teams that had used it for explosive training.

Within a few weeks, our camp had been optimized. We shifted our focus to laying the groundwork for the months ahead. The nature of our mission necessitated relationship-building within the local community and understanding the complexities of the dynamics at play so that we could gain an advantage. But those dynamics proved to be far more complex than any of us had anticipated. Despite our training for the environment we were stepping into, nothing could have prepared us for the impact of the civil unrest between the Sunni and Shite communities in Baghdad.

Although the vast majority of the Iraqi population identified themselves as believers in the Muslim faith, two major religious sects divided them—those commonly referred to as Shiites and those referred to as Sunnis. The key theological difference between Sunnis and Shiites, as I understand it, primarily lies in their beliefs regarding the succession of the Prophet Muhammad. Sunni Muslims believe that the Prophet did not explicitly name a successor, while Shiite Muslims believe that he publicly designated his cousin and son-in-law, Hazrat Ali, as the first in a line of hereditary imams from the Prophet's family to lead the community after him. Additionally, Sunnis have a simpler religious hierarchy compared to Shiites, and the two sects also interpret Islam's schools of law differently. I'm not qualified to explain the complexities between the two branches, nor am I able to clarify the nuances of the history that led to my involvement in the area. I'm an operator, not a religious expert. But what I can tell you is that although we did our best to prepare and train amidst the tension between the groups, we drastically underestimated the dangerous environment we were walking into due to the tension between the two sects. Not only was there a war being waged between the American military and a rising insurgency, but there was also a full-blown civil war being waged between the local Sunnis and Shiites. During the reign of Saddam Hussein, the Sunnis gained power as Hussein placed only Sunnis in positions of authority within the government. As a result, over the course of his reign, the Shiites suffered many acts of violence, aggression, and oppression. Once Hussein was overthrown, the Shiites grasped at the chance to rise up and enact retribution. This kicked off a full-blown civil war.

On February 22, 2006, just after our successful honey trappin' operation, a massive bomb shattered the golden-domed mosque in the city of Samarra, one of Shia Islam's most revered sites. The attack on the mosque in Samarra, located sixty miles north of Baghdad and home to a large Sunni community, occurred shortly after dawn. Up to ten gunmen dressed as police commandos burst into the compound, tied up the guards, and triggered a series of explosions that brought the golden dome crashing to the ground. All that remained was the wall of the mosque, flanked by two minarets. As a result, protests in Samarra were magnified in the Shia heartlands of Baghdad and cities throughout the south. In the capital, residents woke up to shouts booming from the Shia mosques. Over twenty-five Sunni mosques were attacked nationwide as protestors took to the streets shouting, "I will burn the Abu Hanifa Mosque [a revered Sunni place of worship in Adhamiyah] to the ground. It is time to take revenge for the martyrs!"

A prominent journalist wrote, "Despite the violence and horrific attacks on the civilian population, it's difficult to imagine an act more designed to stoke civil war than the destruction of one of Shia Islam's holiest shrines." We couldn't have agreed more.

This was our first initiation into the area, and it was gruesome. Unidentified bodies began popping up in vacant lots in contested neighborhoods. Others were dragged out of the Tigris River where they had been dumped. At first, we thought these might be isolated events. But as time progressed, sections of the river transformed into graveyards as murder victims were callously disposed of and left to float downstream. These victims were usually found stripped of any form of identification, blindfolded, handcuffed, or bearing gunshot wounds to the head. Cities across the country, particularly Adhamiyah, were plagued by the horrifying sight of bodies strewn across the streets. Sometimes the bodies were rigged with explosives, endangering anyone who responded to the scene. No one wanted to take that risk. Often, bodies would remain uncovered for days before being retrieved and properly buried.

Reports from local police in the town of Suwayrah, located south of Baghdad, substantiated this disturbing trend. But the news reports of it seemed to be severely lacking in accuracy to capture the extent of the violence. The city's nine districts became battlegrounds where Sunni insurgents and Shia militias targeted each other's populations, leaving the civilians trapped between two warring sides. This period marked the deadliest summer of the Iraq War, with sectarian violence significantly impacting the daily lives of the city's residents beyond imagination. Even our coalition leaders were gradually recognizing that Baghdad was caught in a cycle of communal violence fueled by Shia and Sunni militants seeking to purge each other from key areas in and around the city. This was a stark contrast from the hopeful period following the December 2005 elections.

Our location in Adhamiyah was at the epicenter of the Civil War, giving us a front-row seat to the severity of the situation. The Abu Hanifa Mosque that many wanted to "burn to the ground" was in Adhamiyah and in close vicinity to Camp Apache. All the suburbs around Baghdad had undergone an extreme transformation from being populated by a Sunni majority to being populated by a Shia majority—except for Adhamiyah. This posed a significant challenge for us. Local contacts were on high alert and hesitant to meet. No Shia contact wanted anything to do with Camp Apache. Even Sunnis from other parts of Iraq were reluctant to travel in or around Adhamiyah because of the danger involved. They didn't want to be the next body handcuffed and dumped in the river. Due to this reluctance, we often had to convoy to meet them in the Green Zone, which was significantly safer. The Green

The Carnage of War

Zone offered enhanced security measures, and the fact that many Iraqis worked there allowed our contacts of interest to blend in and provide a solid explanation if anyone asked why they were there. We found ourselves making trips to the Green Zone frequently as we began to build relationships with local partners and informants in the city. We always made the most of our trips to the Green Zone. We used the opportunity to not only connect with national-level assets but also take care of various tasks, such as internal ODA and company business, resupplying, and drawing money through the finance department.

On one particular day, I assembled a convoy to go to the Green Zone with a list of things to accomplish. We departed Camp Apache by late morning. Approximately an hour into our trip to the Green Zone, I received a call from Dave.

"Hey, D. Uh, we got a pretty big problem here back at camp."

That's never a good thing to hear. I didn't waste time. "Tell me."

"Abdul was murdered today in Adhamiyah. Hussein, the Iraqi family, and the guards are devastated. I've never seen people act like this. They are beating their chests, screaming, and uncontrollably sobbing. This could go south, D."

I took a moment to process the information. Abdul was the nephew of the Iraqi family that lived with us. His dark eyes and boyish face momentarily flashed in my mind before fading away. My mind had been programmed for war, an effective program that suppressed any feelings of empathy or emotion. Instead, a cold, procedural logic had taken its place, designed to maintain composure under pressure. We were already well into our trip to the Green Zone, and I didn't want to deviate from the plan. I felt sorry for the family, but it didn't seem that the young man's death was connected to us. I wasn't certain if there was anything we could do to help.

"Look, Dave, I'm not there, so you're going to have to make this call. If you think we should head back, we'll leave now," I said. Dave was one of the best young operators I had ever had the pleasure of working with. He was calm, brave, and steady. I'd bank my life on his instincts.

"I've never seen Hussein this erratic. You have a good relationship with him; I think it would be best if you were here to deal with him," Dave said.

"Roger that." I hung up the phone. No further discussion needed.

The drive back to Camp Apache was a blur. We were well aware of the constant threat of IEDs in and around Baghdad. We also knew that if you drove fast enough, the damage could be reduced if you were able to throw off the timing of the person detonating the IED, so we smashed the gas pedal to the floor and didn't let up. *Always aggressive, never reckless.* Within twenty minutes, we were back at camp.

As we approached camp, a scene unlike anything I had ever seen before unfolded in front of my eyes. The mother, along with all three daughters of the Iraqi family as well as the female cooks living with us, were lying on the ground. I heard their screams even before I exited the vehicle. With their knees in the dirt, they pulled at their hair and beat their chests, moans and screams escaping their lips in between bouts of tears. The father and a few other men were there too, ripping their shirts open and wailing with fists in the air. *What the fuck is this?*

Before jumping out of the vehicle, I pulled out a plastic can of Copenhagen snuff from my cargo pocket and placed a big Fat Nasty between my cheek and gum. Chewing tobacco was a habit of mine, my way of preparing for the storm ahead. I exited the truck and immediately walked up to Hussein, whose face glistened with tears as strange-sounding grunts and screams came from his mouth. I opened my right arm to embrace him in a half–man-hug. I wasn't sure what else to do. He buried his face in my shoulder.

"Hussein, I'm very sorry for your loss. I'm here for you. What can I do to help?" I asked.

"Abdul was murdered in Adhamiyah this morning." Hussein could barely choke the words out. "But the Nu'man Hospital refused to release his body to us for a proper burial. I called, and they laughed and taunted me. Disrespectful pigs." Hussein spat on the ground.

We both knew that the morgue was run primarily by Sunnis. Given that Abdul and his family were all Shiites, this belligerent attitude was explainable. I looked from Hussein to the screaming women and men. Their extreme reaction actually surprised me. Death surrounded us day and night. We were living in one of the most violent places on Earth. How could they be surprised? Why were they reacting so severely? At that very moment, the mother raised her face from the ground. It was stained brown from her tears mixing with the dirt. For a brief moment, I caught her eye. She stared past me off into space, but I was looking at her. Suddenly, it was there. A prick of empathy.

I saw her.

We were at war, but this woman was not a soldier, and neither was this young man. She was just an aunt who loved her nephew dearly. She had helped raise this boy, held him close when he was a baby, the one who cheered when he took his first steps. She was the one who held onto hopes and dreams for that young man's life—who he would marry, what he would become, the life he would live. Neither she nor his mother would ever have the chance to see those dreams come true. His mother would never hug him again. His mother would never get to tell him that she was proud of him. His mother would never see him become a father. When his mother said goodnight to her son the day before, how could she have known that they would be the last words she ever spoke to him? I looked away.

And then, as quickly as the prick of empathy came, it disappeared. Emotion clouds clear thinking, and it wasn't a luxury I could indulge. We had only spent a few weeks acquainting ourselves with the local Iraqi family, our guard force, and our surrogate partners in the country. We hadn't undergone any training together, nor did we have the time to establish the same level of trust and respect that we had within our own unit. However, at the end of the day, we were all part of the same team. Each of us had our reasons for being at Camp Apache, with unique circumstances that brought us to that particular moment in time.

As I reflected on the events of that morning, the reality hit hard—how we responded to this situation would test the strength of our bond and shape the tone for the remainder of our time at Camp Apache. I had a quick huddle with Mark to discuss the situation privately.

"What do you think, man?" I asked Mark.

"It's tragic as hell," he said. "Do you think it's worth a drive over to the hospital?"

"Yes. I think we need to go and get that kid from the morgue and return him to his family for a proper burial. This is an opportunity for us."

Whether we liked it or not, the truth was that we had all agreed to be a team at camp. If we were going to function as a team, we needed to act like one when it truly mattered. And I knew exactly how we would respond if it were one of our comrades in that morgue. Some might refer to it as "winning hearts and minds," a concept I had learned during training. It involves not only relying on superior force but also making emotional or intellectual appeals to win over supporters from the opposing side. Our duty extended beyond following orders; we had to win the hearts and minds of the civilians we protected and collaborated with.

Following our instincts, Mark and I gathered the team and our local Iraqi forces. Our mission was simple: retrieve Abdul's body and return him to his family for a proper burial. But before committing to the operation, I asked Hussein to provide me with a brief overview of exactly what the plan would entail. I wanted to know what our next steps would be if the hospital allowed us to take the body. Hussein explained that once we secured the body, we would proceed to a Shia mosque located in Kadhimiyah, a Shia stronghold suburb of Baghdad situated across the Tigris River on the Adhamiyah Bridge. There the body would be washed and wrapped. Following that procedure, our next destination would be his parents' house, where Abdul's body would be returned home so his parents could properly grieve and bury him according to their cultural and religious practices.

The plan sounded straightforward enough, but we all knew the potential risks of signing up for the task at hand. There was always a risk in venturing out into unknown areas of the city—this much we knew. But this situation also brought another worry. What if it was all a hoax? We were headed to an unsecured location. What if we were being lured into a trap? There was no way to know for sure. We knew the risks but pushed forward and began preparing a small convoy to leave.

I quickly briefed the team and surrogates, and then we were off. The morgue was close by. We arrived on site in under five minutes. There were two Iraqi guards posted outside the building—and they were armed.

I dismounted from the vehicle along with Joe Joe. We approached the guards and confiscated their weapons before they had time to react. Up close, I could see the lines etched into both men's skin, deep wrinkles that marked the passing years. They were my grandpa's age. In another life, they might have been in a retirement home playing dominos instead of trying to guard a morgue. They were too old and too weak to put up a fight anyway and seemed to understand our precautionary measures of confiscating their weapons.

Joe Joe and I proceeded inside and were met by a doctor who appeared to be in charge. A look of stress was evident on his face as soon as we locked eyes. He took one look at us and lit a cigarette.

"What do you want?" he asked.

"One of my men has been taken, and we're here to retrieve him. He was killed just a few hours ago. He should be returned to his family."

The doctor's eyes widened in shock and fear. "No, no, no! Do you really think we have a dead American soldier here? That's impossible!"

I leaned in a little closer. "I never said that he was an American. But he is one of our team members, and if he's here, we would like to allow his family to properly bury him."

As the words passed my lips, I felt the meaning they held. Maybe that young man wasn't an American, but he and his family had made the choice to work with my team, and that made him one of ours. A look of understanding dawned in the doctor's eyes.

"Look, I don't want any trouble. If you can positively identify the body, I will release him to you, and you can be on your way," he said.

I assured the doctor that we wouldn't be long and walked back outside to get Hussein. With his help, we would be able to positively identify Abdul and transport him to the waiting gun trucks. I returned with Hussein a few minutes later and the doctor pointed us in the direction of an overflow morgue that was adjacent to the hospital. After the events of February 22, it was clear that the morgue had been forced to repurpose an old storage space due to the significant surge in killings.

It was the smell that hit me first, a peculiar odor that I couldn't quite place as I descended the stairs into the makeshift structure. It smelled like rotten eggs, shit, and decaying meat. With every step, the smell grew stronger until I could hardly breathe. Some say they are haunted by the images they see on the battlefield. I am still haunted by that smell. The smell of rotten humanity. The smell of death.

At the bottom of the steps, I froze for a minute to take in the scene in front of me. Nearly 150 dead bodies lay stacked in piles all around the perimeter of the room, all uncovered and exposed. It was difficult to comprehend what I was seeing. There were bodies of men with deep cuts through their arms, still wearing the bloodstained clothes that they died in. There were bodies clearly marked by the evidence of torture. There were dismembered limbs and arms on the ground. There were limp bodies of females, a sickly color of white, covered in bruises. And there were children. Tiny bodies stacked one on top of another. I looked away.

All that humanity just piled in an old storage unit, rotting. Vomit rose in my throat, hot acid burning my esophagus, pushing to escape from my mouth. I clamped my jaws shut, forcing the putrid liquid to stay inside my body.

Get the fuck out of here, D. It was the only thing I could think about. Running, leaving, and getting as far away from that little room of horrors as soon as possible. It was humanity on display at its absolute worst. Visions flashed in my mind of the pain, agony, blood, and terror that each of these individuals must have felt during their last moments on Earth. It was hard to fathom the strength, the mental fortitude, the *conviction* that the terrorizers possessed to do such a thing.

The carnage of war.

I had grown accustomed to seeing death on the battlefield, but I had never seen it painted across the bodies of the innocent. The small bodies, the old bodies, the blameless bodies. Discarded like carcasses.

What a waste of human life.

I wanted to look away. I wanted to close my eyes to block out the sights and smells. They were imprinted into my memory and nostrils with such precision that I knew it would be impossible for me to ever forget a single detail of what I experienced that day. My eyes tried to escape the scene in front of me without success.

Get through this, D. They need a leader right now, and it's got to be you.

I took a deep breath and started at one side of the room to begin the search for Abdul, looking through the stacks of bodies one by one.

Hussein was the first to break the silence. "This is him," he said. I turned and saw him too, laying in a pile of limp bodies. He had been shot once through the head and several times through the upper body. His clothes were soaked in blood. Hussein crouched down, face contorted with emotion as he looked at the body. Then he sucked in a deep breath and stood up. "I'll get the others to help me move the body," he said.

While Hussein was getting the others, the doctor prepared the paperwork for releasing Abdul's remains.

Within minutes, a few members of the Iraqi force returned with Hussein to assist in transporting the body. I stood back out of respect. My job was to stand beside our local allies so that they would have the power to take back what had been stolen, to grieve what was lost, and lay the boy to rest in a way that honored their customs and beliefs. I was only there to provide safety and protection, not to interfere.

The men transported him back to the waiting convoy and placed the body in the gun truck, an unarmored vehicle with an open back. All the local men let out low cries of grief at the sight of his lifeless body covered in bullet holes. Each of their faces told a story of sadness, anger, and disbelief.

With the body under our protection, it was time to take him to the mosque in Kadhimiyah to be cleaned and prepared for burial before returning him to his family. But before we started, I pulled aside Hussein, who had just finished speaking to his contact in Kadhimiyah, to ask him several security questions.

"Trust me," he said after I'd voiced my concerns. "There will be no problems."

My intuition told me that Hussein was serious. I could see it in his eyes. He knew beyond a shadow of a doubt that we'd be safe. But his confidence was unsettling. How much influence did he have to ensure our safety with one phone call? Kadhimiyah was a known Shia stronghold in the city, and it was clear that Hussein was a powerful man in the community. I filed the question away for another day. I thanked Hussein but emphasized the importance of remaining cautious. There had been multiple instances of vehicle-borne IED (VBIED) incursions into Kadhimiyah, which were beyond the control of the Shia community and likely the work of al-Qaeda. We could not afford to be complacent.

"I understand, I understand," he nodded. "But please, *please* do not direct your guns towards the Mosque. Please."

I reassured Hussein that unless there was an immediate threat, we would exercise extreme care and show respect. With that, we returned the confiscated weapons to the hospital guards, wished them luck, loaded up into the vehicles, and drove into Kadhimiyah.

We crossed the Adhamiyah Bridge over the Tigris River and soon reached the mosque in Kadhimiyah. I carefully surveyed the area, keeping my mind alert. However, true to Hussein's assurance, there was nothing to validate my apprehension. The surroundings exuded an unsettling tranquility. The local surrogate force unloaded the body and escorted him inside. I knew that the burial rituals in the Muslim faith were an important aspect of the Shiite tradition. They followed specific practices and guidelines to bury the dead according to their religious customs, from the *ghusl* (the ritual washing of the deceased's body), to the *kafan* (wrapping the body in three white burial shrouds), to the *Janazah* (a special prayer said as a supplication for the deceased's forgiveness and mercy).

As I stood outside of the mosque with the rest of the group, I couldn't help but notice a subtle yet profound change in the demeanor of the local Iraqi surrogates and guard force members. There was a newfound sincerity in their gazes, a sense of trust, and a shared understanding. They looked at us as if we were brothers. They were fully aware of the risks involved in our mission. They knew that we had willingly taken on those risks to bring one of their own back and ensure that he was treated with respect according to their customs and rituals. Their brother had become our brother.

It took about an hour for the body to be prepared inside the mosque. We waited patiently outside, ensuring that everyone remained safe. I sat lost in thought as the minutes ticked by. I thought of my reaction when Dave called me that morning, how guarded my humanity was behind a thick and calloused wall. I hadn't felt even a prick of empathy or compassion during that call. *We are at war and he's not one of my men.* That had been my initial thought.

But then I had seen the face of the grieving woman in the dirt. I saw the confused and grieving faces of our local Iraqi force. It was at that moment that I realized we couldn't truly unite unless I embraced them as part of our own team. Within the span of a single day, we achieved just that.

The jaded shades of war had fallen from my eyes, and I could see the situation with the eyes of a human, not just an operator. I saw my fellow Special Forces brothers in the faces of the men carrying Abdul. I realized they loved that young man, they dreamed for him, they wanted so much more for him than what he got. Abdul deserved better.

Within an hour, Hussein and the others carried the body outside of the mosque and gently placed it in the back of the open gun truck. This time, the body was inside a wooden box. Before leaving, I spoke with Hussein again regarding the next and final phase of our journey. Together, we made a plan to go from Kadhimiyah and make our way to Abdul's family home, which was situated just outside the Green Zone. With Hussein and our surrogate force being familiar with the precise location, I allowed them to guide us to the house. When we reached the destination, Hussein and his team unloaded the body from the gun truck and carefully brought it inside the family's home.

Several grieving family members were ready to receive the body, raw emotions on display for us to see.

The atmosphere was heavy with sadness. It was both uncomfortable and humbling to witness such an intimate and solemn occasion. We found ourselves in a delicate moment, silent observers amidst their mourning. We wanted to help in some way, so we gathered the emergency cash that each of us had brought with us from camp that morning. Altogether it was nearly $1,000. We entrusted our interpreter, Joe Joe, to deliver the funds properly and respectfully to Hussein along with our sincerest condolences in an effort to help the family. It was the least we could do. The family and Hussein were deeply appreciative of the gift.

While the family grieved in their way, we kept a vigilant eye out, knowing that the best thing we could do was provide a safe space for them to say goodbye to their beloved son without fear of danger. We all found ourselves in a city that was riddled with uncertainty and violence. A city filled with political and religious complexities. A city filled with mistrust and violence. My team and I couldn't solve those complexities. We couldn't eliminate the danger and violence. But we did have the power to stand guard for a few hours so that the family could have a moment to safely grieve the death of their son. And that's what we did. As a result, an unbreakable bond of loyalty formed between each and every person living at Camp Apache.

We wouldn't realize the full extent of this loyalty until a few months later when our bond would be put to the ultimate test.

CHAPTER 6
PSYCHIC INTELLIGENCE

March 2006

On January 7, just days after we arrived in Baghdad, we received an unsettling report that an American reporter for the *Christian Science Monitor* by the name of Jill Carroll had been kidnapped. The report garnered widespread attention. Her rescue became the priority of elite special operators and the Intelligence Community.

Jill Carroll had been living and working in the area, determined to shed light on the complexities and daily realities of the war, until things took a turn for the worse. She was ambushed while en route to meet an Iraqi politician. Her interpreter was shot on the spot, and she vanished without a trace. Now nearing the end of March, it had been eighty days since Jill was last seen. Her captors were demanding the release of female prisoners held by the US military. We, along with the rest of the world, watched the situation unfold with anger and disgust as the young journalist's life became a bargaining chip in the hands of merciless extremists. The kidnapping sent shockwaves throughout the journalistic community; it was a grim reminder of the danger faced by those who reported from the front lines. We all knew of several kidnappings that had resulted in grizzly outcomes. Rape, beheadings, mutilation, and torture were clearly marked on the discarded remains of dead victims. Even the ones who managed to live still bore the scars of unthinkable travesties.

The outlook for American hostages in Iraq during that time was grim. Several hostages, such as Nick Berg, had been beheaded on video two years prior—nothing but theater for the world to witness. Other victims included Tom Fox (a peace activist from Clear Brook, Virginia), Margaret Hassan (the director of Care International in Iraq, who held citizenship in Britain, Ireland, and Iraq), Ronald Schulz (an industrial electrician from Anchorage, Alaska), Jack Hensley (a civil engineer from Marietta, Georgia), and Eugene "Jack" Armstrong from Michigan. The story of Jessica Lynch, a US Army soldier who was taken as a prisoner of war and subjected to rape by her Iraqi captors in 2003, was also still fresh in our minds. Time was of the essence to find Jill Carroll, but no matter how hard we tried, every clue to her whereabouts proved to be nothing but a dead end.

On Wednesday, March 29, the subject weighed heavily on my mind as I paced around camp. I was angry at our lack of progress and desperate for anything that could lead us in the right direction. Every passing day felt like a failure. Then an idea popped in my mind. *Why not ask Hussein?*

I made my way to where he was sitting and struck up a conversation. Then I shifted to the topic of Jill Carroll, expressing my frustration that we had not been successful in gathering any human intelligence on her or her captors. I remained skeptical of Hussein, unsure if he harbored a secret agenda of some kind. However, given that Jill Carroll's kidnapping was believed to be the result of aggression from a Sunni faction, and considering that Hussein belonged to the Shia side, I concluded that there was minimal risk in discussing it with him. Perhaps he had some knowledge or connection that could assist us in this situation. Desperate times called for desperate measures.

Hussein listened intently. Something had changed about him since our trip to the morgue, but I still didn't fully trust him. His eyes grew dark when I spoke about Jill Carroll, intently taking in every word.

When I finished, he was quiet and thoughtful for a while. When he did speak, I was woefully underprepared for what he had to say. "Have you considered using a psychic mind reader to get more information?"

It took me a minute to process what I was hearing. "A psychic mind reader? Are you serious, Hussein? You don't really believe in that shit, do you?"

I searched his face for a hint of humor even though the situation was anything but humorous. Psychic mind readings, fortune telling, and belief in magic isn't common among devout Muslim believers or mainstream in the Iraqi culture. He had to be kidding me. But Hussein's face was stone cold. He was serious.

I sat back, thinking. His suggestion was ridiculous. If anyone else had advocated such a ridiculous idea, I'd have shrugged them off and ended the conversation in a second. But Hussein was no idiot. He was choosing his words very carefully as he spoke, that much I could see. He had an angle. But what was it?

Several possible explanations for his unusual behavior came to mind as I studied his face. My first thought was that it could be a big ploy for money—maybe he wanted us to believe that he had a valuable asset so he could ask for money to facilitate a meeting. Second, maybe he was trying to appear useful while he wasted our time. Or maybe, just maybe, Hussein had some reason to believe that the meeting would provide valuable intel on Jill Carroll's whereabouts.

I ruled out the first possibility. Hussein is financially well-off, and he didn't strike me as one for a cheap scam. Whatever his agenda was, he was playing a long game. The second option also seemed unlikely considering Hussein's intelligence and my low tolerance for nonsense. That left only the third possibility: maybe Hussein was actually trying to feed us valuable intelligence and had come up with a unique cover story to protect himself and whoever else was involved in sharing the information. Maybe he knew someone who actually had information on Jill Carroll's whereabouts but was too scared to report it as a "regular" Iraqi citizen. A psychic mind reader might just be a creative cover to deliver information without putting the informant in danger.

Our battalion commander, Lieutenant Colonel Sean Swindell, had encouraged all teams under his command to actively engage with the local network by employing the strategy of "pinging the network," as we called it. This approach involved the ODA's reaching out to every Iraqi intelligence source to gather any information related to the kidnapping of Jill Carroll—her whereabouts, captors, treatment, and any other relevant details. Lieutenant Colonel Swindell specifically instructed the ODA to do this in response to any significant events taking place in Iraq during that time, and the abduction of Jill Carroll unquestionably fell into this category. With more than 80 days in captivity, even our darkest imagination couldn't fathom what the young woman was enduring—if she had even managed to survive that long.

A crucial part of implementing the strategy of pinging the network involved what we referred to as "tickling the spider web." Chief Steve Dayspring, one of my mentors, had taught me about this technique, and I realized it might just work. The spider web represented our existing official human intelligence (HUMINT) network. Tickling the spider web meant activating that network by initiating meetings or calls and requesting information about Jill Carroll.

Hussein served as an unofficial link to the Shia militia's network. The hope was that Hussein would contact someone and raise inquiries regarding Jill Carroll. Subsequently, that person would contact another individual, potentially leading us to the group that held her. Additionally, there was a chance that this call would be intercepted by national-level assets, who monitored signals intelligence (SIGINT), such as mobile phone traffic and location tracking. This was all part of tickling the spider web. It was about time to call a Hail Mary.

"Alright, Hussein, bring him."

Hussein nodded and disappeared immediately. I headed off to explain to my team why I had just made a tactical decision to call a psychic mind reader to our camp for an impromptu reading in the middle of a kidnapping hunt. To their credit, they listened intently without suggesting I check myself into a mental clinic.

Hussein arranged for the psychic mind reader to visit us just before curfew. The entire city of Baghdad was effectively sealed off, with strict restrictions imposed on vehicle access and a nightly curfew beginning at 8:00 p.m. In light of this, we planned for him to arrive at Camp Apache between 7:00 p.m. and 8:00 p.m. and then spend the night with Hussein until his departure the following day.

Once he arrived, the psychic mind reader appeared to be in his mid-forties to early fifties. He sported a light-colored, two-day-old beard and casual clothes. He looked nothing like any psychic mind reader I'd seen in the movies. I was cordial but not friendly as I greeted him and led the way to a place to sit outside.

The evening was picturesque. The temperature was perfect, accompanied by a gentle breeze that made the palm trees inside the compound sway. Hussein, trying to make the strange encounter more comfortable, had arranged for chai to be served. The surroundings only made me more uncomfortable.

What the fuck did I get myself into?

Just as we settled into our seats, a loud noise cracked through the air. The psychic mind reader snapped his head upward in alarm.

"Nothing to worry about," I assured him, patting him on the shoulder calmly even though we had everything in the world to worry about. An explosion had detonated not far away—that much was clear by the sound.

I didn't waste time and dove straight into the topic at hand. I gave the psychic mind reader a brief background on Jill Carroll, including her kidnapping and the duration of her disappearance. I ended with a plea toward his humanity. This was a woman who deserved to be returned safely to her country and united with her family.

The psychic mind reader listened attentively as I spoke. Then he asked his first question: "So what does Jill Carroll look like? Do you have a detailed description?"

I stared at him without flinching, but his first question struck a nerve. "Well, fuck, *you're* the psychic mind reader. Why don't *you* tell *me* what she looks like?"

My eyes bore a hole through the guy as I waited for Hussein to translate. The psychic mind reader didn't show a strong reaction when

Hussein finished speaking. It was clear that Hussein had taken it upon himself to soften my wording a little bit in an effort to keep the conversation friendly. Gauging the reaction, I decided to shift my strategy from hardball to helpful.

I stood up. "Give me just a minute, and I'll go get a picture of her for you to see."

I walked inside and tinkered with the computer and printer for a few minutes and then returned with a colored picture of Jill Carroll. In reality, I had no earthly idea what this whole psychic mind reader process was supposed to be like. The entire thing was ludicrous. I had worked my ass off to become a member of the Green Berets, to become an elite fighter and defender. Never in my wildest dreams had I imagined that I'd find myself sitting with an Iraqi psychic mind reader discussing an American hostage while having a cup of tea.

This is just fucking weird, I thought. *If he pulls out a Ouija Board, I'm going to punch him in the face.*

But I was in it now. I wasn't about to back off. I sat down and handed the picture to the psychic mind reader and looked him straight in the eyes.

"Please help us get her back," I said with deep feeling, allowing him to see a hint of emotion in my plea. I needed to appeal to any sense of empathy he might have.

Although I had my doubts about the man's claimed "psychic mind-reading powers," a small part of me couldn't help but wonder if he did indeed possess some kind of valuable information. This whole charade gave him plausible deniability, as he presented himself as a psychic mind reader and I played along. If he was sitting on valuable information, I'd employ any means necessary to get it. Any detail, no matter how small, could potentially contribute to a larger puzzle being assembled by national-level assets.

The psychic mind reader looked at the photo for a while and then asked a few more questions. The conversation remained casual. We didn't discuss anything of great significance for over an hour and a half.

God, I hope I haven't just wasted my time with an idiot looking to make a quick buck, I thought. To my relief, he didn't burn candles, chant, or do anything out of the ordinary. But finally, he was ready to share his insights from the "psychic mind reading," which had pretty much amounted to nothing more than three dudes chatting over chai outside on some stairs.

But suddenly he had a lot to say about Jill Carroll.

He started by assuring me that she was being treated well, without any instances of physical abuse or assault, and that she was in good health. He said that a Sunni group (whose name he did not disclose) had taken Jill to western Baghdad, where she was being held in an ordinary residential setting that was not heavily guarded. He said the ultimate intentions of this Sunni group were unknown. Their eventual plans for Jill and their specific desires remained a mystery. He spoke for a while, mostly in generalities—nothing too specific.

I could only hope that this psychic mind reader had reached out to a wide network of sources to gather this information before our meeting and attracted the attention of national-level resources. I took diligent notes and played along with his narrative and ended the meeting by expressing my gratitude for his time and effort. I paid him before proceeding to our office to craft a comprehensive report for higher headquarters.

After completing the report, I sat staring at the empty section where the source of the information should be listed. My hands hovered over the keyboard, thinking. I wanted to be forthcoming about how I had gathered the information, but I couldn't bring myself to write "psychic mind reader" as the source.

Recognizing that labeling it as such would likely result in the dismissal of the report, I decided to seek guidance from my trusted advisor and mentor, Chief Steve Dayspring. As a seasoned combat veteran and the primary person in charge of reviewing all reports within our battalion, Chief Dayspring's opinion held great weight. After recounting the situation and expressing my dilemma, Chief Dayspring advised me to omit the reference to a psychic mind reader altogether. Instead, he suggested that I attribute the information to an anonymous individual who walked in too frightened to disclose their identity, which was technically true. I was thankful that at least Chief Dayspring hadn't discredited my unconventional methods for gathering intel.

After finishing the report, I sent it to Chief Dayspring at battalion headquarters. I knew that it was a desperate move, a shot in the dark. But we had to do everything we could for Jill Carroll. We needed to get her back, no matter the odds. Unconventional as it may have been, I was determined to do whatever it took.

After the report was sent, deep fatigue settled in. Finally, well past midnight, I crawled into bed, hoping for a few hours of uninterrupted sleep. But the sound of rockets exploding in the distance tore through the silence and sleep did not come. While these attacks were not uncommon, they still managed to disrupt our fragile peace. The night was restless. By the time morning finally arrived, it all felt like a cruel joke. I struggled to open my eyes and my body felt heavy with exhaustion.

As I descended the staircase, my tired eyes met the gaze of our army guard from the 101st Airborne Division.

"What's the damage?" I asked, exhausted.

"Nothing too bad, sir. Nothing we can't handle," the young army sergeant replied.

"Please don't call me sir. Call me D," I said as I headed to the kitchen to grab a can of Rip It. Rip It was the cheap, local alternative to Red Bull or Monster energy drinks. It can only be described as liquid, atomic energy. There's something about twenty-five grams of sugar and one hundred milligrams of caffeine that makes you ready to face the day. The vibrant green cans stood out against the dullness of the refrigerator, and I felt a tiny surge of adrenaline just looking at them. Rip Its were more like a drug than a drink. They're my secret source of energy; each sip was like riding a lightning bolt. I couldn't help but wonder how much easier Ranger School would have been with a healthy supply of Rip Its by my side.

As I cracked open the can, Dave Roten walked in wearing a Viking helmet on his head (the horns of which extended impressively from the sides), no shirt, black Ranger panties, and flip-flops. *Why am I not surprised?* He actually looked the part of a Viking soldier. Dave was muscular, blessed with the genetics that made him look like he'd been chiseled by a fucking sculptor. He'd also grown an impressive beard that stood in sharp contrast to his bright green eyes. Somehow the Viking helmet seemed to fit. I didn't even bother asking where he'd gotten it or why he was wearing it. Dave swirled a large Styrofoam cup of black coffee in his hands, whistling into it to cool it down. It was a habit with him.

Dave was the newest and youngest addition to our team. He was brand new and had zero combat experience. He arrived just before we departed to a shooting school at the Gunsite Academy in Arizona. The day before we were scheduled to fly out of Colorado Springs Airport, I decided it was time to commence our customary hazing practices to "properly" welcome Dave to the Special Forces and our team. As soon as I saw him, I walked up to him and handed him a bright red hat.

"Dave, this is for you. Wear this hat and your best suit when you show up tomorrow."

I'd walked away without another word, grinning to myself. It was my new favorite hazing practice, forcing the new recruit to wear a suit and red hat for the civilian flight while the rest of us sported a casual jeans-'n-polo style, making the new addition feel like the misfit and newcomer that he was. The whole set-up would be just humiliating enough to get on his nerves. Too many guys seemed to think that they were the greatest thing since sliced bread just because they'd made it through Special Forces training. It was my job to keep them humble right from the start. I wanted low-maintenance, high-production, and respectful operators next to me. I didn't have time for the overconfident sort who was prone to showboat or go rogue because he thought he knew best. And while Dave didn't exactly hit me as the arrogant type, I didn't hold back. It was tradition. I couldn't wait to watch his discomfort the next day.

But the moment I saw Dave the next morning, I knew I'd made a mistake. Dave looked even better in a suit than he had in a uniform, the jacket fitting snugly around his muscular shoulders and bulging biceps. Chest out and neck tall, he even made that goofy red hat look good. His swag was in overdrive. I hardly acknowledged him, hoping that he'd grow more uncomfortable on our flight from Colorado Springs to the Phoenix airport.

But boy, was I wrong.

As we all filed onto the plane, the eyes of a pretty flight attendant glided down Dave slowly from head to toe, taking in every inch of him. He looked her in the eyes and gave a serious nod, not even cracking a smile. She was melting under his gaze.

Good God, man. I've created a monster. Fuck.

After takeoff, two more beautiful flight attendants emerged for the in-flight drink service. As they pulled the cart toward the front of the plane to make their way down the aisle, their eyes went straight to Dave. They'd already spotted him. The blonde's lips turned up in a coy smile, and the brunette tossed her head in the opposite direction after giving him a quick wink. Hell, even the lead male flight attendant checked Dave out.

"Dude, they didn't even give the rest of us a second look," Brian said. He was already laughing at the situation.

This was not going according to plan. No one even bothered to ask Dave why he was wearing a red hat while dressed in a business suit. It looked like he was making a fashion statement. The flight attendants were eating it up. Instead of being embarrassed, Dave was out there living his best life.

When the pretty flight attendants arrived at our row of seats, Dave was waiting with a winning smile, chest pumped out in that suit and big red hat. He was rewarded with free drinks, lingering conversation, and overly enthusiastic bouts of laughter at his jokes. The rest of us rolled our eyes. Dave was visited constantly throughout the flight as the attendants returned multiple times with special food and drinks just for the man in a red hat and a suit. The blonde even left him with her phone number and the promise of a good time.

By the end of the day, my irritation had turned to amusement. All my efforts to humiliate the guy had only worked out in his favor. Even still, he wasn't arrogant or conceited. He was just the kind of guy who held his head high and took on any challenge with unshakable confidence. That's the kind of guy I wanted on my team. We all patted him on the back and laughed about it for the rest of the day. Dave was officially welcomed to the team that day. So, when he stood in the kitchen with nothing but a dinky pair of shorts and a Viking helmet, I didn't ask questions. If anyone could look comfortable in such an outfit, it was Dave.

"Hey, D, did you hear the news?" he asked.

"What news?" I wondered if he was referring to the hit we'd taken during the night.

"Jill Carroll has just been released! They found her!"

I nearly dropped the can of Rip It. "Are you fucking kidding me? Are you sure?"

"Yep, it's on the news."

Relief flooded me and I started walking quickly to the nearest computer to read the reports. Dave fell in step beside me.

"D, you gotta stop drinking so many Rip Its with fucking cookies for breakfast," Dave's face was far too serious for someone who was walking half-naked in a Viking hat. "When you're ready for some protein powder, just let me know."

"Yeah, thanks," I mumbled under my breath. I wanted to make a witty comeback of some kind, or hit him with a good burn, but *shit*—the dude was parading around like a Viking.

Over the next few hours, I read the reports. It was true—Jill Carroll was alive and safe. We were overjoyed at the news.

That evening, we celebrated Jill's release with a game of Texas Hold 'Em and discussed the bizarre events of the past twenty-four hours. *No one will ever believe this story,* I thought. The entire situation was so bizarre, so convoluted, and so outrageous that I wasn't entirely sure that anyone would believe me if I tried to explain what had happened. While I have my theories, conjectures, and ideas about how the events may have been connected, I'll never know for certain. No one will. The important thing was that Jill Carroll was safe, and we did everything we could to ensure that she made it back home alive.

Is it even legal to have this much swag as a three-year-old? Pic taken right across from Kellogg Elementary School on Piedmont Road, Huntington, WV, in 1975.

Vinson Youth League Football. Learned valuable lessons on the football field—mainly how to take an ass whoopin' because we typically lost every game. But I was a glutton for punishment.

Of course, I'm wearing overalls. It's a West Virginia thing. Don't let the face fool you—I was as mean as a rattler.

Little League Baseball at League #1. I played for Tradewell (a local grocery store in Westmoreland) well before name, image, and likeness (NIL). Otherwise, I'd be wealthy.

Me and my mom after I graduated from basic training at Fort Benning, GA, in 1990. See how my fist is prepared to defend myself or issue a first strike if warranted. Yes, my mom was one of those #FAFO before that was even a thing.

Eighteen-year-old Darrell Utt rocking the infantry blue cord in 1990—something I was extremely proud of. The infantry blue cord is a US Army decoration worn over the right shoulder of all qualified US Army infantrymen.

Me and my battle buddy "Walker." I wish I remembered his first name. He was a good dude.

Me and one of the best pieces of army gear in the inventory: the poncho liner. It's lightweight and will keep your ass warm on a cold night. Pic taken in my barracks room in 1990 at Fort Ord, CA.

Infantry Team Leader Utt at Fort Hunter Liggett in Jolon, CA. One of our mottos back then was, "Pack light, freeze at night." We all put some serious mileage in at Hunter Liggett.

Multinational Force and Observers in Sinai, Egypt. Due to a medical emergency, I was elevated from team leader to squad leader during this rotation. To my immediate right is SFC Don Yarian, a badass platoon sergeant who took me under his wing and showed me the way. SFC Yarian took the liberty to shoot live rounds in our proximity during our squad live-fire maneuvers (no shit). This type of exposure was invaluable to me when it happened for realsie in Kosovo and Iraq.

Who else do you know that can make a tracksuit look this damn good? Me posing for the camera somewhere in Israel in 1995.

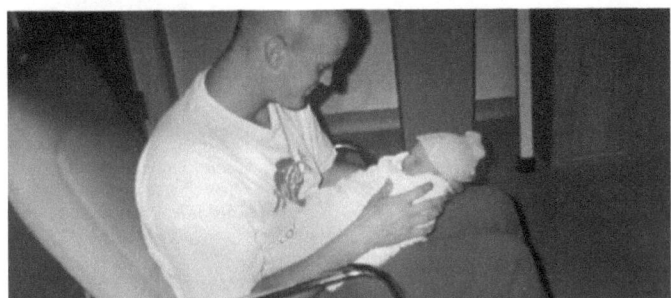

Luckily, my unit really took care of me. I pulled staff duty for twenty-four hours right before my son was born on July 1, 1995. Then, as a special touch, I deployed for six months to Sinai, Egypt, three weeks after he was born. We were too hard-core for parental leave back then.

Me and Rod Bennett ready to conquer some white water rafting on the New River Gorge in West Virginia. This was the summer of 1998 (after graduating the Special Forces Qualification Course and language training at Fort Bragg, NC). We had a helluva good time!

Working with the Secret Service and performing counter sniper security for President Clinton in Sarajevo, Bosnia and Herzegovina, in July 1999. We were overlooking the presidential route on "Sniper Alley." Pictured with SFC Chris Algiere.

Preparing to do combat search and rescue (CSAR) after lifting off from Camp Eagle in Bosnia and Herzegovina near Tuzla in 1999. During one of these missions, we were almost shot down by an SA-6 surface-to-air missile. I was part of 1/10 SFG(A) out of Stuttgart, Germany. The guy with glasses is SFC Mike Toth, a great role model and mentor for me. Mike has one of the funniest basic training stories that I've ever heard.

Counter sniper security team for President Clinton. L to R: me, SFC Chris Algiere, and SFC Mike Toth. Both Chris and Mike took care of me and showed me the right way to do things. Little-known fact: we were adjacent to the team who had the "shot heard around the world."

Special Operations Target Interdiction Course (SOTIC) (a.k.a. sniper school). Spotting for my sniper partner, SFC Logan Powelson. Send it!

I'm humbled to even be in this photo. Pictured here to my left are the 1 percent of the 1 percent and the best special operators in the military (not me—them). L to R: Rob Elliott, Conrad Gilbert, Liam Collins. Rob, Liam, and I were all on the same team. I would follow these guys anywhere.

Hands down, some of the toughest work I ever did in Special Forces was special reconnaissance (SR) along the border areas in Kosovo. It was exhausting but gratifying work. I spent most of my summers while assigned to 1/10 in the Balkans (primarily doing SR work). L to R: CPT John Fravel, me, Robert "Rob" Elliott.

Working with the Secret Service and leading joint SF/SEAL Teams doing counter sniper security for President Bush 43 in Kosovo in 2001. This mission would come full circle decades later in Arlington, Texas.

"Liberating" Altun Kupri, a town in the Kirkuk Governorate, Iraq, in 2003. We met no resistance, but I would be attacked by a friendly mob later while giving out candy to "my fans." I also liked to pretend to talk on our satellite phone to President Bush back in the States and report on our "progress" in front of the Iraqis. I think we all enjoyed it. The Iraqis always had a big smile and tried to thank Mr. Bush in the background.

Operation Ugly Baby in March 2003 (initial infil into Northern Iraq). You can see how fired up I am while reading a Dean Koontz novel. (Hey, this was way before Jack Carr arrived on scene writing bestsellers.) This flight had been canceled and rescheduled so many times, I thought for sure we'd never make it to Iraq. Off to my left is our 18C and my good buddy, Jason Maglathin.

This tank had seen better days. A lot of these Iraqi tanks were abandoned. Still great target practice for our big brothers in the sky, the US Air Force!

We tried to destroy every piece of round, ammunition, RPG, etc., that we could get our hands on, but there was simply too much. Our engineers did a great job of handling and destroying all this shit.

Britney and D on that special trip to NYC. Fortunately, I was able to give them that memory and many, many more.

Britney and D on the same special trip to NYC. Yes, it was cold as hell, but we didn't care. We had a great time and took in all the sights and shows!

Brit and I sliding down a slide in Colorado! She was (and always will be) Daddy's girl!

Deciding whether I should throw D in with the zoo animals (1996). We had a pretty good day, so I decided to keep the little guy.

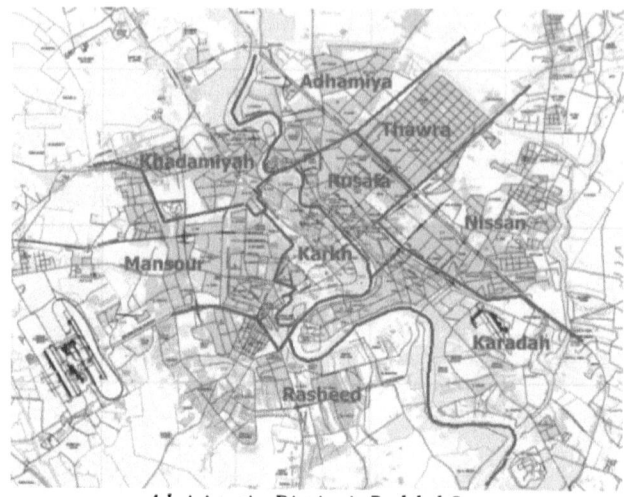

Administrative Districts in Baghdad, Iraq

After the fall of Iraq and Saddam, the Shia quickly moved in and pushed many of the Sunni out of Baghdad. The last remaining "true" Sunni stronghold in Baghdad was Adhamiyah. The Sunnis would never give up Adhamiyah because one of their biggest mosques (Abu Hanifa) was located there. We had a front-row seat to one of the most violent time periods of the entire Iraqi War in Adhamiyah.

A lookout from our buildings to the bustling city of Adhamiyah. Our generator is front and center and was a favorite target of mortars and rockets (which usually pissed us off).

A calm and peaceful day would often turn violent with a VBIED, firefight, mortar/rocket attack, or someone wounded and killed. It was a violent place that was very unforgiving.

Russ Hiatt wasn't just a communications guy. He was all-around solid on driving, gunning, shooting, moving, and being a great teammate. He was always cool under pressure—never rattled. He drove Gun Truck #2 on April 17, 2006, and performed exceptionally. Russ was the definition of a guy who was "low maintenance, high production"!

ODA 043 all kitted out and in our desert flight suits. No one ever told us we could wear flight suits, but they never said, "Don't wear them." I took that as a positive. We never had problems with what we wore or with our beards. Of course, it helped that we had contractor ID badges when we were around the big army guys. That prevented comments or corrections on what we wore, the sunglasses on our heads, why we didn't salute, ballcaps, clearing weapons—any and all jackassery that would come our way.

Ryan Land feeling the cool breeze on BIAP! Dude could rock a beard. Dude could also rock a .240 and lit many bad guys up on April 17, 2006.

Doing some medical training with Brian Rainwater in the background kinda supervising while my "patient," Russ Hiatt, prepares to be my needle cushion. Medical training is critically important.

An iconic picture of Dave Roten in Adhamiyah. Dave was one of those guys who remained calm and cool even in the most stressful of situations. He was also a force to be reckoned with on the .50-caliber and .240 machine guns.

My face when it's time to go because I have shit to do and the guys aren't ready. Serious!

This is my best friend's happy face. You DO NOT want to see him when he's angry! My guy Matt Girard. This is right before Matt chased a dude off the top of a three-story building.

Me and Ryan and the lime green Iraqi tracksuit top! Yep, someone is going to get fucked up! Who blends in better? Me or Ryan? Me, right?

My company sergeant major, Howard "Howie" Massingill. Man, it was so nice to have a solid SGM whom I could talk to and receive wise counsel from—especially with the rocky start that I had in the rotation. Howie (along with my company commander, Phil Mahla) had my back from day one, and I'll never forget that. Great command team. And no disrespect to the Marine Corps with my T-shirt. I never served in the US Marines, but I'm a supporter.

April 17, 2006. We linked up with the Iraqi Army at Antar Square. We then circled around to the east and linked up with the 101st Airborne Division a few blocks northeast on RTE Absolut. We ended up doing a very bold maneuver and played a dangerous game of leapfrog on RTE Absolut while engaging the enemy to the west (in the engagement area) down the side streets. Our early actions changed the momentum of the fight.

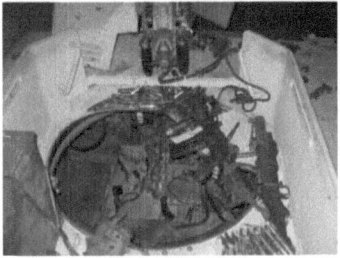

Truthfully, our vehicles often looked exactly like this. We were not scared to leave the wire and get into firefights. We often "trolled" for firefights and drove slow through Adhamiyah, hoping someone would engage us so we could destroy them.

Yes, we used incendiary grenades on the engine blocks of multiple vehicles. Yes, before we arrived back at our compound, that regular army battlespace owner had already initiated a 15-6 against us. Serious. Good thing we had a trump card up our sleeve! We detained a top five Multi-National Division – Baghdad high-value individual on this target. You're welcome!

Our modus operandi—shit is on fire or billowing smoke. This picture illustrates the difficulties of urban combat at close range. We fought in a 360-degree environment that was often deadly, violent, complex, and chaotic. This is the definition of an unforgiving environment.

L to R: Jody Thrasher and Dave Roten bonding over cold sodas at the compound after a long day of work. Dave is holding the Hard Hitter sledgehammer!

Back in the Green Zone after confiscating a shitload of vehicles. It was a joyous occasion all around . . . then, things got serious when a time-sensitive target (TST) presented itself.

One of the very few pictures that I have with a Green Beret on my head. I wasn't a guy who took pictures downrange with my beret. Always thought that was a little weird. Check out that clean-shaven face.

Me and my boy Matt. He took me elk hunting for the first time in Chama, New Mexico. He even let me get the first shot/first elk. Now, that's a friend right there. Looking back, I think he was happier than I was. Great dude here.

Took the kids back to NYC and received a tour from the Port Authority officers (his partner is taking the picture) of One World Observatory and the 9/11 Memorial & Museum. We felt like bosses being escorted around like VIPs. That was a great moment, and I'll always be a supporter of the Port Authority folks. Great Americans!

My wife, my rock, Misti, and I in my hometown of Huntington, WV, at the Marshall University Memorial Fountain. It stands just outside of the Memorial Student Center at the heart of the Huntington campus—a visible reminder of the seventy-five lives lost in the November 14, 1970, plane crash.

Doing tourist stuff in San Antonio with my wifey! A fave place to visit for us.

Me, Brit, and D a day or so before Britney's wedding in the mountains of North Carolina. What a gorgeous place.

L to R: Me, Misti, Patrick, Britney, Hailey, D. Family picture! What a proud day for me. Patrick and Britney's wedding in North Carolina. Hailey is D's wife and part of our wolfpack!

Man, I really worried about not having this moment with my daughter, but it all worked out and I got to walk my little girl down the aisle at her wedding. I used up all my superpowers NOT to cry while doing this because I didn't want her to start crying and mess up her makeup and all that. But it was tough. I was an emotional mess.

Daddy-daughter dance. The last time we did this was when she was in fourth grade. Thankfully, we didn't have to do the chicken dance. This was just a magical moment and magical wedding. My heart was full.

Misti and I welcoming a new wolf cub to our family. Hailey and D brought sweet little baby girl Eliza into this world. Another super proud day for the Utt family!

Having a great time at the NASCAR track in Fort Worth, Texas, with Medal of Honor recipient James "Doc" McCloughan. What a great, great man Doc is. Most know about his MoH action, but they don't know he was a teacher and coach for forty years and positively influenced thousands of lives. He's a great friend and mentor to me, and I love the guy!

Me and Medal of Honor recipient Salvatore "Sal" Giunta at a function in Dallas, Texas. Sal is the first US Army soldier and the first living person since the Vietnam War to receive the Medal of Honor. Talk about a lot of pressure. And this guy handled it like a pro! Another guy I have so much love and respect for who helped me out and gave me advice on projects that I was working on. He's a great American, patriot, and human. I'm so honored to call him a friend.

I met President Bush 43 and the First Lady at a Texas Rangers baseball game when they visited our suite in 2023. Check this out—true story. I told the president that, back in 2001, I was a member of his counter sniper security team when I was a Green Beret, and he remembered the event/trip. (He obviously didn't remember me because we never met.) I told him how worried I was because of the First Lady's outfit, and the guy remembered what she was wearing that day—all white in a sea of camouflage! Needless to say, I'm a huge supporter of the president and First Lady.

Medal of Honor recipient, author, speaker, world traveler, marine, country boy . . . Kyle Carpenter! Another guy I love so much. One of the most genuine and humble dudes you'll ever meet in your life. I was so fortunate to meet many of our nation's greatest heroes while working as the chief of operations (COO) at the National Medal of Honor Museum Foundation. Kyle and I became fast friends, and I'm looking forward to what the future may hold for us. Watch out, world!

I really enjoyed speaking for the Rotary Club, Daughters of the American Revolution, VFW, MOWW, and many, many more. It was great experience, and I got to meet a ton of great Americans who are serving their community and doing great things for their fellow citizens.

As a lifetime introvert, I got a lot of practice speaking to groups while I was the COO at the National Medal of Honor Museum Foundation. You know what they say: practice makes perfect!

Really fun speaking engagement here with Convergint Technologies. One of the Grit Code principles you can see on the screen is "Calm Breeds Calm." I was able to bring in a few thousand dollars to the foundation with this speech.

I had the privilege of working with the very talented Kevin Basik and Chris Cassidy at the Frontiers of Flight Museum at Dallas Love Field in Texas. As a guest speaker, I was able to share leadership lessons as a Green Beret that really resonated with the audience. How can I not do a good job with a huge American flag in the background? What an honor!

CHAPTER 7

ALIVE DAY

April 17, 2006

A soldier's intuition... is it real? Some describe it as a visceral sensation—a gut feeling or a premonition nestled deep in the chest, a whispering indication of impending ominous events.

I call bullshit.

When I opened my eyes on the morning of April 17, 2006, I didn't feel any premonitions or superstitions that the day ahead would someday etch itself into my memory. I would later name that day my Alive Day and celebrate it in the years that followed with more dedication than a Catholic on Easter morning.

I woke up to the sound of gunfire. By that time, I'd grown accustomed to hearing explosions in the distance. But this was different. This was sustained gunfire, clearly from machine guns and rifles, punctuated by the occasional explosion of a rocket-propelled grenade (RPG). I bolted out of bed.

We might just have a fight on our hands.

I quickly made my way down the stairs to get a pulse on the situation and learned that our comrades from the 101st Airborne Division had come under heavy fire during the early morning hours. Hearing the report was like catching wind of a rave party that you hadn't been invited to. After three months in Adhamiyah, we were addicted to the adrenaline rush of action, and we wanted to be involved. We offered our assistance, but it seemed that the 101st had things under control. With no further responsibilities on that front, I shifted my attention to our scheduled plans for the day, which entailed an administrative convoy. I was responsible for coordinating outgoing convoys from the compound. The night before each convoy, I gathered the necessary information and identified the team members who would be joining me. To ensure everyone was well-informed, I utilized a whiteboard located at the end of the stairwell. In the event of any unforeseen circumstances, this would enable the team at the compound to have a clear understanding of every person's position within the vehicle.

Gun Truck #1 was equipped with a .240 machine gun. Gun Truck #2 boasted the formidable .50-caliber machine gun, our most powerful weapon, designed to penetrate armor and incapacitate targets with overwhelming force. Given the high-risk nature of traveling through the streets in and around Baghdad, I strongly believed that it was essential for me, as the team sergeant, to accompany every convoy. Additionally, I frequently assumed the role of the gunner, taking up the most exposed position in the vehicle's turret. This approach made me somewhat of an anomaly, as few team sergeants shared my philosophy. My guiding principle was to lead by example, adhering to the mantra of "Don't ask your team to do anything you wouldn't do yourself."

For that day's convoy, I would be in Gun Truck #1 as the gunner. Ryan would drive, and Keith, the newest member of the team, would be the TC (truck/track/tank commander). Joe Joe would sit behind Ryan in the back seat. Gun Truck #2 would be manned by Brian Rainwater, our most experienced .50-caliber gunner. Russ Hiatt would drive and Rick Townsen would be the TC. Luke Roberts, our senior 18B, occupied the back seat, right behind Rick.

We never fell into a discernible pattern and often changed our rollout times in order to maintain unpredictability. Our scheduled administrative day would involve a trip to the Green Zone in Baghdad to drop off Luke and check in with the leadership team. Afterward, we would convoy to Baghdad International Airport (then known as BIAP) to pick up supplies and upgrade our turrets. Then we would drop off our interpreter, Joe Joe, allowing him to fly out for some well-deserved time off. While Joe Joe was not officially a member of our Special Forces team, we counted him as much. Joe Joe had been with me since 2004, and we'd gotten through more than a few scraps together. Born in Baghdad but an American citizen for many years, Joe Joe was dedicated to his job, fiercely loyal to our team, and never blinked when things got dangerous.

As we loaded up the two gun trucks for the trip to the Green Zone and BIAP, Joe Joe emerged from his room dressed to impress. He sported a snug pair of jeans, a floral button-down shirt, ASICS shoes, and hair slicked over with enough gel to ensure an impenetrable crust when it dried. The wind had no chance of blowing it back and revealing the bare patch hidden beneath it. Joe Joe was pulling out all the stops to get ready for a rendezvous with his lady, and we didn't hold back on giving him shit for it.

"Jesus, Joe Joe, you smell like Bigfoot's ass," I said in mock horror as Joe Joe took his seat, all dolled up and smelling like a half-priced strip club after midnight.

"That's not what your mom said last night," he shot back at me without missing a beat. "Your mom" jokes were always a favorite among the team.

I stared at him in stone-cold horror. "That's fucked up, man. My mom is fighting cancer right now."

Joe Joe's face dropped in shame, horrified for offending me and dishonoring my mother. No one in the vehicle dared to breathe.

"Ha, fucker! Got you!" I broke out into laughter when I was certain that I'd scared him enough.

Everyone snorted with laughter. Give us an audience of immature teenagers and any one of us could have become a full-time comedian. Branch out of that demographic and we'd be fired on the spot.

Laughter has a way of lightening the mood and taking stress down a notch. Even in the most dangerous and intense moments, you can always count on humor to get you through, guaranteed. At least, that's how we looked at it.

The sky was overcast with low-hanging clouds as we left the compound. "Not a bad day for a drive," I muttered under my breath as I performed a 360-degree check of the turret.

It didn't take long before we were off. After taking care of business in the Green Zone and dropping Luke off for his scheduled meeting, we prepared to drive into BIAP. As we approached what we referred to as Route Irish for BIAP, my embassy-issued cell phone started ringing in my jacket pocket. It was our team leader, Mark.

"Pull off for a sec," I told Ryan, who quickly pulled off the road and parked the vehicle so I could comfortably take the call.

"Looks like the 101st needs support after all," Mark said as soon as I answered. Mark informed me the 101st had been engaged in a firefight for the past five hours and were running critically low on ammunition. This particular engagement was far from typical for Adhamiyah; our previous experiences had mostly involved sporadic harassment fire and hit-and-run attacks. We all knew that the sustained nature of this firefight suggested the presence of a substantial number of well-armed fighters. The fight had lasted much longer than expected and they needed backup, Mark informed me.

"Roger that, Mark. Give me five minutes to talk with the guys and I'll call you back."

After hanging up, I quickly relayed the limited information I had to the team, conveying the gravity of the situation. As a former 101st guy myself, I felt a personal connection to the men and their mission. It was my responsibility to offer them support in their time of need. Besides that, we had a gentlemen's agreement with the 101st: If we ever needed help, they would assist. If they ever needed help, *we* would assist. Understanding the significance of a potentially life-and-death decision, I made a point to involve every member of our team. If we were going to offer our help, it was vital that each person understood the risks involved. Even though I had a good sense of what the answer would be, I wanted to ensure everyone's buy-in and create a sense of shared responsibility.

Without exception, each operator gave a resounding "Hell yes." We all realized this was high-risk and extremely dangerous, but we saw it as an opportunity. We had come to relish the fight.

I gave Mark a quick call back on the embassy-issued cell phone. "Hey man, we're fucking down. Tell the 101st we're headed their way."

"Roger that, will do," he said.

"You have the link-up location?"

"Antar Square. Enter from the east. Enemy activity appears to be west of Route Absolut."

"Okay, Antar Square, entering from the east, enemy west of Route Absolut. I have seven men with me total. I'll be TC'ing Gun Truck #1. Ryan will be gunning. I have three in Gun Truck #2," I said.

Mark knew that this was my way of letting him know to update the whiteboard. If things went south and we hit an IED, knowing those positions would be vital information.

"Roger, good copy."

"Pass on our internal freq. They can reach me at ROWDY 7."

"Roger that, we'll be monitoring the situation if you run into trouble."

"Cool, talk soon."

During my conversation with Mark, the team gathered around, overhearing most of the discussion. Once I ended the call, everyone was already shifting into gear to prepare to move from the Green Zone to Antar Square in Adhamiyah.

In Gun Truck #1, I made a seating change for this particular mission. Keith assumed the role of the driver, while I shifted from being the gunner to being the TC. Ryan, in turn, transitioned from driver to gunner. This rearrangement allowed us to adapt and optimize our positions for the task at hand.

Typically, when I was the TC'ing or gunning, Ryan got behind the wheel. I liked his driving style and assertiveness. But given that we were about to enter a firefight, I needed to take the responsibility of TC'ing, and I needed Ryan, one of our most aggressive operators, behind the gun. That left Keith as the driver with Joe Joe behind him. Ryan's eyes lit up like a child on Christmas Day when he heard the news. His collarbone injury was finally on the mend, and he was aching to get back behind the gun.

We rolled out, calm and confident. We were poised, focused, and ready to get shit done. We were fighting to win and had zero reservations about killing our enemies.

"Time to roll deep and bring the heat!" I said as the engines roared to life. Instead of saying, "Stay safe" or "Be careful" or "Go get 'em," we had a habit of saying, "Roll deep and bring the heat." It was more than a phrase or a statement. It was a mindset.

Our engines roared to life as we left the safety of the Green Zone. "Take this exit," I said to Keith just outside of Adhamiyah. It would put us on the best route to Antar Square. But Keith just stared ahead and didn't react.

"Take the fucking exit," I said again, louder this time, pointing to the turnoff.

Keith was confused by the road system and what I had just asked him to do. Although he had driven many times before, he wasn't used to my style and my direction didn't register until the last moment—just before it would have been too late to take the exit. Suddenly, he swerved to the right in an attempt to save the situation. But the massive overcorrection nearly flipped the vehicle. We teetered dangerously on two wheels for what seemed like an eternity before regaining our balance.

"Goddamn it, man, what the fuck are you doing?" I yelled. "We're no good to anyone if we don't arrive alive!"

Keith's mistake could have easily cost Ryan his life and maybe the lives of everyone in the vehicle. The gravity of the situation hit like a slap in the face. It was a humbling reminder of our fragility and the weight of every small decision we made. Keith's eyes were wide with stress and a thousand apologies that he couldn't find words to communicate. I knew that look. We'd all felt it at one time or another. The truth was that all of us had the potential to make a mistake that could jeopardize the team if we weren't careful. That thought scared us more than anything. It was one thing to die in the heat of battle, to be wounded by an enemy, or to sacrifice your life to save a brother in arms or defend your country. But losing your life because of a careless mistake—or even worse, jeopardizing the safety of your teammates because you let pressure get the better of you and lost focus—that was unthinkable.

I knew that dwelling on the incident wouldn't serve any purpose. I needed everyone to be fully focused and perform at their best.

"Keith, forget that shit. It's done," I said.

Keith nodded in appreciation. I knew he was sorry, and my yelling had certainly not helped anything. I needed him calm. I shoved a big Fat Nasty in the side of my mouth, leaving the responsibility of calming *my* nerves to a lump of Copenhagen.

That's how you kiss and make up on the battlefield.

The air was filled with the deafening sound of AK-47 fire and PKM machine gun rounds. The explosive impact of RPGs at close range rang in my ears as we entered Adhamiyah, Baghdad, from the east and began the drive to Antar Square. An inexperienced soldier can't distinguish between these sounds; he'll duck in fear of an explosive miles away. Hell, I did once too. But it doesn't take long before you become attuned to that song of war and learn to differentiate one instrument of destruction from the other and gauge the distance and viability of a threat just from the sound.

Damn. I didn't like the tune of this one.

We pulled into the area with two gun trucks—*MacGyver* Special Edition—proudly touting steel I-beams as front bumpers. I peered out the side window and got my first look at the local Iraqi Army caught in a heavy crossfire. Their eyes were wide with fear. They'd been in a sustained firefight against a well-equipped enemy for hours, and things weren't going in their favor. The weather was bad, and the low ceiling had emboldened the insurgents who damn well knew that our air support was grounded for the day. It was clear they intended to take full advantage of that fact.

I watched the expressions of the soldiers go from terror to surprise to relief at the sight of us. We were the salvation they'd been praying for, and the weight of responsibility sat squarely on our shoulders. We didn't look anything like the 101st guys they were accustomed to seeing. We sported full beards, chest rigs, and unique helmets. It would be their first time witnessing our team of Green Berets in action during daylight hours.

After identifying what appeared to be a hastily established Iraqi Army command post inside a small building, I directed the drivers to position themselves outside the line of direct fire. I needed to establish contact with the command post to understand what kind of situation we had on our hands and how we could help turn things around. I also needed to know the exact location of the Iraqi Army members and the 101st guys who were pinned down to avoid a "blue on blue" incident, better known as "friendly fire." The tough thing about urban warfare is that you can't tell shit about where the enemy is positioned just by looking.

But there was one problem. The distance between where my ass sat in the front seat of the gun truck and the Iraqi command post was approximately 100 to 150 meters. Not so far under normal circumstances, but a mile-long death march when you're under heavy fire from an unseen enemy. Given the complex, urban environment, it was challenging to pinpoint the exact source of the incoming rounds as gunfire and explosions reverberated from all directions. I stared at the open space between me and the command post for a second before opening the truck door.

Now I had a choice to make. I could run the distance and attempt to minimize the danger. Seemed like the obvious thing to do. But at the first sight of me doing a Tom Cruise sprint to the command post, everyone watching would switch to full panic mode, and that's never a good thing. I couldn't afford to have a bunch of panicked men on my hands not thinking clearly. Panicked people do strange things, and strange things get people killed.

That left option number two: I could walk quickly but calmly to the command post. No sprinting, just a nice, smooth pace like I was headed into Gino's Pizza on Fifth Avenue back in West Virginia before the college crowd hits after a football game.

Stepping out of the gun truck, I made my decision. I needed everyone to stay clearheaded and calm. Experience taught me that if a leader was strong-minded enough to stand up and display courage, others would follow suit. And as the team sergeant, it seemed that leader was me. I might have looked more confident than I felt, but feelings don't matter much in the heat of combat—just action. Head held high, I dismounted the truck and took my first step. Joe Joe, my faithful interpreter, fell in lockstep beside me.

Ten feet tall and bulletproof, D. You're ten feet tall and bulletproof.

It was the smell that hit me first. The air was thick with the acrid odor of gunpowder and burning tires from vehicles set ablaze. Nothing good ever happens when that smell is in the air.

Another step. Another loud crack of gunfire sounded in the air like thunder, and the roar of gunfire echoed through the concrete canyons, assaulting my ears and reverberating through my bones. Unfortunately, I *was* well attuned to the songs of war. I *could* differentiate one instrument of destruction from the other and gauge the distance and viability of a threat just from the sound.

Fuck, that one was close.

Another step and then another and then another.

I lifted my chin and squared my shoulders, eyes never moving from the command post ahead. The sound of a PKM belt-fed machine gun with bursting fire bounced off the buildings. Bullets whizzed past, sounding more like bees than bullets as they moved through the air. Only three steps to go.

I ducked inside the command post. After consulting with the Iraqi commander, I gathered more information on the situation. There was a slight delay in communication due to the language barrier, with Joe Joe acting as the intermediary, but I soon learned that they had been engaged in a direct firefight for several hours against well-equipped, highly trained insurgents. The enemy's tactics were aggressive, indicative of good training. That was never a good sign. He estimated the number of insurgents to be between fifty and one hundred. When I asked about the positioning of the 101st guys, the Iraqi commander provided a detailed description, using gestures to indicate that they were positioned roughly between Antar Square and Route Remy on Route Absolut. With that information, we had our bearings. Now it was time to move on to an MWE assessment: men, weapons, equipment. Basic ranger school stuff.

The Iraqi commander had several injured soldiers with him inside the command post. Their faces were contracted tightly in pain, necks slumped in fatigue. One of them clutched a limp, bloody arm. The man locked eyes with me. He didn't say a word, but he had that same expression on his face as though he was looking into the eyes of the savior himself.

"Got any KIAs?" I asked, pulling my eyes away from the injured man.

"No," the commander shook his head.

The wounded soldiers displayed gunshot injuries and shrapnel wounds as far as I could discern. While their conditions were not critical, I recommended to their commander that they be transported back to Camp Apache for proper treatment. I also suggested that he check on each soldier's fighting position to ensure sufficient cover, ammunition, and proper equipment. Before exiting the command post position, I leaned my face close to the commander, Copenhagen breath and all, looked him in the eyes, and said quietly, "We're here now. Let's go kill these motherfuckers."

He nodded furiously, a light in his eyes that hadn't been there before. Joe Joe and I calmly made our way back to the gun trucks just like we had before.

Instead of opting for the fastest and easiest route, which would have been Route Absolut, I decided to take the narrow alleys that ran parallel to it on the east side. This strategic decision would allow us to link up with the 101st guys while maintaining an element of surprise. We'd also gain protection from the area where most of the enemy fire seemed to originate.

As we left, the Iraqi Army soldiers rose to their feet and erupted in applause, vigorously waving their arms in the air, celebrating our arrival. Their radiant smiles and heightened morale stood in stark contrast to the fearful atmosphere when we initially arrived.

Courage is contagious.

Upon linking up with the 101st guys, we were briefed on the situation, which closely aligned with the report provided by the Iraqi Army commander. The enemy force was substantial in size, well-equipped, and displayed advanced combat tactics. It was made clear that it was not an ordinary group of neighborhood watch boys trying to protect their territory. We were dealing with hardened insurgents determined to engage in combat. I couldn't have been happier with the news. *All bets are off. No mercy. No hesitation. No remorse.*

Now we could pound the hammer of power, force, and violent action until the enemy was obliterated. I briefed the team on the engagement area and threat level, and we worked out a plan of action on the fly. The men from the 101st were stationary due to concerns over getting sucked into an enemy-controlled area and being surrounded. But we were a small unit, which gave us the ability to operate unilaterally. Maybe we weren't big in numbers, but we packed a heavy punch with the .240 and .50-caliber machine guns.

The plan we devised was straightforward. I would lead our two gun trucks on Route Absolut (which ran north to south) and stop on the X. The X refers to a location where enemy forces have positions of superiority and tactical advantage to surprise and overwhelm a friendly force. In our case, the X referred to all the side streets to the west of Route Absolut. That was the area that posed the most threat. It was clear that the enemy was hiding there and waiting to attack the moment we approached. They had a positional and tactical advantage. Most forces caught on the X do everything to get off the X and out of the kill zone. But our approach was different. This situation called for surprise, speed, violence of action, and overwhelming firepower. And that just happened to be our specialty.

We planned to head straight for the X. They would think that we had unwittingly entered their trap, only we had a plot twist waiting. It wouldn't be us getting killed on the X—it would be them.

If we ran into enemy forces on the side streets, Brian and Ryan would let loose. If the street was clear, we would proceed down the road. *Surprise, motherfuckers.*

Before starting, I confirmed once more with the leader of the 101st guys the location of the friendlies and the enemy. While facing the area to the west of Route Absolut, I stuck out my left hand to the far left and my right hand to the far right and confirmed that no Iraqi police, Iraqi Army, or American units were in that area. He gave another full confirmation. That made my job simple. If the enemy moved on any west side streets, kill them. Simple.

Let's roll.

Our trucks barreled down the street and halted to a stop at the first west side street to our left. Nothing.

We inched forward. At the second side street, a vehicle throttled toward us and then came to an abrupt halt upon spotting our gun trucks. The 101st had remained stationary throughout the gunfight, so our tactics had caught the insurgents off guard just as we'd hoped.

Five armed insurgents swiftly disembarked, approximately fifty to seventy-five meters away from us. One was holding an RPG. Without hesitation, Ryan unleashed a barrage of fire from the .240. The man with the RPG prepared to engage, but he was no match for Brian, who responded with a burst of fire from the .50-caliber. His rounds were absolutely surgical. He was our most experienced .50-caliber gunner due to his previous military occupational specialty and training, and it showed. The sheer intensity and intimidation of the .50-caliber firing resonated through the air.

The images of a human body being ripped apart by that much force is something that can't be easily forgotten. Brian's shots tore through the insurgents like fruit being shredded in the blades of a juicing machine. The bodies disseminated into large chunks and a red mist appeared in the air. Some chunks were bigger and more identifiable than others. I watched as an arm flew up in the air at least fifteen to twenty feet and then disappeared behind a vehicle. Ryan and Brian stayed focused, not letting up until the vehicles were destroyed as well. Onto to the next street. We moved forward, leaving the street littered with pieces of the insurgents and blazing vehicles behind us.

Later, I would recount each detail in slow motion. But that initial engagement was over faster than the blink of an eye. No remorse. No regret. Combat is ruthless. Kill or be killed. If you don't act first, it'll be you, not the other guy, lying in chunks on the street.

We kept moving up the street. Our approach varied. Sometimes we halted both gun trucks on the same side street and fire. Other times we'd bound individually from one side street to another, like a high-stakes game of leapfrog. I kept things simple as we exchanged instructions over our internal frequency.

"Gun Truck #2, this is #1. Go past us and move on to the next side street."

"Roger that."

"Gun Truck #2, this is #1. We're all clear. Go ahead and move to the next side street."

As we traveled north on Route Absolut, we noticed a significant decrease in enemy presence. Once we approached the Tigris River, we turned and headed back down the street on Route Absolut. We continued to employ the same tactics during our return journey. During our first encounter, the enemy engagement took place at close quarters. The remaining insurgents fired and quickly sought refuge across the street or in nearby buildings in all subsequent engagements. To ensure efficiency, Ryan operated the .240 machine gun while I took on the role of ammo bearer, providing him with the 7.62 ammunition whenever necessary, allowing us to save precious time. The hot brass of Ryan's machine gun ricocheted inside the gun truck. The only thing between my eyeballs and the hot casings was my dependable pair of Oakley Magnesium M-Frame glasses. And they fucking saved the day.

Our tactic of heading straight into the middle of the kill zone with surprise, speed, violence of action, and overwhelming firepower had indeed caught the enemy off guard. We had successfully gained the upper hand.

After sweeping the western side streets along Route Absolut, we regrouped with the 101st and another QRF team that arrived around the same time as us. Together, we assembled a nice lineup, including gun trucks and assets from the 101st, members of the Iraqi Army, and our two *MacGyver* special-edition gun trucks. Positioned on Route Absolut, we faced westward down the side streets, ready to clear the path. Our primary focus was on the areas west of Route Absolut, where the highest concentration of remaining insurgents were located. With friendly elements on our left flank, our two gun trucks stayed together, and we started moving toward the west. We encountered intermittent fire right away, making it challenging to pinpoint the exact locations of the insurgent fighters. Ryan manned the .240-machine gun, and I provided continual updates on the distance and direction of the insurgents. Keith skillfully maneuvered the vehicle to minimize the risk of an RPG attack. This area was teeming with enemy combatants emerging from rooftops, windows, streets, and even alleyways.

By the time I could call out, "one o'clock, 150 meters," I was already overdue for calling out "three o'clock, seventy-five meters" as a new incoming threat became visible. Everything was happening so quickly. My voice was growing hoarse. The insurgents were quick to fire but even quicker to get the hell out of dodge.

Spraying and praying—that's what we called their signature fire-and-run move. We benefited from their tactic. It allowed us to gain an advantage given the fact that our gunners, Ryan and Brian, were stable in the turrets and laying down perfectly aimed suppressive fire. I watched in awe as Ryan acted with perfect clarity and precision, dropping multiple insurgents to the ground.

"D, D, straight ahead! They have the road blocked!" I snapped to attention at the sound of my name being screamed out in the midst of the chaos. It was Keith who was shouting at me from behind the wheel. I had been so focused on identifying insurgents from rooftops for Ryan to kill that I had overlooked what should have been abundantly obvious at street level.

F-U-C-K.

Approximately 150 meters in front of us, stretching across the road, was an array of debris, including trash, barrels, wire, boards, and various other items. There were also metal poles with three-stranded wires interwoven between them positioned on both sides of the road. We'd seen this kind of thing many times before. These obstacles were typically removed during daylight hours and then placed across the street at night to keep American and Iraqi forces from conducting raids in particular neighborhoods. *This could be a real problem,* I thought as we approached.

"Keep moving and I'll tell you when to stop," I instructed Keith.

The roadblock appeared to have been hastily constructed but was nevertheless an obstacle that would have to be eliminated before we could continue. But our options weren't looking good. Going directly through the obstacle would render the vehicles undriveable. The roadblock might have been crude, but it was effective. It was going to impede our progress and put us at a much higher risk of being hit by an RPG. It was clear that we'd done exactly what the insurgents intended for us to do: drive right up to the obstacle and come to a stop. *They planned to eat us up at the intersections when we stopped.*

I had to think quickly. We weren't turning around and leaving the 101st's right flank exposed. And we couldn't go forward without damaging the gun trucks. Someone was going to have to get out and move all the fucking shit if we're going to make it through this. But this posed an enormous risk. It wasn't just the fact that you'd be an exposed and vulnerable target while out in the open—there was also a significant chance that the area was boobytrapped.

"Here's what we're going to do," I told Ryan and Keith. "I'm going to clear the obstacles, and Ryan is gonna cover for me from eleven o'clock to one o'clock. I'll take care of anything on either side of that. If I get hit, drive up and try to get me back in the vehicle. Got it?"

I told Keith to stop a safe distance away from the obstacle to minimize our vehicle's exposure. While we were still vulnerable to threats between the positions of eleven o'clock and one o'clock, I knew that with Ryan covering us, the enemy wouldn't have much time to engage us before they ate .240 rounds. Because of the angles, our gun truck couldn't be engaged from nine o'clock or three o'clock. But that also meant our gun truck couldn't see or support at nine o'clock or three o'clock.

"Listen, I'm going to go move all the shit," I informed Gun Truck #2. They confirmed that they were standing by to support us as needed while we eliminated the obstacle. "Once I move the fuckin' stuff, I'll jump back in and we'll keep moving. Got it?"

I exited the gun truck and sprinted to the obstacles in front of me. *Where to even start with this fucking mess?*

I grabbed the metal pole with the three stranded wires and began pulling it from the left side of the road to the right side to create an opening. I was grabbing my Leatherman to cut through the wire when my entire body jumped as several bullets whizzed past me from multiple directions. I'd only been exposed for a matter of seconds, and they'd already noticed. *F-U-C-K.* They were close, but I had no idea which direction the rounds were coming from. Ryan fired a few rounds just above me as I continued hauling the metal pole across the street. Jumping back into the truck for cover would only waste time. Someone had to clear the path.

Sweat beaded down my face. Another bullet whizzed past my head. Suddenly, an old memory flashed into my mind of the time I accidentally mowed over a nest of yellow jackets in North Carolina. How those yellow bastards had all swarmed around me at once, buzzing across my body and making the hairs on my arms stand up. I couldn't make out a single yellow jacket apart from the vibrating swarm. For a minute, I didn't understand why my mind had decided to play *that* highlight reel in my head at that particular time. *You're in fucking Baghdad, D, not mowing a goddamn lawn.*

Then I realized. The rounds sounded just like that swarm of yellow jackets. And they didn't let up.

I had worked up a nice sweat by then, but I was almost done. Just one more barrel to go. But then, out of the corner of my eye, I saw it: an armed fighter running from left to right, just down the street. Our eyes met, and he halted, raised his gun, and fired.

This is it.

Luckily for me, he wasn't much of a shot. I raised my rifle and fired back, discharging five rounds in his direction, but he vanished into thin air. Did he take the rounds and just keep running? I couldn't be sure.

As soon as I'd finished moving the barrel across the street and there was ample room for the gun trucks to navigate the obstacle, I sprinted back to Gun Truck #1 and we pressed onward.

It seemed that my chances of living long enough to participate in tonight's card game had just increased. I was grateful. I also didn't like the idea that I could have died thinking about mowing lawns and yellow jackets. *Fucking anticlimactic.*

We continued down the street and ran into three more roadblock scenarios, each instance strikingly like the initial encounter. Each time, I hopped out of the vehicle and cleared the junk while Ryan provided cover. Twice, I found myself twisted up and entangled by the mess of barbed wire, struggling to break free. On both occasions, Joe Joe swiftly jumped out of the vehicle to help. Joe Joe wore body armor over his floral shirt and carried Ryan's M4 rifle with him. Technically, it's against the rules for interpreters to bear arms, for many reasons. But nobody gives a fuck about that when you're fighting for your life and trying to survive. And that's why we had trained our interpreters on our weapon systems and ensured they knew what the fuck to do if things went south. Sometimes you gotta do what you gotta do.

But despite the chaos, we didn't waste the opportunity to bust each other's balls a little.

"I'm always bailing you out, D! What would you do without me?" Joe Joe yelled at me as he began to help clear the obstacle.

"Well, for one, I could breathe better. That nasty-ass Iraqi cologne is enough to make a grown man suffocate."

"Not what your mom said," he yelled over the noise. We were back to square one.

To an outsider, it might seem that this untimely and irreverent humor in the heat of battle is nothing but a waste of time and energy. But it helped maintain a sense of purposeful bravado and calmness under pressure. It gave us the feeling that it was just another day on the job. Those jokes gave us an unshakable confidence that we desperately needed in order to think clearly and remain unified in the face of danger.

Calm breeds calm.

My respect and love for Joe Joe grew as I watched him sweating in the heat next to me. The man had woken up with the intention of reuniting with his family but had changed his plans at a moment's notice and volunteered to risk his life to support the 101st. What's more, he hadn't hesitated to jump out in the open to stand by my side when I needed it most. His courage and reliability were unmatched. That man was my brother, and I would trust him with my life.

Once we'd removed the obstacles, we hopped back into the trucks and moved on. The gunners continued to engage any potential threat down the side streets. As we cleared the final obstacle at a major intersection, I checked in with Rick Townsen in Gun Truck #2. Rick Townsen was one of the most seasoned members on our team and excelled in coordinating with other elements while maintaining communication with ROWDY Base.

"You know what I was thinking about down there?" I asked with a smirk. "Yellow jackets. Those fucking rounds sounded just like the swarm that got me once when I was mowing the lawn."

He threw his head back and laughed. *Calm breeds calm.*

But our conversation was cut short. Brian Rainwater was firing the .50-caliber weapon. I booked it back to Gun Truck #1, crouching low to avoid attracting attention. As I opened the door, my eyes caught sight of a figure peering over the parapet, positioned strategically atop a nearby building. We had a twenty to twenty-five feet height difference with no more than fifty to seventy-five meters separating us in distance. The guy had a perfect vantage point—he was in a position to fire directly at Brian, Ryan, and myself. My heart rate spiked and adrenaline coursed through my blood. I slammed the door shut and sprinted toward Gun Truck #2.

Before I got there, I spotted a group of five insurgents emerging from the parapet, armed with AK-47s. While most of their bodies were shielded by the wall, their upper chest area and heads were exposed when they stood up. I fired three rounds in succession at the first insurgent that lined up within range. The first shot was too low. The next two rounds found their mark, striking the man's chest area with precision. The impact seemed to immobilize him, and he reacted as if he had been shocked by electricity. He dropped and vanished from sight. Meanwhile, the remaining insurgents retaliated by discharging multiple rounds in my direction while I continued to engage. A few of my rounds grazed the lower portion of the parapet, only causing minor damage.

"*BRIAN!*" I shouted, trying to alert him of the danger. But he couldn't hear me over the roar of the .50-caliber.

Taking cover behind the engine block of Gun Truck #2, I waited, ready to engage whenever the insurgents resurfaced again. As soon as I detected movement on the parapet, I unleashed a barrage of fire. I could tell that I hit at least two insurgents, as evidenced by their twitching bodies. But to my frustration, they seemed unaffected by the hits and continued to fire on us before seeking shelter once again.

Damn it, I cursed silently, realizing the limitations of the 5.56 green tip round I was using. The 5.56 green tip round is notorious for ripping small holes without stopping power. Pausing to collect myself, I took a deep breath. Another insurgent, having just emptied his magazine, stood motionless and dazed. Seizing the opportunity, I unleashed a controlled burst of rounds into his upper chest and head. He crumpled to the ground. *What the hell was he thinking?*

"*BRIAN!*" I shouted again as I dropped down to change magazines. No answer. He still couldn't hear me over the noise.

To avoid exposing myself from the same firing position, I shifted a good foot or so away from my previous spot behind the engine block, preparing for the next engagement. The wounded insurgents also changed their positions and started firing again. This time, they were right on top of me. When I opened fire, I finally got Brian's attention. With one motion of my muzzle, I signaled him to watch where my rounds landed and fire on the targets accordingly. No words necessary. Brian positioned the .50-caliber and unleashed a barrage of fire at the middle and top of the parapet. The sheer power of the .50-caliber rounds made a slapping sound as they tore through the cinder block and reduced the wall and the upper part of the building to rubble.

Dust, large fragments of brick and mortar, and remnants of bodies cascaded down the building's facade. Suddenly, I heard a woman's voice speaking in Arabic and spun around. Then I saw it. A woman shouting and moving in our direction from one o'clock. *What the fuck?* I aimed my rifle at her instinctually, waiting for confirmation that she posed no danger. When she showed no signs of being a threat, I lowered my rifle. I ran for Gun Truck #1 and knocked on the window, desperately trying to get Joe Joe's attention. I needed to know what the woman was shouting about and if there was some unforeseen danger that we'd neglected to notice.

"Joe Joe, what the fuck is she yelling about? She shouldn't be out here. She's going to get herself killed!" I said as soon as he jumped out of the vehicle. Joe Joe began speaking with her in Arabic.

"She's looking for her husband!" he yelled.

"If he was one of the dudes on the roof back there, he's dead as fuck," I said, making sure the woman couldn't hear what I said.

Joe Joe nodded grimly and directed the woman to return to her house and wait for her husband. She obeyed his orders and half-walked, half-jogged away from us, looking over her shoulder back at us every few steps before disappearing completely. *That's fucking odd*, I thought to myself.

Joe Joe and I climbed back into the gun truck and prepared to push forward. The relief of feeling the cool air conditioning revived me. The temperature hadn't reached the scorching levels like it would once summer came, but my sweat-drenched body and parched tongue were a clear reminder of the hour I'd spent with nothing but a dip of Copenhagen in my mouth. Disposing of the tobacco, I rinsed my mouth with water from the available supply in the truck and gulped down several sips. I checked for any signs of personal injury and made sure I had a fresh magazine. All good.

The road stretched out ahead of us, devoid of any obstacles. For a minute, things were looking good. But our relief was short-lived. As soon as the nose of the gun truck moved into the open space, we were met with a barrage of enemy fire. Ryan positioned the .240, ready to unleash a retaliatory response toward the incoming fire. But right in the middle of the escalating situation, my comms lit up with a frantic voice.

"ROWDY 7, ROWDY 7, you guys are leaking fluids like crazy."

It was Russ Hiatt, the driver of Gun Truck #2, reaching out to me over the radio.

Russ had maneuvered Gun Truck #2 amidst the chaos and effortlessly handled internal communication within the team like a rock star. He'd kept up with relaying critical information to ROWDY Base and coordinating with the 101st guys while exposed and under intense enemy fire like it was a walk in the park.

But his tone had changed, and I knew that could only mean one thing—we were in trouble. Before I could open my mouth to relay the message to Keith, he was already speaking loudly.

"D, I lost power. The engine is dead. I got nothing." Our engine block had suffered multiple hits. That's when I felt a sense of intense pressure wrapping its gnarly fingers around my throat.

"Fuck, we're in a kill zone and we have no power," I said loudly to Keith, trying to process the information myself. "Guys, our engine block has been shot out. We need to get the tow straps going."

Rick jumped out of the vehicle without hesitation, connecting the tow straps. Gun Truck #2 began pulling and we started moving again. I contacted Camp Apache to inform them about our situation.

"This is ROWDY 7. Our engine block was shot out. We are returning to camp to get another gun truck along with double the basic load of ammo so we can get back out here as quickly as possible."

After receiving confirmation, I made a call to the 101st, updating them on our status.

"We'll switch trucks and be back ASAP," I promised. We made it back to Camp Apache and swapped out our battle-torn vehicle for a new one. A bit of friendly tension ensued between those of us who had been out versus the guys who had stayed behind at camp.

"Hey, I'm the Bravo," one of the guys complained to Ryan. "You're the engineer. It only makes sense to let me get on that gun."

Ryan laughed, "Not today, bitch! I'm gunning for D."

We all laughed. The guys were hungry and relished the fight. I preferred having men who were eager to fight rather than those who lacked the courage. But I decided to retain the same group of men who had first accompanied me when we set out again with our new gun truck. If it ain't broke, don't fix it.

We reconnected with the 101st and the Iraqi Army near the Abu Hanifa Mosque, a location that was familiar to all of us. The mosque was situated close to Aimmah Bridge, which connected Adhamiyah and Kadhimayah over the Tigris River. Less than a year prior, on August 31, 2005, a devastating incident occurred on the al-Aimmah Bridge. Rumors of a suicide bomber had sparked panic during a Shia pilgrimage, resulting in a stampede that claimed the lives of over 950 people. Many were crushed or fell into the Tigris River from a height of thirty feet. As a result, the bridge was closed off and deemed impassable. Occasionally, American convoys, unaware of the danger in Adhamiyah and the bridge's closure, attempted to cross the al-Aimmah Bridge at night, only to realize it was inaccessible and had to turn back. Each time this happened, they faced hostile fire from the vicinity of the Abu Hanifa Mosque.

A dozen thoughts crowded my mind as we faced the Abu Hanifa Mosque. We soon linked up with the 101st without incident and delivered 7.62 and .50-caliber ammunition. We were curious as to what the insurgents' next move would be. The Abu Hanifa Mosque was bustling with a crowd of people. The insurgents had discarded their weapons and were trying to blend into the crowd. No one fired in our direction. It was clear that they had reached a point of surrender, exhausted from the conflict. The fight was over.

I radioed the 101st and told them that we were headed back to Camp Apache now that the threat had been eliminated. While en route back to base, we received a notification informing us of the unfortunate loss of several Iraqi police officers in Adhamiyah. Due to the large Sunni population majority in the area and the predominantly Shia composition of the Iraqi police, fear prevented them from retrieving the bodies and equipment that were left behind. Given our presence in the vicinity and our familiarity with the suspected location of the vehicles, we willingly took it upon ourselves to investigate and assist the Iraqi police. Although we did not come across any deceased or injured officers, we successfully recovered several Iraqi police trucks and weapons. We returned to Camp Apache just over two hours later.

Within half an hour after returning to Camp Apache, our compound was greeted by a First Group team, along with Luke, who we'd dropped off that morning. Luke had been collaborating with the First Group team on the Taji target set since it fell within their area of operation. First Group, like the rest of our company, heard about the intense firefight in Adhamiyah over the radio. They had offered to drop off Luke at Camp Apache since it was conveniently located on their route back to Taji. Shortly after their arrival with three gun trucks, the 101st called in an update that the insurgents in Adhamiyah had reemerged on the streets and prepared for battle. We welcomed the news now that we had an additional Special Forces team and a total of five gun trucks.

After a quick huddle with First Group's team sergeant, we headed back out. While patrolling the streets, we encountered a few minor altercations, but they paled in comparison to what we had just experienced. With no imminent threat, we had a chance to survey the damage in the aftermath of the battle—charred vehicles, raging fires, fallen power lines, and scattered brass from all the rounds fired. We hardly spoke as we took in the sight with reverent silence, knowing full well that those dirty streets could have been any one of our deathbeds.

When we returned to Camp Apache, I expressed my gratitude to the First Group team for bringing Luke home and for volunteering their help to support us. When they left, I instructed everyone to clean weapons and work on getting the gun trucks back in fighting shape.

Later, we discovered that a coalition of Sunni groups, including Ansar al-Sunna, al-Qaeda, the 1920 Revolution Brigades, and the Adhamiyah Omar Army, had masterminded a well-thought-out assault on the Iraqi Army positions in Adhamiyah earlier that morning. Equipped with PKM machine guns, AK-47s, and RPGs, around fifty insurgents executed their mission with the aim of seizing control of Adhamiyah and instilling fear in both the Iraqi Army and American forces.

April 17, 2006, was one hell of a close call, the kind of experience that makes you realize just how fragile life can be. But against all odds, we made it out alive. Every year since, I've made it a point to celebrate that day, to raise a glass to remember the day we danced with death and lived to tell the tale.

CHAPTER 8

SKI MASK TERRORISTS

Throughout history, every major war era is marked by a unique set of characteristics. These characteristics not only shape the outcome of the conflict but also how battles were fought, which is a testament to humanity's resilience, innovation, and propensity for destruction. In the history of human conflict, warfare is a chameleon, adapting not only to technology and strategy but also to the cultural, social, and political landscapes of each era.

In ancient warfare, there was a time when swords and spears in the hands of brave warriors were the greatest force on Earth. Forged from bronze, iron, and eventually steel, these were the tools of destruction to be feared. Battles were mass coordinated as armies in formations like the Greek phalanx or the Roman legion advanced with discipline and unity. Siege engines like catapults and battering rams were the artillery of this era, and strategies were all about maintaining that formation, exploiting terrain, and using close combat weapons effectively.

Then came an era marked by guns thundering onto the battlefield—a seismic shift in the art of warfare. The emergence of firearms and gunpowder disrupted everything. The musket's extended range and firepower forced us to rethink our tactics. Linear formations became the norm, with rows of soldiers firing in unison. Cannons were made, bringing down entire fortresses. The dynamics of warfare were never the same.

Then another page turned into the deafening explosions and trench warfare of the World Wars. This was the era of explosives, where dynamite and other deadly concoctions controlled the game. Artillery shells filled with explosives wreaked havoc on the battlefield. Then came chemical warfare, which brought yet another horrifying dimension: poison gas choking the air. This led us to an era of precision. Guided missiles, precision airstrikes, and powerful explosives have turned warfare into a science of destruction. Guerrilla warfare and insurgency evolved, with IEDs becoming effective weapons against conventional forces.

The war we were tasked with fighting was no different. It came with its own set of characteristics, strategies, and challenges. One of the most prevalent characteristics was the use of IEDs, which became a significant threat in Iraq, particularly in the mid-2000s. They were often employed by insurgent groups primarily against coalition forces, including US troops. At times, they were used to target Iraqi civilians and infrastructure. The use of IEDs in Iraq escalated around 2004 and reached its peak in 2006 and 2007, just in time to welcome us to the scene.

So, when we got word that after completing a stint at a US military school, it was time for the final member of our team to join us at Camp Apache, we had a grand idea. Aaron Gallagher brought a lot of energy, experience, intelligence know-how, and advanced special operations competence to our team. From the sunny shores of California, Aaron was an avid surfer and looked the part. But beneath his SoCal charm was a hell of a warrior. This dichotomy defined Aaron as the guy who effortlessly blended the laid-back cool of California with the intense dedication of a warrior on the field.

We felt that it was only fitting to give him a proper welcome to Baghdad in a celebratory style befitting the era of war in which we found ourselves. What better way to give him a warm welcome than to stage an IED just outside our perimeter fence and trigger it as Aaron approached in one of the gun trucks? Since it was Aaron's first time in Baghdad, he was unfamiliar with the compound's layout and would be completely oblivious to the fact that this mock IED was strategically placed right outside our perimeter. The moment I shared my bright idea with the rest of the team, they were in. Just the idea of it made us grin like hyenas. Dark military humor at its finest. For days, we conspired to pull off the prank perfectly. We invested all the collective strategic planning and meticulous execution skills that we'd spent years cultivating into a single prank. It was going to be epic, of that much we were certain. The simulated IED wouldn't do anything harmful; it would just create a minor explosion with a substantial amount of white flour to give the appearance of smoke. It would be harmless but intense enough to scare poor Aaron shitless. We couldn't wait to see his face.

To help Aaron acclimate to Baghdad and gain a better understanding of our operational surroundings, we decided to have him ride in the TC seat of Gun Truck #1. This position would allow him to have a front-row view of our movements and get a feel for the city's dynamics. As the time approached for the gun trucks to depart from the Green Zone, we began making our final preparations for the prank. It was one of the rare occasions when I wouldn't be part of the convoy, which meant I could stay back and watch the prank from a distance.

I tuned in to the radio communication, carefully monitoring the convoy's progress as it got closer. Through the radio traffic, I caught wind of when the team was nearing our compound. The excitement among the team was palpable as we all anticipated the big moment. The more we talked about it, the more we couldn't contain our eagerness. Humor was often the best outlet for all the pent-up and suppressed emotions that we compressed within ourselves.

Finally, the moment we had all been waiting for had arrived. Aaron, stationed in the TC seat of Gun Truck #1, drove right up to where our meticulously planned fake IED was positioned. We could hardly breathe, all crowded around waiting for the big moment.

But that big moment never came. The explosion was a pathetically small, barely audible little poof. The "smoke" was nothing more than a goddamn unicorn fart. The entire thing was a dud. A total flop of a practical joke. To make matters worse, Aaron was completely oblivious to the entire ordeal. He neither saw nor heard anything out of the ordinary and emerged from the vehicle wearing an expression that seemed to say, "I thought it was dangerous as hell here. Seems peaceful to me."

Our prank, which we had hoped would be a memorable and hilarious welcome, had fallen flat on its face. Nothing but a couple of flour farts on the road. The collective groan of frustration and disappointment among us was louder than our little explosion.

Dark Special Forces combat humor: 0

Lame/shitty engineer sergeant who built our fake IED: 0

California cool dude Aaron: 1

I had served alongside Aaron during previous rotations, both in Iraq from 2004 to 2005 at FOB Caldwell within Kirkush Military Training Base and in Kosovo in late 2003. I had a deep appreciation for his qualities as a teammate. Aaron was solid; his talent and reliability were unquestionable. He was the final piece of the puzzle, and I was happy to have him with us. While our personal efforts to welcome Aaron to Baghdad with a little danger and action seemed to have initially failed, a handful of insurgents in Adhamiyah saw fit to make up for it that very day.

"Hey, D, you might want to take a look at this." It was Jody Thrasher who first alerted me to the situation from the security cameras at the base of the stairs. In March, we had welcomed another member to our tribe: Army Sergeant of the Guard Jody Thrasher. Jody was recalled back to active duty, thrown into a mixer of bodies, and luckily ended up on assignment to our team. As a Special Forces team, we needed someone to man the cameras 24/7, answer the phones, and handle administrative tasks that came along, allowing us to maintain our focus on critical missions. We received this support from our army counterparts, who agreed to send over one of their brightest to stay with us at Camp Apache. This support meant that we didn't have to burn the candle at both ends, conserving our energy.

But integrating a new member at camp is not always a smooth process. Special Forces units operate very differently from the regular military, and that distinction was abundantly clear. We thrived in the gray zone, often far from conventional military rules and regulations. We sported beards, wore ballcaps, and deviated from traditional methods and strategies. Learning to operate alongside us was always a significant change for the regular army guys. We tried to be sensitive to that fact when we had young army guys among us. We didn't want to be viewed as a force of corruption by our army counterparts, but somehow it seemed to happen that way. A young sergeant would arrive fresh-faced and buttoned up and end up on a first-name basis with a bunch of senior guys. This had the tendency to create stress between their unit and ours. I didn't want to cause any trouble or undermine the discipline and training of the young soldiers who were tasked with supporting our team. But I also wasn't going to ask my team to cramp our style because of one new addition. While we had a few soldiers from the 101st with us, there was still a lingering sense of caution when it came to fully trusting them to operate in our unique way. But Jody was different. We dished out a little tough love to Jody for the first few weeks, then welcomed him with open arms. He was a hard worker, and we respected him for it. He was tall, lanky, studious, and had a deep Alabama drawl that made us laugh. "You guys are just a bunch of rattlesnakes and assassins!" Jody remarked in that thick drawl a few days after arriving at Camp Apache, looking more scared than anything. *Rattlesnakes and assassins.* We appreciated the label, and it stuck.

Jody was funny as hell and didn't take things too seriously. On top of that, he was always ready to roll up his sleeves and help in any way possible. As such, Jody quickly became an integral part of the team.

Gathering around the monitors of our advanced forward-looking infrared (FLIR) camera system in front of Jody, a wave of unease washed over me. The FLIR cameras were conveniently positioned on our rooftop, providing a bird's-eye view of Adhamiyah. A scene unfolded before our eyes like a movie.

Our cameras offered a clear view of the Adhamiyah police station located just a few hundred meters from Camp Apache. Unfortunately, we had grown accustomed to seeing it lit up by enemy fighters. The police station was a frequent target, often enduring multiple attacks within a single day. These attacks typically followed a pattern—a dangerous game of hit-and-run. A handful of insurgents or enemy fighters would unleash a brief flurry of rounds at the station and then swiftly retreat. The insurgents were experts at blending back into the civilian population after carrying out these assaults. Both the insurgents and the Iraqi police seemed particularly fond of these cat-and-mouse game tactics. The police, in many instances, were ill-equipped and overwhelmed, making them easy targets. They were the undertrained and underprepared underdogs in the game. The scenario repeated itself frequently.

But the scene unfolding in front of us on the FLIR cameras was far from the typical one we had grown used to. There was something distinctly off about these enemy fighters. They were all concealed behind ski masks, bearing a chilling resemblance to the terrorists from the infamous Munich massacre during the 1972 Summer Olympics in Munich, West Germany. We dubbed our enemy fighters the Munich massacre insurgents. The nickname stuck. *This is certainly a departure from the usual routine*, I thought. I moved closer to the screens for a better view.

The figures on the monitor popped in and out of sight, making it challenging to confirm their exact numbers. Still, it was evident that there were between four and six armed fighters, each wielding AK-47s, and all ominously shrouded in ski masks. It wasn't only the ski masks that captured our attention; it was their tactical movements as well. These fighters displayed a level of training and discipline that wasn't typical among many of the adversaries we encountered in Iraq. Instead of the usual "spray and pray" approach, they methodically aimed their weapons before firing, indicating a degree of marksmanship and calculated aggression that demanded respect. Equally notable was their use of cover, a skill that required both training and experience. This was a significant departure from the rather unorganized fighting tactics we were accustomed to seeing. The entire situation had taken an eerie and unsettling turn. We needed to support the Iraqi police station as best we could.

A fire ignited behind Ryan's and Dave's eyes. I knew exactly what they were going to say before they uttered a single word.

"We're headed to the roof!" they shouted as they nearly broke into a run upstairs. This was a common tactic of ours when things got interesting at the Iraqi police station.

"Roger that, just make sure you're up on comms," I shouted to them. "If you can get a shot, take it."

"Got it. Hell yeah, we will." Ryan's voice was filled with excitement. I couldn't blame him for the enthusiasm; these were the moments we lived for.

Our designated two-man sniper team, Ryan and Luke, had recently completed a one-week sniper refresher training course as part of our pre-deployment preparations. Upon arriving at Camp Apache, Ryan and Luke diligently worked on re-zeroing all the sniper weapons. This standard procedure accounted for climate and elevation changes, ensuring precise and accurate shots.

They had previously been given an opportunity to test out the new gear shortly after our arrival in an incident we later dubbed Operation King's Monument. This operation had been prompted by recurring harassing fire directed at our back civilian vehicle gate from local insurgents during the night. The insurgents would launch rapid bursts of small arms fire at our Iraqi guards stationed at the gate before disappearing into the darkness. Clearly, they didn't know who they were fucking with.

It was time to put an end to the nonsense and establish a powerful presence in the area.

One night, as the sun was setting, Ryan, Luke, Dave, and I had climbed to an elevated vantage point where we could see the area where we believed the insurgents were attacking our compound. As expected, a few hours later, the insurgents had moved into position and started firing on the back gate with their AK-47s before attempting to retreat. *Not so fast, little dudes.* Ryan lifted his weapon of choice—the Mk12 Special Purpose Rifle, commonly known as the MARK-12. With an effective range of seven hundred meters, it was exceptionally well-suited for urban combat due to its compact and lightweight design, giving enhanced mobility in tight spaces while maintaining precision. It seamlessly transitioned from a sniper rifle for long-range accuracy to an assault rifle for close-quarters engagements, eliminating the need for multiple weapons.

Its semi-automatic action and generous thirty-round magazine capacity provided a higher rate of fire and fewer reloads, which was essential in fast-paced urban combat situations. With a built-in suppressor to reduce noise and flash signatures, we didn't have to worry about tipping off our location.

As soon as the insurgents began to open fire, we were in the perfect position to get a straight line of sight on them. When one of the insurgents fired his AK-47, Ryan and Luke executed a synchronized sniper shot, hitting him with deadly precision just as he reached the far side of the road. The other two enemy fighters ran away. It was clear that they should not return to retrieve their buddy unless they were ready to join him on the ground.

Operation King's Monument had showcased the skills and teamwork of our sniper team. But even with a successful win in our pocket, my years of experience in special operations had taught me a valuable lesson—far quicker than we gave them credit for, the enemy had become eerily adept at recognizing our effective engagement areas versus the zones where we couldn't reach them. They had developed an uncanny sixth sense for it that had been refined over the course of three years. As a result, they tended to stay within these "safe" areas. It was a science; they knew precisely where to evade our reach.

So now, as Ryan and Dave ran upstairs, I harbored doubts that they would be able to engage the enemy fighters effectively from our location. As the attack on the Iraqi police station escalated, the team grew increasingly eager to load up the gun trucks and join the fight. But my intuition was sounding a note of caution, urging me to pause and gather more information before making a move. Something about the situation didn't sit right. *Always aggressive, never reckless.* That was my motto as team sergeant.

Still positioned in front of the FLIR cameras, I weighed out our options. I couldn't shake the feeling that this might be a trap, a planned and coordinated ambush intended to draw us into a deadly confrontation. Another possibility was that the insurgents had prepared an IED or VBIED for us, even though such tactics weren't standard in Adhamiyah. There's always a first for everything, though.

Luke voiced his impatience, urging us to take immediate action. "D, let's go kill these motherfuckers," he pleaded.

But before I could even respond, the scene on the monitors took an unexpected twist. One of the ski mask assailants jolted like he'd been hit by lightning.

"Holy shit, that dude just got fucked up," I blurted out as the surreal scene played out before us.

The precision of the shots was undeniable, and the enemy fighter went down hard. Suddenly, another one dropped to the ground. "DAYYYUMMNNN, Ryan and Dave are fucking them up!"

The remaining enemy fighters appeared disoriented. Their confusion was visible as they frantically scanned their surroundings, trying to pinpoint the source of the shots that had taken down their comrades. At first, they huddled around the two wounded insurgents on the ground. But then, they stood to their feet and ran for cover as if a collective realization dawned on both simultaneously—*If my buddy just got hit, I'll be next.*

I would later discover that when Dave and Ryan geared up—Dave with his M4 and Ryan with his Mk12—and climbed to the rooftop, they were still unsure whether the situation called for engagement. However, when it became clear that the insurgents possessed an unprecedented level of audacity and training, they knew what needed to be done. The determination and aggression radiating from their movements posed a greater threat than the typical spray-and-pray bandits who would occasionally show up to harass us.

Over the years, the team house's roof had undergone security and combat upgrades. It featured elevated sniper positions, also known as eagle's nests, as well as a reinforced bunker that housed a .50-caliber machine gun. However, the Iraqi police station and the enemy's escape routes were mostly hidden from these positions. The enemy fighters seemed to be aware of the visual limitations of Camp Apache. They deliberately moved in a pattern that minimized the risk of encountering our ODA from any clear vantage points we had.

But the insurgents made one big mistake—they continued firing on the Iraqi police station for an extended period, which allowed Ryan and Dave to get creative. Ryan spotted a precarious position on the roof, offering a narrow line of vision to engage the insurgents as they moved between their fighting positions. This makeshift sniper position was vastly different from the established sniper nests. It lacked the stability, cover, and concealment that our usual positions provided. Moreover, it posed significant safety concerns as it perched on a precarious arch-like structure with a forty-foot drop below. To get in position, Ryan had to navigate an obstacle course of wires, pipes, and other obstacles while carrying a sniper rifle and extra magazines. Ryan didn't mind. He crawled out on the ledge and positioned himself, belly down against the concrete, ready to fire. It was the only vantage point that offered a clear shot.

The distance from Ryan's perch to the insurgents was approximately 350 to 400 meters. The high winds, coupled with the sporadic movement of the enemy fighters, made it a difficult shot. It would require constant adjustments, timing, and precision, especially since the position lacked the stability and safety of conventional sniper nests.

Ryan and Dave wanted to provide the Iraqi police with a little relief—and the risk paid off. Ryan lined up a shot with perfect precision and took it. The rest of us witnessed the instant effects of it on the FLIR cameras like a movie.

As Ryan and Dave continued to fire on the insurgents, they began to move with less predictable force, indicating that the intended psychological effect had taken hold. In the blink of an eye, panic set in. The ski-masked insurgents scattered in every direction, leaving one fighter behind to aid his injured companion in a desperate attempt to escape the area. *Gotcha.*

Seeing the hits land on the enemy fighters, I knew we'd just gained the upper hand. The initiative had swung firmly in our favor and the tables had turned. Now it was our turn to dictate the course of the engagement.

Ski Mask Terrorists

"Come on, guys. Let's roll," I called.

While the rest of the ODA prepared to roll out in gun trucks, I directed Ryan and Dave to stay in position. They'd be able to maximize damage on the enemy and provide crucial support as the team moved to engage the threat. I told them to shift their line of fire above ground level as soon as we came into their view. Second and third floors only to avoid friendly fire.

While Ryan and Dave remained on the roof to provide sniper support, I assigned Aaron the driver's seat in Gun Truck #1. We headed toward the Iraqi police station through a winding neighborhood road just a few hundred meters away.

As we cleared the gate of our compound, Aaron unexpectedly turned right instead of heading straight to the exit through the main gate of Camp Apache. In anger, I yelled over the roar of the gun truck engine, "Hey, what the fuck are you doing? Where are you going? Stop!"

Aaron, caught up in the intensity of the moment, yelled back, "Fuck, I don't know! This isn't the exit. Which way am I supposed to go?"

That's when it hit me that this was Aaron's first time driving in this environment. He didn't have a clue where to go. I kicked myself silently for my outburst, for my failure to prepare my fellow team members, and for not being a better TC, navigator, and leader.

"We need to exit here," I said, pointing him in the direction of the main gate.

Even in the heat of the moment, the incident served as a tough reminder of the importance of continuously improving as a leader. I knew immediately that the mistake belonged to me, and I took ownership of that fact. I had failed to equip my teammate with the necessary information to properly execute the job at hand. Even though it was just a small mistake without any serious repercussions, I couldn't let it happen again. "My bad, man. We're straight now. Let's go."

As we rolled up to the X, the focal point where the enemy fighters had been firing at the Iraqi police station, it was evident that they were retreating down one of the main streets. Gun Truck #1's

.240 machine gunner continued to engage them until they vanished down the side streets.

The atmosphere in the area was tainted by a strong and pungent odor of diesel fuel, likely from a major leak in one of the neighborhood generators. *Fucking stinks.*

My immediate priority was to assess the situation in the vicinity before our team ventured deeper into the Adhamiyah neighborhood. A member of our local Iraqi force named Sami, who was seated behind the driver in Gun Truck #1, joined me for a quick reconnaissance.

Although there was no more gunfire in our immediate vicinity, the distant sound of AK-47s continued to echo just a couple of streets away. I reckoned that was probably a celebratory fire from the retreating enemy fighters, who were putting on a show in front of their neighbors and friends.

As I moved closer to the area where we believed the downed enemy fighter to be, I caught sight of a ski mask lying on the street, surrounded by pools of fresh blood. The blood hadn't even dried. My attention shifted to a blood trail leading away from the mask. The sweltering heat caused sweat to stream down from my helmet into my eyes—it was already getting hot and summer wasn't even in full swing.

I stayed fixed on the blood trail as it led me approximately one hundred meters, right up to an old school bus that was riddled with bullet holes and left abandoned in the street. I couldn't see anyone on the bus, but I had a gut feeling that one of the enemy fighters had sought refuge inside. The blood trail pointed straight to it. I radioed our team using our internal call signs, informing our senior weapons sergeant, known as "Three-Five," that I was moving to investigate the school bus.

Accompanied by Sami, I stepped onto the bus and quickly scanned the floor from front to back. Then I saw it: halfway down the bus, two legs were visible, and blood was everywhere. It was clear from the gruesome scene that the fighter had bled out after sustaining a serious injury. I walked up close to inspect the body. There was a gunshot wound on his back and abdomen area, which left no doubt in my mind that it was the same fighter that Ryan had engaged. A pungent odor filled the bus, a mixture of blood and what smelled like urine.

The fighter's left hand was soaked in blood. *Must've tried to stop the bleeding with his hand, but that didn't work*, I thought to myself as I looked at the vacant shell of a man in front of me. *What a way to go.*

The last thing he saw was the inside of an old bus as he bled to death.

I stood there for a minute, surveying the grim aftermath of our engagement with the enemy fighter, thoughts racing through my mind. I couldn't help but wonder about the man in front of me. Did he hear me and Sami approaching and realize that we were just outside, closing in on him? Had he lost control and urinated out of sheer fear, or was it a macabre side effect of his fatal injuries? A sort of dark curiosity had taken over my mind, but I pushed the unsettling thoughts to the side.

We needed to gather any intelligence we could from the scene. I searched through the dead insurgent's belongings and discovered $200 in US currency, a relatively new Nokia cell phone, and a few phone numbers. I put the items into a Ziploc bag for further analysis.

Stepping off the bus, Sami and I quickly devised a simple plan. We would conduct a hasty clearance of the side streets branching off from the main road, the same path the enemy fighters had used to retreat. I assigned roles for our plan: Sami would clear the left side while I took the right side. Based on our knowledge of the area, the layout of Adhamiyah, and the last known positions of the fighters, we calculated that they would likely be hiding on the side streets—specifically, on my side.

Our main goal was to minimize the risk of our gun trucks falling prey to an RPG attack from any of these side streets. I directed Gun Truck #1 and Gun Truck #2 to follow us down the northwest road and offer support as necessary. We all wanted to avoid getting entangled in a complex ambush involving RPGs, PKM machine guns, or AK-47s. Once again, we chose tactics that emphasized surprise, speed, and decisive action. Our plan was to strike with force and swiftness, quickly move to a new position, strike again, and then keep on moving. We didn't have the resources or the capability to sustain a prolonged firefight.

My goal was to stay on foot and assess the situation ahead of the vehicles, allowing us the opportunity to retreat if needed. We adopted a hit-and-run approach—cross the road, engage, and then seek cover. After Sami and I cleared the first street, we would jump back in the gun trucks and move towards the next street. When we approached a side street, the gun trucks would halt, and Sami and I would disembark to clear the street before we proceeded. This tactic served a dual purpose—it baited the enemy into revealing their capabilities while we were mobile and unpredictable. Our experience in previous engagements had taught us that when a firefight erupted, most civilians sought shelter indoors. Those who remained on the streets and armed themselves were looking for a fight, and we were more than willing to oblige. We alternated between firing from the vehicle and dismounting for on-foot engagements.

We had a fight on our hands right from the start. At the first side street, I encountered a group of armed fighters about 100–150 meters away from our position. They seemed taken aback by my on-foot approach, and I capitalized on their surprise by opening fire, discharging ten to fifteen rounds before making it to the other side of the street. They took cover and returned fire in my general direction. That was the signal to bring the gun trucks forward to engage. The gunners unleashed fire. When they were done, no one fired back. We continued to repeat this pattern until we cleared the next five side streets, using the element of surprise, speed, and the sheer violence of action to disorient the enemy fighters and maintain control of the situation.

Throughout the ordeal, Ryan and Dave continued to provide vital support, firing precision shots at armed targets of opportunities. From their elevated vantage point, they had a perfect line of sight to provide a watchful eye over us. Ryan later reported that the moment our vehicles moved out of his line of sight and a sudden and intense exchange of gunfire erupted, he knew that we were getting after it.

On the ground and in the heat of battle, the enemy fighters fired. We responded and continued to move in the same pattern up the street. But conducting a proper battle damage assessment to determine how many enemy fighters were wounded or killed in action proved to be incredibly difficult. This wasn't like the movies, where you fire a few rounds and the enemy slowly crumbles to the ground like a sack of potatoes. There was no instant gratification, no quick kills confirmed. Accuracy and precision are challenging to gauge. Despite our best efforts, we couldn't be entirely certain about the effectiveness of our rounds.

But after some time, it became evident that we had done our duty. Our swift and brutal action had shocked the ski-mask insurgents, whoever they were, and sent them promptly into hiding. We'd made an example of them, leaving no room for doubt in the eyes of the community that the local Iraqi police force was being supported by the American military.

This situation serves as further proof of a truth I firmly hold to: a fixed set of tactics repeatedly employed without variation due to narrow-minded thinking is a recipe for disaster.

This sentiment was especially true during our 2006 deployment, where the ability to innovate and adapt was vital to survival. The insurgency we faced was a dynamic and ever-changing adversary, and failing to evolve alongside it would only have catastrophic consequences. Our encounter with the Munich massacre insurgents, as perplexing as it was, gave us a glimpse into the web of factions, motivations, and interests that defined the national landscape of Iraq in 2006. We never saw them again, and their affiliation remained a puzzle. This uncertainty was emblematic of the broader challenge we faced—understanding the complex interplay of organizations and groups vying for power and influence in Iraq. It was a murky world where loyalties shifted constantly. Perhaps the ski-mask insurgents were connected to the Iraqi army or a militia element within the government, frustrated with the perceived sectarian loyalty of the police force.

Our mission, in part, was to help rebuild and empower the Iraqi security forces, but it was an uphill battle. Corruption, internal divisions, and a lack of commitment plagued these institutions. Society itself was torn apart by historical grievances and religious differences. Amidst this complexity, Iran also emerged as a covert player in the game, operating at a level of strategic sophistication that often caught us off guard. Iran had a knack for transforming enemies into allies, wielding its influence in Iraq effectively. Its ability to provide support to the vulnerable segments of society won the country support in unexpected places. While we grappled with the insurgency, Iran was playing at a pro level right under our noses, often outmaneuvering us in many respects.

On June 14, 2006, Iraq's prime minister announced the immediate commencement of Operation Together Forward. This operation involved the participation of nearly fifty thousand troops from forty-eight Iraqi and coalition battalions. There were thirteen Iraqi Army battalions, twenty-five Iraqi national police battalions, and ten coalition battalions comprising 21,000 Iraqi police, 13,000 Iraqi national police, 8,500 Iraqi Army soldiers, and approximately 7,200 coalition forces. The primary objective of these troops was to implement a "clear, hold, build" strategy in Baghdad. With the Iraqis taking the lead and tackling the most challenging tasks, coalition forces were supposed to partner with Iraqi troops to "clear" various neighborhoods in the city. Simultaneously, the Iraqi police would be responsible for "holding" the areas that had been cleared, while the Iraqi ministries and local governments focused on the task of "building" and developing the areas with the assistance of the coalition. This new phase of the Baghdad Security Plan was supposed to represent a significant step forward in ensuring the safety and stability of the city. With a collaborative effort between Iraqi and coalition forces, Operation Together Forward aimed to create a secure environment for the citizens of Baghdad.

But Operation Together Forward was characterized by large-scale clearing operations that yielded limited intelligence and caused unrest among Baghdad's Sunni neighborhoods. These operations largely overlooked areas controlled by Shia militias like Sadr City and Sha'ab. As a result, when Sunni areas were cleared, they were often left without a lasting security arrangement. In many cases, this left the local inhabitants even more vulnerable to sectarian killings than before. Just ten days into the operation, the Iraqi coalition forces' periodic review acknowledged this fact publicly, saying, "Sunni citizens continue to fear the Ministry of the Interior, Jaysh al-Mahdi [JAM], and Badr death squads. High-profile incidents of intimidation persist, and JAM continues to carry out assassinations. Adhamiyah, Dora, and Mansour remain key areas of violence." This media coverage perfectly summed up the ineffectiveness of the operation, with most reports replacing the term "reconciliation" with "civil war." That was exactly what we were facing.

Our training prior to deployment, although valuable, was only the beginning. Experience on the ground taught us real lessons. We were thrown into a world where we needed to learn about the deep historical and cultural factors that fueled the unrest between the Sunnis, Shias, Kurds, and others.

I think very few Americans fully grasped the intricacies of the situation at the time. Most people back home had a simplistic view of the war—the good guys versus the bad guys. But it was never that simple. Even *we* thought that we'd come prepared and were instead met with a rude awakening once we were on the ground. We were fighting a sectarian web of complexities, a civil war, and an enemy that was far more cunning than we had first anticipated. The more we immersed ourselves in the community and spent time talking with our local partners, the more we understood the depth of the mounting tension in the area and the more effective we became in our mission.

By embracing innovation under pressure in our tactics and strategies, we gave ourselves a fighting chance. We weren't just responding to the insurgency; we were proactively shaping our battlefield. Constant adaptability was the key to our success. It allowed us to stay one step ahead, to outthink and outmaneuver our opponents, and ultimately, to achieve our mission objectives while minimizing risks to our team.

But it wasn't easy. Our run-in with the ski mask insurgents was just another reminder that just when we thought we knew the players and understood the game, everything could change in an instant.

CHAPTER 9

GRAND THEFT AUTO

On March 26, 2006, an event unfolded in the heart of Baghdad that passed through the ranks and served as a grim reminder of the enemy we were up against. Operation Valhalla, as it came to be known, stood as a vivid testament to the cunning and strategic prowess of our adversaries. The news of this operation reached our team swiftly, leaving a mark on every one of us. It served as a stark reminder of the complexities and dangers faced by Special Forces amid the ongoing war.

The incident unfolded as the Iraqi Special Operations Forces (ISOF) and US Army Special Forces engaged in a battle against a JAM death squad deep within the confines of Sadr City. Initially, the operation seemed no different from the countless others targeting those responsible for the merciless killings of Iraqi civilians and American troops.

As the joint forces closed in on the JAM compound, a fierce firefight erupted, resulting in the demise of sixteen or seventeen JAM fighters. Amid the chaotic exchange of gunfire, an unexpected discovery unfolded. The teams stumbled upon an extensive cache of weapons, which they promptly neutralized. They also managed to rescue a severely beaten hostage and apprehended approximately sixteen additional JAM members. It was a resounding victory, a flawless execution of a meticulously planned operation.

However, this triumph was abruptly interrupted when the narrative took an unforeseen and dramatic twist.

By the time ISOF, accompanied by their American Special Forces advisors, returned to their compound at Area Four about an hour after the firefight, they found the media lit up in a frenzy. Photos had been leaked to the press of the aftermath, only the JAM compound had undergone a strange transformation. The photos looked nothing like the scene as they left it.

The bodies of the JAM fighters had been rearranged and their weapons removed. Instead of evidence correctly showing the bodies of the fighters as having fallen in the act of firing weapons, they now appeared to have been killed on their knees in prayer. The bodies were photographed in new positions, and the images quickly found their way onto the internet—accompanied by a press release that accused American soldiers of entering a mosque and killing a peaceful group of men while they were praying. The manipulation of the scene had taken place less than an hour after the operation. The repercussions of the fabricated story were far-reaching. The American and Arab media latched onto the story almost immediately, amplifying the allegations. An investigation was launched, a process which spanned roughly a month. During this period, the Special Forces unit was sidelined and barred from entering Sadr City. Operation Valhalla served as an ominous warning to all of us, a stark reminder of just how quickly the fog of war can blur the lines between heroism and controversy.

Navigating the sectarian tension and political environment of the time was no easy task. At the helm of the nation, Iraqi Prime Minister Nouri al-Maliki, a Shia Muslim, pursued a sectarian agenda, firmly establishing a Shia-dominated state that paid little heed to the concerns of the Sunnis. This disenfranchisement had been brewing since the initial invasion of Iraq in 2003, and tensions had escalated. The situation took a darker turn when Iraqi police resorted to violence against peaceful Sunni protestors, employing anti-terrorism laws to conduct mass

Grand Theft Auto

arrests of Sunni civilians. al-Maliki forged political alliances with violent Shia militias, fueling the flames of Sunni frustration. It seemed as though the prime minister was unrelenting in targeting and eliminating Sunnis. However, a shift occurred when it came to targeting Shia interests. al-Maliki began applying political pressure on the general officers leading the war effort in Iraq. These same officers were already grappling with intense scrutiny from politicians and the media back in the United States. This multifaceted pressure made it even more challenging for us to carry out our duties effectively.

Around this period, we witnessed a noticeable shift in the targeting paradigm. A significant portion of the targets we pursued were Shia. The CIA seemed to be so focused on gathering intel on al-Qaeda that there was very little intel on dangerous targets and militant leaders within the local Shiite community and the Iranian influence. Even at camp, the lines were drawn. Hussein consistently backed us up if our actions were against a Sunni target but refused to support any operations targeting Shia groups. This stance became increasingly apparent after the February 22 Shia mosque bombing in Samarra, and it was a sentiment shared by many Shias at the time. Hussein's anger was notably directed at the Sunnis in Adhamiyah and their revered mosque, Abu Hanifa, which was among the most prominent Sunni mosques in Baghdad. We had to be careful not to discuss any matter that involved Shia groups or potential targets around Hussein.

We were committed to being "equal opportunists" who showed no regard for race or religion when it came to executing targets. But our mission became far more complicated when certain Shia targets or enclaves were declared "off-limits" to us, despite clear data that proved their involvement with terrorist organizations. We had no choice but to innovate and devise creative strategies to draw Shia targets out of hiding and into our operational net. This is far easier said than done. In the face of these challenges, we made a collective decision to redouble our efforts. We viewed the situation not as a setback but as a unique opportunity to demonstrate our resourcefulness.

For several months, we'd been on the trail of a Mahdi Army battalion commander, a shadowy figure deeply entrenched in the heart of Sadr City. His rap sheet included dozens of abductions, executions of innocent Iraqi citizens, and attacks against American and Iraqi security forces. He was also running a car dealership just outside the Sadr City limits as a financial front for his nefarious activities.

Given the sensitivity surrounding operations within Sadr City, we hatched a plan to lure him out in the open in an elaborate ruse. The idea was to stage a raid on the dealership, ostensibly searching for a fictitious character by the name of Omar, in the hope of baiting the Mahdi Army battalion commander into coming on the scene to clear up the supposed misunderstanding. This would put him in a tight spot, with two unequal, unappealing choices on the table. If he chose to show up, we'd take him down, no questions asked. If he didn't, we'd seize all his assets and leave him to face the inevitable fallout from a swarm of disgruntled customers who had trusted him to successfully sell their vehicles. It was all up to him to decide which way he wanted to roll the dice.

The operation was officially known as Operation Loki, but our team gave it the unofficial moniker "Operation Grand Theft Auto." Our plan would require the support of our sister team, ODA 044, the high altitude low opening (HALO) team. During our rotation in 2006, ODA 044 was stationed adjacent to our battalion headquarters at the RPC. They had an Iraqi scout platoon at their disposal, an "action arm" for executing targeted operations. Coincidentally, my best friend, Matt Girard, was their team sergeant. Matt and I had served together for years and even survived Operation Ugly Baby together.

My plan was a little unorthodox, but I knew that Matt would be down to participate. Matt had heard and *seen* just about everything. A few months before, just as I was taking the reins of ODA 043 as the team sergeant, Matt assumed the same role for ODA 044. Before leaving, we decided to have a modest little Christmas gift exchange in the team room. But if you think we were trading socks with reindeer on them, candy canes, and mugs that say "World's Best Dad," you clearly haven't spent any time around SF teams.

Our Christmas gift exchange was not for the faint of heart or the clean of mind. Our gag gifts would have made the front desk clerk at a sex toy superstore blush. After the first few gifts were opened, Randy, our warrant officer, opened a *very* special gift that included two clothing items of interest. Somewhere else in the world, this gift might have kicked off a sexy night for two lovers, a gateway for indulging in a little fantasy role-play.

"Put that shit on!" one of us shouted as Randy held up the garments.

Never one to back down from a challenge, Randy dropped his trousers and tossed off his pants and slid the clothes on. Just as he turned around to reveal his new look, the door suddenly burst open with none other than Matt Girard.

Now, let me clarify that we had a rather strict "no knock, no entrance" policy in place, primarily to keep the riffraff (mostly the fresh-faced, cherry-ass Special Forces rookies) out of our hallowed space. But there were a couple of exceptions to the rule for company leadership and, of course, Matt.

Matt froze at the entrance. The rest happened in slow motion. Matt's eyes glided down Randy, first in shock, then in horror. Randy turned to face him full frontal. And boy, did Matt have a sight to see.

The white elephant gift had been a Hooters outfit set, complete with a tiny white T-shirt and a pair of XXS bright orange shorts. Our red-headed, pale-skinned warrant officer was wearing it with pride. Matt got an eyeful: chest hair poking through the thin white shirt; a full view of his mangina (or moose knuckle, depending on your perspective) in those XXS Hooters shorts; and one inch of pale-white male ass cheek protruding from the back. It was a sight to behold, or perhaps one we all wished we could unsee.

Randy opened his mouth as soon as he saw Matt, trying to form any sentence that would explain what Matt was seeing. Matt's eyes just widened, trying to make sense of the scene: a handful of SF dudes behind closed doors cheering for a warrant officer dressed up like a Hooters waitress. He must have had a lot of ideas cross his mind all at once, none of them pleasant.

Matt just looked from one side of the room to the other and then said, "Never mind, you bunch of weirdos. I'll give you cupcakes some privacy," before slamming the door shut. Thanks to Randy and Matt's reaction to Randy's outfit, Hooters has never been the same for me.

Beyond the laughter, Matt and I shared a deep friendship, and I held him in the highest regard. So, when I gave Matt a call and explained our rather unorthodox plan, I knew he'd be ready. I was right.

Once again, the operation unfolded in broad daylight. When the "car dealership" came into view, we all laughed. It was just a concrete lot adjacent to a dusty, gravel-filled yard with a bunch of used cars parked at various angles. The entire plot was surrounded by a chain-link fence with barbed wire at the top. We rolled up and unloaded with precision, leaving no time for resistance. In less than sixty seconds, we had all nine men lined up in a neat row. Five of the men were the dealership sales force team: one with an enormous unibrow; one in a traditional dishdasha; one in a knock-off brown Vodafone ensemble; the other two in plaid shirts and sandals. The remaining four men were bystanders, or perhaps potential buyers—we couldn't be sure. We lined them up just the same. Then we gave the rehearsed lines that we'd all agreed upon.

"We are looking for Omar," we told the most competent-looking one of the bunch. We asked him over and over. He insisted that there was no Omar to be found in the area. We had hoped that we'd be rewarded by an appearance from the Mahdi Army battalion commander target to clear up the misunderstanding.

The plan didn't work, but his absence left us with a dozen spoils—we confiscated a total of thirteen vehicles in one fell swoop. The Mahdi Army battalion commander was about to have thirteen angry vehicle owners on his hands who'd entrusted him to make a sale. Maybe these angry folks would help us catch him. Maybe they would deal with him. To crank up the pressure, we even left a contact number behind for anyone who wanted to venture into the Green Zone to reclaim their seized vehicles. We then drove out with an entourage of thirteen vehicles plus our gun trucks, all in a row. We even confiscated a bright red Kawasaki motorcycle.

After we successfully transported the confiscated vehicles back to the safety of the Green Zone, we wasted no time in conducting our after-action review (AAR). Our approach to these sessions was blunt and no-nonsense. No congratulations, no words of encouragement. We only pointed out what could have been better and where mistakes were made, no matter how small. To an outside observer, our AAR might have seemed rather brutal, but it was all about getting to the point. These sessions typically lasted between five and ten minutes. They were geared toward making improvements for future operations.

But our AAR was interrupted. One of our interpreters received a call from a trusted contact who claimed to have the current whereabouts of one of our most elusive targets, whom we referred to as "the Viper." This target was not only on our high-priority list but also ranked as a top five target for Multi-National Division Baghdad. We shifted into high gear as soon as we got the news to verify its accuracy. Language and cultural barriers increased the potential for miscommunication and misunderstanding, which could result in fatal consequences. We couldn't afford to act without thoroughly cross-checking the info, but we also didn't want to miss our chance to get the target. We worked quickly and sure enough, our informant had gotten it right.

The Viper and his bodyguards were spotted outside the confines of Sadr City and in the eastern precincts of Baghdad for a meeting. The elusive Viper was known for being a particularly challenging mark—always a step ahead, always elusive. But we had a rare window of opportunity where the Viper seemed to have let his guard down. Maybe he was emboldened by the fact that it was broad daylight—a time when US forces seldom executed pinpoint targeting operations against high-value individuals (HVIs). Because of this reluctance, we had a lot of success with daylight hits.

Our HVI was a JAM commander from Sadr City. He was responsible for a grim litany of crimes, including abductions and executions of Iraqi citizens, as well as orchestrating sophisticated Katusha rocket attacks on US forces. The stage was set for a high-stakes takedown with a rare opportunity to bring him to justice. This operation was undeniably time-sensitive, so we classified it as a time-sensitive target. Our operational package mirrored one we used during the Operation Grand Theft Auto. It consisted of us, ODA 044, and their invaluable Iraqi scout platoon.

"Ready to roll?" I asked Matt as I stuffed a Fat Nasty in my mouth.

He replied, "Fuck yes. Let's go."

We were ready, but there were a few complications that we needed to consider. The Iraqi contact who had alerted us to the target's location was no longer in the vicinity of the house where the Viper was conducting his meeting. We didn't have the luxury of a precise eight-digit grid coordinate. Instead, we needed to first locate our contact and then rely on him to guide us to the target house.

There was always an element of uncertainty when we relied upon our local contacts to direct us to the correct location. While we meticulously checked the intel they provided, we could never be absolutely certain that we weren't walking into an ambush or a house rigged to explode. It was a constant balancing act between risk and trust that we worked hard to build over time.

What's more, linking up with our contact on the way to the target location was not a simple pick-up. To avoid compromising our contact, we'd have to create a scene to make it appear that we'd taken him in by force. Given the fact that he was surrounded by a handful of his lower-level Mahdi militia buddies, we'd need to make it convincing. We knew that anyone involved in intelligence gathering was a high-priority target for insurgent groups, and we didn't want to endanger our contacts. Building trust was difficult enough. Those who helped us were exposed to severe risks, including torture and death, if their involvement became known. Every operation carried inherent risks, and it was our duty to mitigate those risks to the best of our ability while making peace with the fact that some level of risk was inescapable.

We had general information on the location of our contact and a description of his clothes. Only our team and ODA 044 were privy to the plan to make an interim stop along the way to pick him up (or rather, "detain him," as we would make it appear). This information was intentionally kept from the Iraqi scouts to safeguard our local contact.

The strategy was quick and simple. Our team would lead the way, followed by ODA 044 and then the Iraqi scouts. Departing from the relative safety of the Green Zone always carried an underlying concern: IEDs. But the area where we'd been that morning for Operation Grand Theft Auto and our next destination in eastern Baghdad added a new worry: explosively formed penetrators (EFPs). The use of these lethal devices was prevalent in both areas. As the driver of Vehicle #1, I approached the designated location with caution.

Soon, a ragtag group of locals came into view. I quickly spotted our contact among them, wearing a distinctive blue baseball cap. The cap's white visor matched the description of him we'd been given. As we approached, two of the locals attempted to run. But Matt and his team were faster. They jumped out, blindfolded and flex-cuffed all five locals, and directed the Iraqi scouts to load them into the vehicles. This show of force would serve as a protective shield for our contact and ensure his safety.

Amid the chaos, we quickly located our guy and placed him in the lead vehicle so he could guide us directly to the house where the Viper happened to be. Within minutes, we were heading toward the target's location.

As we closed in on the house, I gave the order for our gunner to mark the building using a VS-17 panel affixed to a grappling hook. It would serve as a clear signal for the other vehicles trailing behind. But our gunner, doing his best drunk Tyrannosaurus rex impression, sent the VS-17 panel tumbling awkwardly under a vehicle in front of the target house—exactly where no one would see it.

"For fuck's sake, what the hell was that?" I nearly shouted.

Then I made a snap decision to take our gun truck off the beaten path and steer into an empty lot adjacent to our target house. The other vehicles fell in line like a centipede, the head leading the way and the body following as if it had been a planned maneuver. Matt and his team immediately understood which house we'd be entering given the position of the vehicles. They broke into a sprint as soon as they dismounted and ran straight for the door.

A pair of Apache helicopters—an additional element from our battalion commander, Lieutenant Colonel Sean Swindell—soared overhead. It was one of those days when every possible advantage was on our side. You never know when all that extra "ass" will come in handy.

As Matt and his team charged through the door, the Viper discharged several rounds from his Glock 19—likely either stolen or acquired from the Iraqi police, who carried such weapons—and then sprinted upstairs to the roof to make his getaway.

In response to the sudden gunfire and the sight of the target making a dash for the rooftop, Matt's .50-caliber gunner unleashed a hail of fire that struck the parapets with such force that a deafening thud echoed throughout the entire neighborhood. This was followed by a round of flashbangs detonating inside the house.

"CEASE FIRE! CEASE FIRE!" Matt shouted into the radio over the noise at his gunner. He raced up the stairs behind the Viper in hot pursuit. Matt knew he had him. There was nowhere for him to go—or so it seemed. Just as Matt reached the roof, the unexpected happened—the Viper jumped.

"The fucking dude jumped off the roof," Matt shouted incredulously when I arrived on the roof a few seconds later.

"No fucking way." I couldn't believe it. The ground was a long way down from the top.

In his desperate attempt to escape, the Viper had jumped, landing on his feet on another lower platform just beneath the roof. He made yet another leap to an even lower level before landing hard and injuring himself too badly to stand. He'd failed to realize that we had the entire area surrounded.

As the Viper lay on the ground, groaning in pain, members of ODA 043 approached him, swiftly securing him with flex cuffs and a blindfold. He was loaded into the back of the Iraqi scout platoon's truck while the rest of ODA 044 and the scout platoon conducted a search of the home's interior. With the Viper in custody, I directed our team to perform thorough searches of all the vehicles parked outside. If a guy like the Viper was a house guest, the chances of guns or weapons in the vicinity was high.

Stepping outside, I noticed a group of neighborhood locals under the watchful eye of our Iraqi scouts. I attempted to communicate non-verbally with them, making the universal motion for car keys by raising my hand and mimicking the act of starting a car or unlocking a door. But my attempts yielded no results.

"Car keys, motherfuckers!" I said louder.

My interpreter stepped in, translating my request in much kinder terms: "We're going to conduct a quick search of the vehicles. Where are the keys?"

The group responded with nonchalant shoulder shrugs. It was clear that they weren't about to give up the keys—even more reason to conduct a search.

"So that's how it's going to be," I muttered under my breath. I approached the nearest vehicle. With a quick pop of my rifle barrel, I shattered the driver's side window, reached inside, and popped the trunk open. *Surprise, bitches!* There was a whole collection of Glock 19s and AK-47s.

The rest of my team quickly followed suit and inspected each vehicle, most of which concealed rifles or pistols in their trunks. As a fitting bonus for each vehicle harboring firearms or other contraband, we placed an AN-M14 TH3 incendiary hand grenade on the engine block. This incendiary device packed a punch, containing 26.5 ounces of thermate mixture that burned at a blistering four thousand degrees Fahrenheit. It had a forty-second burn time and could cut through a half-inch homogeneous steel plate like a hot knife through butter, making it the perfect tool to render a vehicle's engine block useless.

With our HVI in tow and confiscated weapons and sensitive documents secured, we made our exit from the target area. A plume of black smoke billowed behind us as the incendiary grenades ignited. Above, the two Apaches circled like wasps ready to strike. It was an unforgettable departure from the scene.

In the days following the successful execution of both operations, we received phone calls from several local Iraqis whose vehicles had been confiscated during Operation Grand Theft Auto. In response, we provided them with a clear explanation, detailing that the confiscations were directly linked to the Mahdi Army battalion commander and his involvement in hostile actions against American and Iraqi security forces. We released several of the vehicles and returned them to their original owners over the course of the following weeks.

We never caught the Mahdi Army battalion commander, but we did receive reports indicating that our operation had dealt a significant blow to his financial resources. It had also resulted in a decline in his status and influence among his associates. We effectively disrupted his operations and diminished his presence in the area, marking a significant achievement in our ongoing efforts. By the end of June 2006, we never received another report about our target for Operation Grand Theft Auto.

We had accomplished something profound. We'd financially crippled the man who'd inflicted untold suffering on his local community, and we had successfully apprehended one of our most elusive targets.

Our motley group of warriors, battle-worn and triumphant, strode through the aftermath of our successful missions Rambo-style. The air was thick with smoke, flames danced on the horizon, and the battlefield echoed with the whirring blades of the Apache helicopters mixed with the distant sound of victory.

That's what you call a damn good day.

CHAPTER 10

DUSTWUN

*Then I heard the voice of the Lord saying,
"Whom shall I send? And who will go for us?"
And I said, "Here am I. Send me!"*

—Isaiah 6:8

June 17, 2006

DUSTWUN: Missing Captured Duty Status–Whereabouts Unknown[3]

On Saturday, June 17, 2006, I was jolted awake at the sound of a close-range explosive blast. The walls began to vibrate. Dust and paint particles fell on my face. A metallic taste spread through my mouth.

Disoriented, I dropped on all fours and began to crawl toward my AK-47, which I kept in the corner of my room for emergencies. As I clasped the cold, familiar grip of the rifle, my mind cleared enough to understand what was happening—we'd been hit, likely by a VBIED.

---

[3] Several details of the events described in this chapter are based on Jim Frederick's account of them in his bestseller *Black Hearts: One Platoon's Descent Into Madness in Iraq's Triangle of Death* (Crown Publishing: 2010).

The only thing I remember is the early morning sunlight filtering through the room, illuminating the debris that fell slowly to the ground. Confetti of war.

With my rifle in hand, I staggered to the door. Each movement was deliberate and automatic. Nothing more than muscle memory and survival instincts in action. In the corridor, I saw my teammates emerging from their rooms. They looked just as shocked and angry as I felt.

"What the fuck was that? VBIED?" I half yelled even though the sound had already died down.

"No, it wasn't a VBIED. Direct hits!" one of the guys replied. *Damn.*

As it turned out, we had been hit with three eighty-one millimeter mortar rounds, directly above my room. An eighty-one millimeter mortar round carries the explosive power of approximately two pounds of TNT, which explained the deafening noise and the force that had jolted me awake. Thankfully, there was minimal structural damage and we were all alive, but our rooftop shower tanks had been shredded to pieces. We weren't happy.

Nobody likes waking up to an earsplitting explosion. Having our shower tanks destroyed just pissed us off. For the rest of the day, the deafening echoes of the explosion still sounded in my ears with a splitting headache. Our compound had already seen its fair share of mortar attacks. It was all too common for insurgents to employ a hit-and-run strategy, launching a few mortar rounds and then blending back into the civilian crowds before we could pinpoint their location. Sometimes they would even mount mortar tubes in the rear cargo areas of civilian trucks, giving them the ability to drive away before anyone had the slightest idea of what they were up to.

But this was different. This crew must have been operating with the precision of all-stars, armed with an almost uncanny knowledge of our precise eight to ten-digit grid coordinates. We had never encountered such a surgically accurate mortar attack, and the potential implications of this newfound threat weighed on our minds. But the unsettling events of the morning were quickly overshadowed by the utterance of a single word: DUSTWUN (pronounced DUST-win).

It's the one word you never want to hear in a combat zone.

DUSTWUN, short for duty status–whereabouts unknown, is a designation assigned to United States service members who cannot be located but have not been officially confirmed as dead or captured.

There are a variety of reasons that a soldier might be given the DUSTWUN status. But in 2006 Baghdad, it only meant two things: missing or captured. We had two soldiers marked DUSTWUNs from the 101st.

The dreaded acronym began to circulate, casting a heavy mood over our camp. Gathering vital human intelligence to help us find the missing soldiers was at the top of our priority list now. We kicked into high gear and reached out to every intelligence source we had. As intel came through, we began to piece together what happened. We pored over every detail, trying to understand the unsettling events that had unfolded.

The trail led back to earlier that very morning. Private First Class Thomas Tucker ("Tucker"), Specialist David Babineau, and Private First Class Kristian Menchaca ("Chaca") of the First-502nd Infantry Regiment, 101st Airborne Division, were stationed at their post near the Jurf al-Sukr Bridge in southern Baghdad. Reportedly, this post was often referred to as "the Alamo" and was in an exceptionally compromised position. The Alamo offered potential attackers numerous angles of assault from nearly every direction. It had minimal defensive sightlines and an absence of man-made or natural obstacles to deter oncoming vehicles.

Additionally, the Alamo was located outside the effective rifle range of other US compounds or bases in the vicinity. It was exposed and isolated. Tucker, Babineau, and Chaca had been sent in a Humvee to stand guard. For an extended period, no one heard from them. No one thought anything of it until a radio check came in at nearly 8:00 p.m. *Silence.*

There was no answer from the trio stationed at the Alamo. Just minutes after the unanswered radio check, gunfire abruptly erupted from the Alamo's direction. A response team arrived by 8:15 p.m. No one was there. Numerous brass shell casings lay strewn about the ground.

The men cordoned off the area and began to sweep the entire scene. They found Specialist David Babineau about thirty yards away, face down in the weeds and water lining the bank of the canal, exposing the exploded back of his skull. He had been shot multiple times up and down his back, and a couple of bullets split his head right open. Tucker and Chaca were nowhere to be found. Total silence.

The whole ordeal was strange: No Mayday signal had been transmitted over the radio. From the evidence of the scene, not a single shot had been fired in defense. The Humvee's turret was locked and its M240B machine gun was still on safety. Tucker and Menchaca had seemingly vanished into thin air. Command issued a DUSTWUN for them.

The location where the soldiers had been was an unforgiving, hostile area we often referred to as the "al-Qaeda rat nest." There were al-Qaeda operatives everywhere, and they weren't easy to dislodge. Two of the largest Sunni tribes in the region, the Quarguli and Janabi (among others), had deep-rooted connections to smuggling networks in the area during Saddam Hussein's era. Al-Qaeda had masterfully exploited these connections, transforming them into a robust recruitment and financing pipeline. Case in point: a Sunni faction of the Janabi clan had a long-standing feud with the Shi'ite Anbari tribe near Yusufiyah. Al-Qaeda, with the Janabi's assistance, had forcibly evicted numerous Anbari families from their homes and converted the buildings into safe houses, training centers, weapons caches, and torture chambers. With al-Qaeda's presence, the already precarious sectarian violence escalated into a systematic, blood-soaked nightmare.

In the frantic race to locate Tucker and Chaca, we immediately activated our network, using every resource at our disposal to unearth any potential clues or information. Admittedly, our assets in the area were limited, but we made the most of what we had. We communicated with our network, making it clear that financial incentives, as well as the well-being of their families, were at stake for those who aided us in the search. Money, closely followed by a deep-seated disdain for al-Qaeda, proved to be potent motivators in our network.

As the search unfolded, a handful of soldiers operating in the vicinity where Tucker and Chaca had been taken made a chilling discovery. There was a trail of bloody drag marks on the road leading to the Yusufiyah thermal power plant—a deserted Russian power plant situated north of Quarguli Village along a route known as Route Malibu. It was a notorious insurgent stronghold and breeding ground for violent activities of every kind.

A few hours later, they stumbled upon fragments of a US body armor vest, a blood-soaked white Bongo truck, and traces of blood on the handrail of a bridge spanning a canal at the plant's entrance. But even with these clues, the search for Tucker and Chaca remained agonizingly slow.

The whole team at Camp Apache worked around the clock. We talked about location. We talked about strategy. We talked about solutions. We did it because we didn't want to talk about the main thing on all our minds: *If the insurgents had our brothers, what were they doing to them?*

If they had been captured and were being brutally tortured, we knew that they would be closing their eyes, hoping, pleading, and begging for their brothers to come for them. Every passing minute without being any closer to finding them felt like a failure. We all felt it. Time was now our most precious resource in the race to locate the missing soldiers from the 101st. A thousand horrid images played through my mind as we worked. I tried to push them from my mind.

All of us had come to grips with the possibility of death. Our greatest fear was not death but being captured by an enemy that had a thirst for brutality and harbored a wicked creativity when it came to exploiting the minds and bodies of the soldiers that they managed to apprehend. We had seen the things they were capable of. More than a dozen times, we'd witnessed the discarded bodies of victims that appeared to have been tortured. Being taken alive by an enemy who abides by no rules was every soldier's worst nightmare.

Approximately forty-eight hours after the abduction, my team received intel from one of our contacts. It contained information on the potential location where Tucker and Chaca were being held—in the vicinity of the Yusufiyah thermal power plant. We kicked into high gear, conducting map reconnaissance and working to coordinate available assets. We'd never been in the area and needed to familiarize ourselves with it as quickly as possible.

But securing air assets proved to be a challenge. It was especially difficult for us to request air support since we weren't directly tied to the missions of the ISOF or the Iraqi Counter-Terrorism Force (ICTF). For a mission of this nature, air support was critical due to the pervasive threat of IEDs on the roads. The roads to get there were classified as black, meaning the likelihood of encountering an IED was extremely high. While we did have several Iraqi partners who could offer support, they weren't our first choice for such a high-risk operation. Besides, we fully realized we weren't the first choice for this sort of mission either. We were just trying to do everything in our power to do *something*.

Despite our captain's persistent requests for air assets through the company and battalion, we were ultimately told that air support wasn't feasible based solely on single-source HUMINT reporting. We raced back to the drawing board to come up with an alternative plan. We couldn't lean on Matt and his team for support; just days before, their Iraqi counterparts had refused to accompany them on an important mission and were sent back to their main unit. Matt had a tough job as a leader, navigating the tension of a local Iraqi force that was unwilling to participate in the mission at hand. We devised a new strategy involving a convoy of five vehicles, consisting of two up-armored Humvees and three open-back vehicles with no armor. The fact that three of our vehicles had no armor was only one of a dozen serious concerns.

A heavy silence fell in the room as the plan hung in the air, unspoken fears weighing on our minds. No one dared be the first to say what we were all thinking. If we went, the chances of our entire team returning alive were very slim. It wasn't the mission that we'd been assigned, and these were not orders that we'd been given. We would be volunteering for a mission that would quite possibly be our last. Even if we did manage to successfully get to where Tucker and Chaca were believed to be, there was a high likelihood that they were already dead.

But what if they weren't? That was the thought that haunted us all. What if they were hanging on to life, bravely enduring torture and pain, holding onto the hope that their brothers would have the courage to stand up and say, "I'll go. Send me"?

I called up Aaron, who was also continuing to work with his contacts to verify and cross-reference information, and then gathered our team. It was time to have a tough conversation. I didn't speak for a few minutes after we came together in a circle.

"Guys, we've done a lot together, but this mission is the highest risk and most dangerous of all. You need to think about what I'm asking you. Are you sure you want to go through with this?" I asked. It's not like the movies, you know, when moments like these unfold to a moving soundtrack in the background when valiant expressions and dramatic glances are exchanged. In reality, that moment was quiet, heavy.

It's one thing to say that you'll risk your life to save someone you care about. It's another to do it for someone you've never met. It's another to face it. A thousand thoughts flash through your mind in an instant. You think of your family, your life, and your dreams.

The moment weighed on me heavily. I wanted to be there to walk my little Britney down the aisle on her wedding day. I wanted to see Lil D grow from a boy into a man. All of us had so much left to do. We were husbands, fathers, sons, friends . . . but we were also *brothers*. And if there was even a chance that our brothers were still alive, we had to come for them.

The only shred of hope that Tucker and Chaca had left was faith in the resolve of the American military to leave no stone unturned in the quest to get their boys back home. We were ready to go all the way.

Each member of the team responded with a resounding, unwavering "yes."

While Mark worked on the Concept of Operations (CONOP) process, which is essentially a commander's strategic blueprint of the operation, I worked on orchestrating the order of movement for our five gun trucks. Then I began to work with Ryan, Dave, and Russ to run through a weapons, gear, and communications check. While they were busy with the check, I worked on preparing the seat positioning of our team and the Iraqis who had volunteered to participate in the mission.

In the middle of my planning, I couldn't help but notice an increasing number of our Iraqis gathering around the vehicles. Given the limited capacity of our armored gun trucks, the open-back gun trucks were the only vehicles capable of carrying most of the team. They weren't nearly as protected, but they were our only transportation option, and we needed as many men on target as we could.

I placed my equipment and gear into one of the open-back gun trucks. It was one of the more dangerous positions, but I wasn't going to ride in an up-armored gun truck if any of my guys were going to be riding in an open-back gun truck. But a few minutes later, I returned to the truck only to see that someone had moved my gear to the up-armored gun truck. *What the hell?* I returned my gear to its original position in the back of the open-back gun truck. When I returned, it had been moved again.

Suddenly, I understood. The Iraqis were relocating my gear so that I could ride in the up-armored gun truck. They were taking my seat in the open-back truck, trying to give me the best chance of surviving.

I stood outside, staring at my gear inside the up-armored gun truck, deeply moved by their actions. They were the same men who accompanied us to the morgue when we volunteered to help bring home their brother and friend. We had recovered their brother's body from the morgue; now they were going to help us save *our* brothers. This action profoundly demonstrated their willingness to sacrifice their lives for us.

I was not only humbled and deeply touched by the moment, but I also felt a profound sense of respect welling up within me. I damn near teared up on the spot.

I didn't say anything, but when I caught eyes with the Iraqi who had moved my gear, a look passed between us that communicated more than words ever could.

We were brothers now.

As the time for our departure neared, I forced myself to focus only on the mission and the logistical details involved—positions, gear, rehearsals, and strategy. *Just another day on the job*, I told myself. *Just another mission.* But even I couldn't fool myself. My son and daughter's face flashed in my mind. For a brief second, I felt a pain in my chest like a blade. *Don't do that, D. You can't fucking go there. Just get the job done.*

I forced the thoughts from my mind. At midnight, I checked in with Mark. We just needed the green light from command and we were ready to roll.

"D, I don't think the CONOP is gonna get approved," Mark said wearily.

I wasn't sure how to feel. I was pissed at command for not approving our plan. But as a leader, I also understood they had the full picture of what was going on whereas we only had a small view.

We had exhausted every possible effort within our control to bring home Tucker and Chaca. We'd done everything we could.

My phone rang fifteen minutes later. It was my battalion commander, Lieutenant Colonel Sean Swindell, on the secure line. He thanked me for my team's effort but informed me that national-level assets were now overseeing the situation. "There is nothing more to be done on our end," he said.

And that's when a terrible sinking feeling came over me. It was clear that this had shifted from a rescue operation to a recovery operation, which likely meant that Tucker and Chaca were no longer alive.

"Tell your guys to stand down and go get some rest," he said. He sounded exhausted.

There was nothing left to say. "Roger that, sir."

As I hung up the phone, there were two thoughts on my mind. *I hope it was fast for Tucker and Chaca.*

We did all we could. If they were dead now, at least they would be at peace, no longer in pain or being tortured. I could only hope that they hadn't suffered.

The day following the disapproval of our CONOP, other assets received critical intel from two detainees who helped pinpoint the location of Tucker's and Chaca's bodies. It was just before 8:00 p.m. when they located them approximately two miles northeast of the power plant. Due to the possibility that their bodies had been booby-trapped with IEDs, they had to exercise extreme caution and have them examined by an Iron Claw team before moving in close. The process took several hours before they could safely recover their remains.

What they discovered haunted us all.

The bodies had been mutilated with sickening creativity. The insurgents later released a videotape that had been shot in the same area where the bodies were mutilated. The video made me feel nauseous. In the recording, a dozen men milled around the already dead and desecrated bodies. Both soldiers appeared eviscerated and half-naked, bodies caked with blood and mud, probably from being dragged behind a truck. Tucker had been decapitated. The head that had been kissed by his mother and that held his thoughts, dreams, and memories was being paraded by an insurgent like a hunter with a carcass. The insurgent placed the head back on Tucker's body. Then another man stepped forward and attempted to light both soldiers' uniforms on fire.

But the worst part about the video was the faces of the insurgents as they took turns mutilating and desecrating the bodies. They wore a nonchalant—not worried, hurried, or anxious—demeanor the entire time. Against the backdrop of the setting sun, their faces lit up with celebration. "Allahu Akbar! Allahu Akbar!" they chanted.

I joined the military to serve and protect. And I learned the skills necessary to do just that. But as I watched the scene unfold on the video before me, I was fucking furious. *Those fucking savages.* I wanted to use every skill I possessed to hunt down and bring justice to those who did this to our brothers Tucker and Chaca.

Following this tragic event, Major General William Caldwell provided a public briefing on the situation and made an appearance on *Larry King Live* to discuss the response. In the aftermath, coalition forces undertook a massive effort. They conducted over twenty-five combat operations, clearing twelve villages and executing eleven air assaults within a span of just seventy-two hours. The air force contributed significantly, logging approximately four hundred flight hours for fixed-wing aircraft and around two hundred hours for unmanned drones. Sadly, one coalition force member lost their life, and twelve others were wounded during these operations. Additionally, one armored vehicle was destroyed, and seven others sustained damage. Throughout these operations, troops encountered a total of twenty-nine IEDs, seventeen discovered and twelve detonated. They also eliminated two al-Qaeda operatives, interrogated numerous individuals, and apprehended thirty-six suspects.

Once we processed the devastating news, reality set in. My heart ached for Tucker and Chaca, their grieving families, and their comrades from the 101st. Tucker and Chaca were young soldiers just doing their jobs, trying to fight for their country. Sadness didn't even begin to describe our feelings about the entire situation. It was clear that when we submitted our CONOP on the night of the eighteenth that Tucker and Chaca were most likely already gone. The location where we'd planned to go was in the vicinity of where their bodies were eventually found. The entire ordeal was tragic and maddening.

But in the midst of the sorrow, I felt overwhelming pride for the dedication and courage displayed by my team throughout it all. Their strength, honor, decency, and unwavering commitment to helping our fellow soldiers were beyond commendable.

No one on ODA 043 questioned the justification. No one on ODA 043 challenged the value of these two soldiers from the 101st against the greater good of the mission. Although this was a mission that we never went on and never executed, it was one of my proudest moments as a Special Forces team sergeant.

CHAPTER 11

KIDNAPPED

July 2006

July 1, 2006, was a laid-back Saturday morning at Camp Apache, the kind that allowed us to go about our usual business without interruption. Everyone had a different idea about how to use the time. Russ was cleaning his firearms and triple-checking his gear. Aaron paced around shirtless (as usual) in the weight room with headphones blasting death metal.

Of course, Ryan and Dave decided it was the perfect time to get a little target practice in. We'd created a makeshift shooting range on the compound using steel targets. It was the perfect spot for letting off some steam and keeping our shooting skills sharp. But every single shot made a loud pinging noise given the material of the target. This turned out to be a big problem for the guys who decided to use the downtime to catch up on a little sleep. None of us had the luxury of getting more than a few hours of sleep at a time, which meant that when it was a quiet day, you'd have a handful of guys in their beds attempting to play a little catch-up.

But just when they were getting comfortable in their beds, the inevitable *ping, ping, ping* of target practice would echo loudly around the compound. And when sleep deprivation was high and patience was low, like it was on that day, someone would inevitably bitch and moan. "D, please tell Bonnie and Clyde to take a fucking break!"

I'd say to Ryan and Dave, "Come on, guys. We still have dudes sleeping."

They'd respond, "D, those lazy fuckers should be up and taking care of business. Little princess ass bitches."

Around and around the banter would go. It made me smile. It also made me think back to one of my mentors, Pat Quinn, an absolute *legend* in the Tenth Special Forces Group. I'll always remember one particular day in northern Iraq back in 2003 when I saw Pat walking around with torn and blood-soaked cammies, a Soviet SVD sniper rifle slung over his shoulder. Pat was awarded a Silver Star for heroics during our initial invasion of Iraq. Pat was one of my team sergeants. He often said, "D, you're going to be a great team sergeant one day. Just remember this: being a great team sergeant is like being a kindergarten teacher. You're gonna have to learn to strike a balance between having high energy and a constant need for patience." Pat had wisdom, no doubt.

Another day in paradise.

Life in Adhamiyah was a rollercoaster of emotion. Sometimes, in a moment of quiet, you'd find yourself in a moment of deceptive calm, nearly forgetting the fact that you were stationed in the heart of one of the world's most dangerous cities, facing an enemy that wanted nothing more than to see you meet a gruesome end. During those brief reprieves while watching a World Cup soccer game or catching an American show on the Armed Forces Network channel, you could almost imagine you were somewhere else, far from the chaos of Baghdad.

But those moments were few and far between. Reality would always rear its ugly head and snap you back into the grind of the mission ahead. Reality was a pendulum swinging between nostalgia and urgency, forcing us to stay constantly alert and focused.

We didn't talk about it, but we all knew. We offered each other an outlet for tension, stress, and even emotion in raw forms within the safety of our brotherhood. The shenanigans, the banter, and the extreme practical jokes were just part of the process. And in this unspoken understanding, there was an unbreakable connection.

Finally, Ryan and Dave got hungry enough to pause their target practice and get something to eat, letting some of the other guys catch up on their beauty sleep. Our slow day picked up in a hurry when one of the interpreter's cell phones rang.

At approximately 10:45 a.m., we received a call from one of our trusted Iraqi contacts. His voice crackled through the line as he reported an incident that was unfolding. A female Sunni parliamentary member in al-Shaab had been kidnapped. Our contact provided no details about her name, leaving us with only her tribal affiliation: al-Mashhadani. The information had yet to be released or reported in the news, putting us at the forefront of an unfolding situation.

We immediately alerted our higher headquarters. Our first task was to confirm the authenticity of the information we had received while working to get more accurate details. Our suspicion was that the Mahdi militia or JAM were involved. The alternative theory was equally grim—the notion that off-duty members of the Iraqi police might have moonlighted as criminals and kidnappers, driven by the promise of a quick ransom payout.

My initial assumption was dour: the female Sunni parliamentary member had likely been abducted, while her security detail met a brutal end with a gunshot to the back of their heads in the streets of Sadr City. This was the way many similar situations had played out in the past.

We worked on dual-source verification to ensure the accuracy of the information we were gathering by making phone calls to our local contacts. As we continued to get fed details, it became evident that our initial assumptions were off the mark. The situation was far more complex and had escalated further. The abductors, now identified as members of the Mahdi militia, had moved the Sunni parliamentary member and her security detail to northern Baghdad. They were being held in three adjoining houses. Within hours, we teamed up with an Iraqi platoon responsible for the sector in northern Baghdad where our target was located, as well as a regular army unit that was supplying soldiers and a Bradley Fighting Vehicle. The Bradley Fighting Vehicle is a lightly armored, fully tracked transport vehicle that provides cross-country mobility, mounted firepower, and protection from artillery and small-arms fire. For armament, it has a 25-millimeter M242 chain gun; a tube-launched, optically tracked, wire-guided anti-tank missile; and a 7.62-millimeter M240 machine gun. In other words, it can spew a lot of hate (i.e., firepower) in a pinch. The Bradley we teamed up with had three crew members and a six-man infantry squad. To us, it was a helluva lot of firepower. We were thankful to have them work with us on this mission.

And then came the big surprise: a mighty, seventy-ton M1 Abrams battle tank affectionately known as "Beast Mode." I couldn›t help but feel revved up at the sheer firepower at our disposal. It was an arsenal of epic proportions, and that was reassuring. The M1 Abrams, with its 120-millimeter main gun, armor-piercing capabilities, and advanced targeting systems, was a force to be reckoned with. We all knew its historical significance as the tip of the spear during the 2003 invasion of Iraq, leading the legendary thunder runs into Baghdad. It felt good to have Beast Mode on our side.

But while we were backed by tremendous firepower, I had never met or trained with these vehicles or soldiers. When you haven't learned each other's fighting styles, communication, and unspoken language that naturally develops within a team, it's a big step to jump straight into a dangerous situation loaded to the hilt with weapons. To reduce the risks, our plan was to position them at the rear of the formation and utilize them as an outer cordon. They would handle threats outside our perimeter, including potential hostiles or vehicles approaching our location. Meanwhile, we'd handle the threats inside. If we ran into something catastrophic, we could call them in to provide backup. When you're operating in North Baghdad, especially in a place like Sadr City, you need to have a lot of ass (i.e., firepower) with you, or you could easily get fucked up. For this mission, two things we had in abundance were firepower and manpower. We had a *lot* of "ass."

Receiving all these assets on such short notice left me and the guys scratching our heads. We were all thinking the same thing: *What the fuck is going on in northern Baghdad?* They were throwing assets at this mission from every direction.

And if that wasn't enough, we got one more addition to our convoy of death and destruction—the Air Weapons Team (AWT), consisting of two Apache helicopters. These bad boys were our secondary source of firepower, expanding our field of vision and ready to deal with any squirters (our nickname for anyone who decided to make a run for it and escape the scene or target of a mission). The Apaches were a flying arsenal equipped to unleash devastation upon anything that stood in their way—enemy armor, personnel, or even materials. With an M230 30-millimeter cannon, Hydra 70 2.75-inch rockets, and Hellfire missiles at their disposal, they spewed destruction.

All together, we had one hell of a rescue package en route to the location our Iraqi contact had provided.

But as we got about 1,500 meters from the target houses, we lost our AWT to a troops in contact (TIC) at another location in Baghdad.

"ROWDY 7, this is REAPER 1," the Apache helicopter sounded into the comms. "We need to respond to a TIC southeast of your location. We'll rejoin the party once complete, over."

TIC was the military's version of a cop calling for backup. TIC typically meant a firefight but could also refer to an IED or suicide attack. In our case, they needed to reroute some of our assets to assist in another developing situation at another location in Baghdad.

"REAPER 1, this is ROWDY 7. Roger that. We've been directed to hold fast and wait for your return to station before proceeding further, over."

"ROWDY 7, this is REAPER 1. Good copy, over."

"REAPER 1, this is ROWDY 7. Happy hunting. On stand-by here, out."

Since we had been ordered to halt the convoy due to the loss of air support, I took a moment to check in with the vehicle TCs to ensure our security posture was as tight as possible. We were only about a mile away from the target buildings; maintaining vigilance was crucial. Once

I knew security was locked down, I made my way back to my gun truck, positioned third in the order of movement, and pulled out my embassy-issued cell phone. I had a call to make.

The phone rang a few times before I heard a familiar voice over the phone. "Dad?" A thousand thoughts and feelings hit me all at once at the sound of that one word.

"Hey, D! Happy birthday!" I kept my voice upbeat and even. "It's your birthday, buddy! You're eleven years old today!" A swell of pride rose inside me. I could almost see the grin spreading across his face.

"Thanks, Dad!" I could hear the happiness in his voice. "How are you doing?"

"Doing great, buddy. Nothing much is happening here. We got to hand out some school supplies and soccer balls to some local families, which was cool. Other than that, it's been quiet." I left out the part about being halted in a convoy waiting for our air assets to return so we could execute our mission. I never talked about those parts. Just soccer balls and school supplies. My son probably thought I had the most boring job in the world. "I just wanted to call you and say 'happy birthday' and tell you how much I love you. You're growing up so fast." I choked out the last words, struggling to contain the feelings rising inside me. It was always hard, being far away on such an important day. I promised him that we'd have a big celebration when I got back.

"Thanks, Dad. I love you, too," he said.

"Can I talk to your sister, please?" I asked.

There was a rustling on the other end as he called for my daughter, Britney, whose seventh birthday was just around the corner.

"Hey, Boo Boo!" I greeted her by her nickname. "How are you, sweetie?"

"Daddy, are you coming to D's birthday party? I want you there for cake and presents. It's going to be so fun!" Her voice was so hopeful. Her question was like a dagger to my heart.

"I wish I could, Boo Boo, but Daddy's far away, and I can't make it today. I'm working, but I promise I'll be back soon. When I get home, we'll have a big celebration, and we'll open lots of presents and eat cake together. You be a good girl for Mommy, okay? And don't forget how much I love you."

"I love you too, Daddy. I miss you."

"I miss you too, Boo Boo. Love you!"

I stood there for a minute without moving after I hung up the phone, thinking about Britney. Even at six years old, she always had an intense connection to the American flag, which touched me deeply. In her young mind, she associated it with "Daddy's work."

"Daddy, what do the colors on the flag mean?" she'd asked me once.

I crouched down to her level and said, "The red on our flag represents valor. It means being strong, brave, and always ready to protect the people we love. That's why we have red on our flag."

She looked up at me with small, innocent eyes. I continued, "Now, blue, that represents something very important too. It stands for justice, which means making sure everyone is treated fairly. It also means we must be really watchful and strong. We need to be vigilant, always looking out for one another and protecting the good things we believe in. That's why there's blue on our flag."

"And what about white, Daddy?" she asked.

"And white," I smiled, "stands for purity and innocence. It's like saying that America wants to be pure and good. We want to be independent and stick to our own ideals, to always do what's right. That's why there's white on our flag."

I stood still for a moment with the phone in my hands, remembering. Calling home was like touching a memory from another life, pulling me back into the body of another man. Those innocent voices had a profound effect on me. They made me *remember*.

Remember being a father.

Remember the life waiting for me back in the United States.

Remember all the feelings I'd chosen to push deep down inside and forget.

And that's exactly why I didn't call home as often as the other guys did. It reminded me of my vulnerability, the fragility of my life. It stirred up all the feelings and emotions that I couldn't afford to indulge in while there was a mission at hand. There was too much riding on my ability to make sound decisions unclouded by emotion. Vulnerability, fear, sadness, anxiety, longing—they would have to wait for another day. This was an environment where logic, calculation, aggression, and swift action prevailed. My mindset had been created through years of systematic training, like hardware installed in my brain that could be relied upon to make calculated decisions in high-pressure situations. Every time I spoke with my son and daughter or touched on some part of my civilian life, the program was temporarily interrupted or short-circuited.

So, while some of the others called home as often as possible, I didn't. I found solace in compartmentalizing my personal life from my duty. It allowed me to focus on my mission without distractions. Sometimes guilt tugged at my heart. Maybe it appeared to the other guys that I didn't feel as bonded to my children as they did to theirs. Maybe my children will ask me someday why I didn't call more often while I was gone. But I knew the gravity of my responsibilities while on duty, not just to my family but also to my fellow teammates who relied on me to make sound decisions. I couldn't get rid of the full weight of that burden. I carried that daily.

If I had learned anything from my experience, it was that no matter how invincible you felt, no one was untouchable. War shows no mercy to the young, strong, and talented. It shows no favoritism for the fathers with children counting down the days until they return. War is cruel and unwavering. It slaughters and destroys. It creates carnal damage from those we call heroes.

The greatest chance of survival did not lie with those who said a prayer at night or tried to remind the Almighty of all the loved ones counting on him to return. The greatest chance of survival came with a clear mind and swift execution. It was as simple as that.

I shoved the phone into my pocket. I forced myself to forget.

Forget being a father.

Forget the life waiting for me back in the United States.

Forget all the feelings I'd chosen to push deep down inside and forget them again.

Just as I did, the security team reported a few motorcycles and mopeds in our vicinity. It was a sight we were all too familiar with, a typical tactic employed by the enemy. These two-wheeled scouts served as their early warning network, keeping a watchful eye on our movements and reporting back to their leaders. Despite their presence, they remained at a safe distance, posing no immediate threat. Frustratingly, there was little we could do, as we couldn't engage them. We settled for observing them as they observed us.

After about twenty minutes, our AWT returned, and we were finally ready to begin advancing toward the target. Leading the way was an up-armored Iraqi Humvee, followed by our team's leadership in the second gun truck. Mark, our Special Forces team leader, was at the helm. I had the responsibility of leading the third gun truck, setting the pace for the overall operation.

As we rumbled along a bumpy dirt road, I couldn't shake the nagging hunch that crept into my mind. *We're fucking burned.* I just couldn't shake the feeling that we'd been compromised, that the mission was going to result in us finding absolutely nothing. A dry hole.

About five hundred meters from our target, a deafening explosion pierced the air, accompanied by an intense flash of light and a billow of smoke near the lead Iraqi vehicle. My heart rate picked up speed.

Those rat bastards got us.

From my vantage point in the third vehicle, I noticed that the Iraqi soldier who had been manning the machine gun in the turret of the lead vehicle had suddenly vanished. Where the hell was the gunner?

Amid the chaos, time seemed to stretch out as I stepped out of my gun truck. Every step was wracked with worry. Was I walking into the path of another hidden explosive? The thought was enough to freeze me in my tracks, but I kept going. I approached Mark and inquired about the status of his vehicle. He confirmed that everyone was all right; no injuries or damage to be reported. Together, Mark and I cautiously approached the Iraqi vehicle together, which was totally incapacitated. They weren't going anywhere tonight.

The Iraqi gunner had been blown out of the turret and was lying on the ground, severely wounded. *FUCK.* The gunner had borne the brunt of the blast. The rest of the Iraqi soldiers had sustained minor injuries. A shiver ran down my spine as I quickly assessed the vehicle's damage and the condition of the severely wounded soldier. We had clearly been hit by an EFP.

Self-forging warheads, or fragments from the EFP, are designed with the singular goal of piercing armor effectively. They do so from a significantly greater standoff range than conventionally shaped charges, which are limited by how close they can be to their target. As the name implies, the explosive charge's power resides in its ability to reshape a metal plate into a lethal slug and then propel it with devastating speed toward its intended target. These devices are *undeniably* lethal.

The EFP was positioned on crash barriers at the level of our vehicle's windows. This was a common setup, aimed at targeting the head and neck area of a seated person inside the vehicle or the groin and stomach area of someone standing, particularly a turret gunner. These devices were positioned strategically along roadsides at choke points where vehicles were forced to slow down, intersections and junctions being prime locations. This positioning gave the operator ample time to judge the right moment to unleash the deadly payload when the targeted vehicle was moving slowly. EFPs could be detonated through cables, radio control, remote arming using a passive infrared sensor, or even something as basic as a pair of everyday cell phones. Whether a vehicle was crawling along at ten miles per hour or hurtling at sixty, EFPs had an uncanny ability to strike their target. They could be deployed individually, in pairs, or even in arrays, depending on the tactical situation.

Fortunately, we'd taken only one EFP hit instead of a full array of the deadly devices. Had our AWT spent more time dealing with the TIC, it would have afforded the EFP placers (who had most likely collaborated with the motorcycle scouts) more time to set up their lethal traps. Our situation could have escalated dramatically.

With our priorities clear, Mark and I made the call to leave an element behind to tend to the disabled vehicle and the wounded Iraqi soldier. The rest of the assault force would push forward toward the target buildings still five hundred meters away. At this point, we had nothing to lose; the whole area knew we were there. That's when we brought Beast Mode up to lead us the rest of the way to the target buildings.

Once we arrived, we decided to use a call-out approach instead of forcibly breaching gates or doors. We directed the Iraqi soldiers to take the lead and engage with anyone inside the three target buildings. They were to attempt to gather information about the kidnappers or the whereabouts of the missing female Sunni parliamentary member and her security detail. But we could read the signs and were under no illusions. This was nothing but a dry hole.

As our vehicles came to a halt and we dismounted, a few men from the target houses had already gathered outside. They seemed well-versed in this routine, indicating an efficient early warning network. The Iraqi soldiers spoke with the homeowners briefly and secured permission for a cursory check inside and outside the residences. As anticipated, everything appeared normal, with no trace of kidnappers or victims.

Before departing the target buildings, we made a point to speak with each Iraqi male from the three houses. We apologized for the disruption and offered them compensation for their trouble and time, though it wasn't much money. The gratitude in their eyes was evident. We reassured them about the nature of our mission and commitment to pursuing the kidnappers and resolving the situation. Before leaving, we made sure each Iraqi was aware of the individual of interest we believed was ultimately responsible for the kidnapping. We delivered a stern warning: Anyone working with or associated with the individual of interest would be held personally responsible for the safety of the female Sunni parliamentary member. There would be severe consequences should any harm befall her.

They nodded intently. Our message was clear; there was nothing more to be done. With that, we climbed back into our gun trucks and began the journey back to Camp Apache.

The drive back to camp was heavy with thoughts of EFPs and the severely injured Iraqi turret gunner. I couldn't shake the feeling that he wasn't going to make it through the night; the extent of his injuries and the rapid blood loss I'd seen wasn't good. Those EFPs didn't discriminate—they were an equal-opportunity instrument of death. As we rode in silence, my mind drifted back to a conversation I'd had in 2005 with an Iraqi detainee in Diyala province. At the time, I was only authorized to interview him, not interrogate him. The conversation that took place is one I'll never forget.

"You fight like cowards!" I chided. "Why not engage in honorable, face-to-face combat? Instead, you fucking cowards use IEDs."

He looked me straight in the eyes and then said, "Oh, so we should fight with honor like you Americans, you mean? With all the planes and drones that drop bombs from the sky? Is that the honor you're talking about?" His words hit me like a gut punch that day. And for some reason, I couldn't stop thinking about that conversation as we drove in silence.

My daughter's face flashed in my mind again. Those innocent green eyes looking up at me. "What do the colors stand for, Daddy?" she had asked me once.

The sound of my voice on replay echoed in my mind. *"The red on our flag, Boo Boo, represents valor. It means being strong, brave, and always ready to protect the people we love. That's why we have red on our flag. Now, blue represents something very important too. It stands for justice, which means making sure everyone is treated fairly. It also means we must be really watchful and strong. We need to be vigilant, always looking out for one another and protecting the good things we believe in. That's why there's blue on our flag."*

"And what about white, Daddy?" she asked.

"And white," I smiled, *"stands for purity and innocence. It's like saying that America wants to be pure and good. We want to be independent and stick to our own ideals, to always do what's right. That's why there's white on our flag."*

That's why there's white on our flag.

When I spoke those words, it had been so easy to define. The meaning of the red, white, and blue; the divide between the good and the bad, the right and the wrong—it all seemed so clean, so straightforward. But war was never clean, never straightforward—that much I'd learned. War was brutal, chaotic, and never easily definable. I liked to think that America was always on the right side, always holding up the ideals that our flag stood for. On most accounts, I believed it did.

But as I stared down our last month of deployment, there was one thing I knew with total certainty: my team and I fought with honor. We fought to uphold the ideals that our flag stood for. We fought to protect the rights of the innocent and remove the oppressors of the weak. We were putting our lives on the line in support of the country we love. And for that, I felt proud. As we passed through the gates of Camp Apache, it marked the end of another long day and night in Baghdad.

Later, in the *New York Times*, we would uncover the details of what had transpired that day when the female Sunni parliamentary member was finally released after nearly two months of captivity. Her captors, as she described them, were religious Shiites, a revelation that immediately discarded any theory of the government's involvement with the kidnappers.

The kidnappers captured her, blindfolded her, and took her to a house in Baghdad, where she remained for four days. She was then transferred to a plain two-story house in another part of the city. She reported that her kidnappers tried to reassure her that she was under their protection, attempting to provide her with some semblance of comfort amid the terrifying circumstances. They repeatedly emphasized that they were Iraqis just like her and swore that they wouldn't harm her. When the *New York Times* journalists questioned the motive behind the parliamentary member's abduction, her kidnappers offered a chilling explanation: they wanted the release of Shiite detainees, and her abduction was justified solely based on her being a Sunni.

CHAPTER 12

RATTLESNAKES AND ASSASSINS

August 2006

August 2006 marked the final month of our tour in Iraq. It signaled in me a mixture of excitement, relief, and apprehension. But after months of working tirelessly, it was hard to leave. We'd only just begun to understand the intricate dance of sectarian tension. We'd established a rhythm, learned the players, and built the infrastructure to gather and verify intelligence. We were finally gaining a foothold in a game where the stakes were higher than we'd even imagined. And now, it was nearly time to hand over the reins to an incoming team. That's the part that filled me with apprehension.

Most teams in our position saw the last month as a time to wind down, prepare for the journey home, secure the gear, handle paperwork, and plan for the upcoming year. It's tempting to want to lay low for those last few weeks. Whether or not we admitted it out loud, we all had a streak of superstition, a little voice in the back of our minds that taunted us with what-ifs like, *What if my story ends by taking a hit on my last week here?*

We all entertained those dark thoughts. We played out conversations in our minds between those we'd leave behind if we died. *"Such a shame, he would have been heading home in a week. It's always the good ones that go too soon."*

Each operator had their unique rituals and superstitions to fend off the whims of fate. Some prayed; others clung to talismans on the battlefield; some dialed home to reconnect with their loved ones. A few remained silent about their fears. The topic of death was a mixed bag; some openly discussed it, while others steadfastly refused to acknowledge its existence. The finish line was now in sight, and it seemed that we were about to cross it together, intact and alive. Yet we hardly dared to utter or even contemplate this notion. Of all our hypotheses about why some operators were spared while others were not, we collectively agreed that there were various factors that influenced one's survival in combat: training, strategic decisions, equipment, individual skills, and sheer chance. It's a complex interplay of these elements that can determine outcomes. War is inherently violent and dangerous, and it often leads to tragic combat deaths. That's just the harsh reality.

This mindset inevitably breeds an undercurrent of fear during the final stretch, a fear of potential injury or even death in those last moments. No one wants to become a casualty in the eleventh hour. Not my team. Not me. We refused to count down the days to departure. The fire in our belly still burned with the same intensity and vengeance as the day we'd arrived. We were determined to stay on the offensive, to extract every ounce of efficiency from our last moments in the country. We had no intention of tiptoeing through the final days, hoping we wouldn't be noticed as we crossed the finish line still breathing. Instead, we intended to leave with a resounding roar, just as we had entered, daring fate to throw its best shot at us. Because we wouldn't have it any other way.

Eight months into our deployment, we were now fully entrenched in the intricate web of loyalties, rivalries, and shifting alliances that unfolded behind the curtain, often hidden from the world's view. The longer we stayed, the more we began to unravel the complexities of this region's politics and the unseen forces that manipulated them.

One noticeable transformation that captured our attention was within the Shia target sets we received. For the first eight months, we closely observed the Mahdi militia and JAM fighters and groups. They initially appeared as a disjointed collection of fighters, each with varying levels of organization. However, as time passed, we witnessed a remarkable shift. They grew more compartmentalized, disciplined, and sophisticated. It was clear they were being expertly trained and well-financed. It was a disturbing realization.

The question that lingered in our minds was whether this noticeable transformation was a product of internal evolution or if there were external forces at play. Rumors and intelligence reports hinted at a deeper involvement. The idea of Iran loomed in the back of our minds. There were undeniable suggestions that Iran was funding and arming militia groups to wage a proxy war against the United States. Reporting and events on the ground in Iraq led us to believe this transformation was a direct result of the Islamic Revolutionary Guard Corps–Quds Force's (IRGC-QF) and the Asa'ib Ahl al-Haq's (also known as the League of the Righteous or the Khazali Network) involvement.

Our perspective from the front lines allowed us to observe these dynamics closely. It led to a realization that the top threats had shifted. It was no longer solely al-Qaeda in Iraq. The Shia militant groups, who were increasingly well-organized and strategically focused, were now taking center stage. Our national-level assets were almost exclusively hunting AQI (al-Qaeda in Iraq), inadvertently clearing the path for most of these Shia militant groups. The strategic implications were profound. Iran, through the Shia militant groups, was seemingly gaining the upper hand in the game, facilitated by compromised Shia government officials within Iraq. Our understanding was growing, but the elusive nature of the war meant that our actions had to focus on what we could control—our targeting efforts and the mission at hand.

This experience underscored the intricacies of sectarian violence in the region and the challenges of deciphering the geopolitics and allegiances at play behind the scenes. The idea of a proxy war, even in the absence of definitive proof, demanded our unwavering attention and adaptability as we navigated the turbulent landscape.

We often encountered the Shia militant groups. These groups had become masters at establishing checkpoints across the country, particularly in Baghdad. Their primary objective was to carry out extrajudicial killings and other violent operations, often targeting the Sunni communities. Experts referred to this as sectarian and factional violence.

A grim pattern emerged in response to the cycle of violence. For every Sunni VBIED attack that rocked Sadr City (a predominantly Shia area), the Shia militant groups responded with retaliatory actions against Sunnis. This vicious cycle of violence created a self-perpetuating feedback loop, intensifying the conflict with each iteration. Tragically, rather than weakening the opposing side or acting as a deterrent, this spiral of violence only served to further fortify the resolve and determination of both factions. The situation resembled a never-ending loop of retaliation. It was roid rage on an unprecedented scale. The violence that unfolded was unimaginable, and both sides became ensnared in a destructive dance of vengeance and counter-vengeance.

One of the most dreaded and active individuals from the Shia militant groups in the vicinity of Baghdad had earned his place as a top-priority target on the Multi-National Division Baghdad's HVI list. Amir Ali had assumed multiple roles within his faction, serving as a leader, organizer, and enforcer for the Shia militant group primarily based in Sadr City. He had gained a notorious reputation for his involvement in a wave of abductions and killings primarily targeting the Sunni community, whom he and his group believed to be responsible for orchestrating VBIED attacks in Sadr City. But his proof for laying this heavy responsibility on members of the Sunni community was grossly lacking; it often reduced to the mere fact of being a Sunni. This kind of hasty verdict typically resulted in horrific acts of torture culminating in death. On rare occasions when a Sunni's life was spared, it was usually a sign that Amir Ali intended to secure ransom money or collect a Shia tax from the victim.

In July, a select few members of my team joined the ISOF and the ICTF as an attachment. Their mission took place at night deep in the heart of Sadr City, with the specific aim of targeting Amir Ali. What they encountered was a firefight of epic proportions, largely due to the sophisticated early warning system that had been established in Sadr City. They had to fight their way to reach the target building and then confront a new wave of hostiles once inside. As if overcoming that wasn't enough, they ran into more trouble on the way back out. They made it out, but the grueling engagement stretched over a two-hour period. The whole ordeal ultimately resulted in the detention of a few individuals of interest, but there was no trace of Amir Ali. He remained a ghost.

Upon returning, my team recognized the need for a more refined approach if we ever got another shot at bringing him in. We needed to catch Amir Ali outside of Sadr City, preferably at a location and time where he felt comfortable and wouldn't suspect US engagement or capture. We needed to neutralize his sophisticated early warning system—a task easier said than done. Finding Amir Ali outside of Sadr City during daylight hours while outsmarting his security measures was going to be a challenge, but we were determined to get it done. It would be our last big win before we left.

As a team, we always adopted the philosophy of making the most of what we had, instead of waiting for everything to align perfectly. As a team sergeant, I was all about taking calculated risks instead of idly awaiting a flawless solution or succumbing to decision-making paralysis driven by fear. Sometimes, you must move forward with a 60–70 percent solution and trust your team to execute and accomplish the mission. It's a balance between efficiency and thoroughness. "A good plan, violently executed now, is better than a perfect plan next week," General George Patton said once. And we found that to be true.

For this mission, we brought in good ol' Daniel Allen, a.k.a. Diablo. He got to work conducting a full pattern-of-life analysis, which involves studying a person's habits and routines to predict their future actions or detect any unusual behavior. The data usually encompassed various aspects of a person's life, such as their travel patterns, companions, clothing choices, gait, and vehicle usage. But since we lacked dedicated SIGINT resources, we went for old-school analysis through HUMINT gathered from our trusted Iraqi contacts. In a streak of luck, Amir Ali visited a gas station in Baghdad two days in a row. *Bad move, bruh.*

We threw together a plan. The third time he showed up at that gas station, we would be there to slap a little bracelet jewelry (a.k.a. zip ties) on him and bring him with us before he had a chance to blink. To bypass his early warning system, we planned to use a civilian bread truck driven by our interpreters with twelve operators in the back to execute the target. To ensure our security and mitigate risk, we had the bread truck marked on top with a large VS-17 panel, which was designed to aid in marking locations and increase visibility from friendly elements. This would allow our AWT, comprising two Apache helicopters, to maintain a distant but responsive presence.

Elements from our company headquarters trailed behind us in two armored gun trucks, stationed five to ten minutes along a designated route. This distance not only prevented us from prematurely alerting the target's early warning system, but also provided a quick response option in case the situation took a turn for the worse.

The mission had received clearance from higher headquarters for a unilateral hit (US team members only), a rare occurrence given the usual insistence on incorporating Iraqi involvement in operations. Yet here we were, set to execute a mission in broad daylight, targeting a top five adversary—all in a civilian bread truck.

Undertaking such a mission was a testament to the trust and confidence earned from our leadership.

We'd come a long way from where we had started in January—from the underdogs who had nearly gotten benched to preparing a team for one of the highest-risk operations of the year. I was very proud and grateful. We were fucking *stoked*.

Concealed within the truck were twelve seasoned Pipe Hitters—two guys for left-side security, two for right-side security, and eight assaulters. We prepared the vehicle by fitting a metal pole from front to back, enabling each operator to maintain balance and avoid creating unnecessary noise during the operation.

Our tactical setup was straightforward, sticking with the KISS (keep it simple, stupid) principle. The order of movement was orchestrated with left side security, led by me, being followed by right side security and then the assault team, which would swiftly adjust to the target's location. For this particular mission, I made a deliberate decision to entrust one of our valued team members who wasn't in a leadership position to lead the assault team. There's a first time for everything. This choice was grounded in the commitment to pass on combat leadership and experience to the younger members of our team who would carry the torch far after the "older" guys were out of the game. Giving them real-world experience was an important step in preparing them for their future roles as leaders, enabling them to confidently execute missions under intense and stressful conditions, especially in close combat. This emphasis on mentorship and hands-on training is one of the cornerstones of building a resilient and capable force, ultimately contributing to the safety and effectiveness of our team in the long run.

Our Trigger (the local Iraqi operative who had been covertly monitoring the target and the site) was effectively hidden from sight amidst the hustle and bustle of the crowded city. The urban environment provided ample cover; a sea of pedestrians, traffic, street vendors, and daily activity concealed his true purpose. When he called in confirmation of the target's attire and precise location at the gas station, we were ready to fucking roll.

Approximately a minute away from the target, we received a final update from the Trigger. He informed us that the target had moved to a small building adjacent to the gas station. *Even better.* The assault team had no problem switching gears.

The scene was set, and as we moved in, the AWT flew overhead along with us. I looked up for a moment and watched in awe through a crack in the doors. "Glad I'm on your side.... *goddamn*" I muttered under my breath as I looked up to the sky. It was an intimidating sight.

The two gun trucks, along with our bread truck, collapsed from their location to the target and positioned themselves in the correct order of movement facing toward our exfil (exit from target). The game plan for our speedy exit was clear: first Gun Truck #1, then the bread truck with target once apprehended, then Gun Truck #2.

Being the first one out, I took a quick look around. Lo and behold, right in front of me was the target. *What the fuck is he doing over here?* I thought, feeling a surge of adrenaline at the sight. I closed the distance between us, ready to fight. I was wearing my favorite Oakley leather assault gloves with carbon fiber knuckle plating. I always wondered what would happen if I punched someone with those gloves on.

But to my surprise, the target promptly raised his hands in surrender. *Smart move. I guess you want to live today.* With his hands raised high and face etched with fear, I looked from his trembling hands to his waistband, where I noticed a Glock pistol tucked to his right side and a large pouch in his right front pocket. Before I could open my mouth to say anything about it, Dave Roten already had him disarmed and flex-cuffed, and he was beginning to search him. Dave managed this without even putting the target on the ground all in a matter of about thirty seconds.

"Damn, Dave. Solid," I commended.

Dave just laughed under his breath. He discovered a wad of cash, two Nokia cellphones, and a plastic bag full of SIM cards. We'd just hit the intelligence motherload.

"Jackpot," I radioed the team just as the right-side security was getting into their designated positions.

It was the fastest and smoothest takedown I'd ever experienced. *Lightning fast.* Dave's and my hands embraced in a hold that was equal parts high five and handshake. He broke out in a wide smile, exposing a little Copenhagen in his teeth. I shot back the same broad, brown-stained grin. It's not often that everything goes down just like you practiced and every movement is textbook perfect. But in that mission, it did.

"We've got the main target secured. Anything else we should be looking for? Anyone else around?" I asked Dave.

Alongside the main target, we also managed to apprehend another Shia militant who worked for Amir Ali. There was also a red Chevy truck in the vicinity that our Trigger identified as belonging to the target.

"Check the ziplock," I nodded to Dave. He had already read my mind.

"Guys, you won't believe this," Dave called out as he triumphantly displayed the keys, his huge grin still plastered on his face. "We've got ourselves a bonus."

The keys to the truck were nestled inside the target's large sensitive site exploitation (SSE) plastic Ziploc bag. The SSE bag allowed us to consolidate things that may be of importance to allow the interrogation team the ability to exploit sensitive site materials and detainees (such as their phones, money, pocket litter, computers, etc.). As Ryan slid into the driver's seat, he exchanged a knowing look with Dave, who had settled in the passenger side. Ryan inserted the key and turned it. The engine roared to life. They both checked the truck's interior, making sure everything was in order.

Then Dave motioned toward the windshield. "Hey, D," he said with a smirk. "Check this out."

I leaned in and squinted to read the sticker. "Jiffy Lube . . . Nashville, Tennessee?" I raised an eyebrow in disbelief. "What are the odds?"

I chuckled to myself. *Even bad guys need a good oil change to keep their vehicles running smoothly, I guess.*

The target and the collected SSE materials were transferred to the professionals at Baghdad International Airport. We also submitted all the relevant information about the red Chevy pickup truck, including its vehicle identification number, model, and the details from Jiffy Lube.

Amir Ali's detention proved to be an intelligence gold mine, significantly aiding our efforts in countering the Shia militant groups. His capture had far-reaching impacts, disrupting leadership in Sadr City and diminishing the group's ability to coordinate attacks. This increased security for the US, coalition, and Iraqi forces; it minimized immediate threats and acted as a deterrent for other leaders considering the consequences of capture. This, in turn, notably boosted morale, paving the way for more effective counterinsurgency operations.

Rumor has it that a red Chevy pickup truck with a Jiffy Lube sticker was spotted at Camp Apache just a few days later, loaded down with .45-caliber ammo, explosives, trash, sandbags, gravel, and other miscellaneous items—a perfect military vehicle without costing American taxpayers a single dollar. Rumor also has it that the truck was driven by a former professional bull rider from the great state of Texas and his team sergeant, both enjoying the highest grade of award-winning tobacco via King of Denmark cigars, the *best* cigars on the market.

Our last mission in Baghdad was a great success. The operation was a significant achievement, not only because we apprehended a valuable target who provided us with a wealth of intelligence but also because we did it without losing a single man. This merry band of rattlesnakes and assassins was going to cross that finish line together.

CHAPTER 13

HONOR AND HUMILITY

Late August 2006

It was the second time the young private had whispered to the guy sitting next to him. There was no audible sound at first, only motions to indicate communication between them. Two pairs of eyes looked in our direction and then promptly looked away. Then the words were audible, but just barely. "CIA . . . Special Forces . . ."

Their faces were clean, almost shiny, and round with youth. Hair nearly buzzed to the scalp; clean uniform with no patches besides name tape and "US Army." Couldn't be older than nineteen; looked more like sixteen. I tossed a sideways glance at Dave, whose lips turned up in the corners almost imperceptibly but enough for me to see. We sat down in ball caps, blue jeans, and T-shirts with two backpacks beside us. We'd scored seats at the back of a C17 aircraft for the long flight to Peterson Air Force Base in Colorado Springs, Colorado. Small talk wasn't on the agenda. The cabin was packed with soldiers from the Fourth Infantry Division all coming back from Iraq. We were all headed to the same location: *home.*

Thirty minutes into the flight, we'd pop an Ambien and be out cold until we stepped foot on American soil again. We were old pros at this by now. Never take the Ambien too early; you never know when your flight might get canceled or delayed, and it's a real drag to lose a whole day floating around in a fog.

A week prior, we'd departed from Baghdad International Airport under the cover of night for Morón Air Base. Even after more than three years of American and coalition forces' presence in Iraq, large parts of the country still held danger with the constant threat of rockets and mortars. Fortunately, our trip had been uneventful. Our usual travel kit included a poncho liner as a makeshift bed, quality ear protection to drown out the noise, a foam mat for a bit of cushion, and the ever-beloved Ambien, courtesy of our 18Ds who had the authority to carry and dispense controlled substances. These essentials ensured that we could stretch out on the cargo deck and catch some shut-eye during the flight.

Our time in Spain revolved around sleeping and eating. After eight months of combat, and with the added jet lag, sightseeing and tourist activities weren't a top priority. Now it was time for the final stretch of our journey back to the United States and eventually to Colorado Springs.

"Are you guys CIA? Special Forces?" The question was loud enough for everyone to hear. Curiosity had clearly gotten the better of the young private.

I sat up and smiled. "Yep."

He waited expectantly for me to continue, but I just smiled. I could see the pictures playing behind his eyes, images created by the movies he'd seen about our line of work. "Really? What's it like?" His eyes were bright, hungry for a good war story, food for his imagination, proof that this war that we had all trained for did exist.

"Honestly? Just a lot of paperwork and writing reports." I wasn't interested in storytelling. But there was something about the kid. Maybe it was his eagerness, maybe it was his innocence, maybe his bright-eyed dedication . . . I liked him. "How about you?" I turned the tables instead. It was our typical ruse to downplay everything and deflect.

He sat up a little straighter and launched into a long description about being a mechanic stationed here or there. Maybe he hadn't directly engaged in combat, but he'd been close to the action, he assured me.

"And do you like being a mechanic?" I asked. I liked hearing him talk.

He was all too happy to oblige. He droned on for a while, eager to share his experiences. I listened with genuine interest. Irrespective of our branch or unit, we all shared a common identity as soldiers for the United States of America. We were all part of the same military family, bound together by a collective commitment to a singular mission. Our differences in roles and responsibilities seemed insignificant in comparison to the common purpose that brought us together. It is a powerful bond that forges a tightly knit community of brothers and sisters. I felt a deep sense of appreciation and respect that I was counted among them. The kid in front of me had decided to stand up and volunteer to risk his life for his country. It didn't matter what our roles were or how much experience we had. At the end of the day, we belonged to the same family and were dedicated to the same mission.

When the conversation dwindled, I popped the Ambien. As the subtle drowsiness took hold, my mind wandered through the events of the last few months. They had gone by fast and our time was up; we had no choice but to leave. Work in combat zones can consume you if you're not careful. It was our time to take a step back and let a new group step in and make their mark at Camp Apache.

As luck would have it, the team moving into Camp Apache was the same one from Fifth Group that we had relieved back in January. I held a lot of respect for that team and knew they'd do a great job. However, I didn't feel like our job was finished. Then again, it never truly is. The sense of absolute mission accomplishment is always elusive; closure was a luxury we seldom experienced.

As the hum of the plane began to draw me into a deep sleep, the thoughts kept running around in my mind about what would come next. Would Tenth Group send us back to Camp Apache in 2007? Would we be deployed north to Mosul, or even as far as Basra down south? We were due to return to Iraq in early 2007, but the location remained a mystery. Our next move was not ours to decide, yet I found myself thinking obsessively about possibilities that were beyond my control.

After a while, I took a deep breath and pushed the thoughts away. There would be no answers to these questions today. My only concern now was ensuring the safe return of my team and our equipment back to Fort Carson, Colorado. The next trip would have to wait.

As we touched down in the evening at Peterson Air Force Base in Colorado Springs, I could already see a vibrant crowd gathered to welcome home the soldiers. A lively band began to play as loved ones hoisted up colorful signs. Families with children perched on their shoulders waited with anticipation. Even a news crew stood ready to capture the moment. I smiled as the Fourth Infantry Division exited the plane. As they disembarked, basking in the long-awaited reception, my team and I stayed aboard in the quiet of the rear section of the plane.

About an hour after the Fourth Infantry Division concluded their welcome home ceremony, gathered their gear, and boarded buses for Fort Carson, it was our turn to deplane. We stood up, slung our backpacks over our shoulders, and walked out into silence. No cheering, no band, no balloons—just a handful of family members below to greet us.

I stood by myself as a handful of the other guys hugged their wives and children, breathing in the fresh Colorado air. After months of playing roulette with death and constantly facing danger, it was strange to suddenly be back on American soil. I could say that I felt a thousand things, but the truth is I didn't feel much of anything at all. The stark contrast between the world we'd lived in for eight months and the one I'd come back to was disorienting.

Transitioning from the high-stakes, adrenaline-fueled world of combat to everyday civilian life is a disorienting shift. After dealing with constant stress, maintaining perpetual vigilance, and making split-second survival decisions, civilian life was a jarring experience. One moment, I felt thrilled to be alive and back in the States, enjoying the simplicities of daily life. Then, I felt like I'd lost my sense of purpose, like everything was devoid of excitement and meaning. The idea of watching a college football game or completing a typical routine just didn't carry the same thrill anymore.

Combat isn't just a job; it's a lifestyle that rewires your body and mind, molding it to the demands of survival. Engaging in intense combat situations, like eliminating the enemy with multiple rounds from your rifle, creates a surge of adrenaline that is unmatched by anything else in life. At least, that's how it feels to me. In those intense moments of action, your senses hit one hundred on the adrenaline scale in a second. The rush of survival and making life-and-death choices jolt your system better than any drug on the market. Back in the civilian world, these life-and-death scenarios are replaced by mundane tasks: filling up your car with gas; tidying up your house; selecting furniture for your new office; deciding what's for dinner. This abrupt shift from high-stakes decisions to normal activities is a difficult transition to make. It took me some time to acclimate to the vast differences between the two worlds.

While working through the transition process, there were still a few things on my team's Baghdad checklist. One of the top priorities was awarding the final winner of the inaugural ODA 043 Hard Hitter Award. It was time to tally up all the votes and see who would win.

We nominated different team members during our deployment for the weekly award—sometimes for recognition of acts of bravery under enemy fire, sometimes for dedication in the face of a difficult task, and sometimes just for a winning attitude. By now, the sledgehammer was covered in inscribed quotes, military coins, and designs. It had been touched by every member who'd had the opportunity to keep it with them for a week. Honor, bravery, humor, resilience, gratitude—each man had discharged his feelings into the sledgehammer while it was his week of ownership. Now it would find its permanent home with one deserving team member.

Upon tallying the votes, the results were clear: Staff Sergeant David B. Roten Jr., affectionately known by various nicknames like Achilles, Snoop, Ba, Dave, or A35X, had received the Hard Hitter Award more times than any other team member.

With pride and honor, Dave was officially recognized as ODA 043's first Hard Hitter Awardee for 2006 and was presented with the coveted and well-deserved sledgehammer, adorned with all the decorations and accessories we'd placed on it over time. Dave's journey, from the early days when he was tasked with sorting brass in the hallway before being allowed into the team room to becoming the Hard Hitter Awardee, exemplified his transformation from a brand-new guy into an all-star operator. It was a well-deserved honor for his outstanding contributions to the team.

"Fucking honor to serve with you, Dave," I said, patting him on the back as he folded his hands around the sledgehammer. "You did a great job, brother."

Dave looked me straight in the eyes and nodded. That's all we needed. We all said it with our eyes, a quick embrace, and a tough pat on the shoulder. There was no further need for words or eloquent speeches. Not when you've faced death alongside a team of your brothers and made it out alive.

Approximately a week later, we gathered at group headquarters in Fort Carson for an impromptu award ceremony. During the ceremony, Brian Rainwater, Ryan Land, and I were bestowed with Bronze Star Medals with valor in recognition of our extraordinary actions on April 17, 2006. Furthermore, Dave, Luke, and Diablo were presented with Army Commendation Medals with valor for their courageous contributions during our 2006 rotation. This collection of six valor awards collectively positioned us as one of the most highly decorated teams within the entire Tenth Special Forces Group for the 2006 Iraq rotation—a significant and humbling achievement.

As the ceremony concluded, I was filled with immense gratitude and humility. I had always been aware of the extraordinary nature of our team's accomplishments within our own Special Forces company, which was composed of five individual ODA teams. But it wasn't until that moment that I really comprehended the extent of our contributions across all of Iraq, especially compared to the achievements of all the teams within the Tenth Special Forces Group.

But nothing could have prepared me for what would come next.

During the Tenth Group Special Forces ball, a formal event hosted to celebrate the anniversary of the group and all the current and past operators, ODA 043 had more accolades coming our way. Colonel Ken Tovo, our esteemed group commander, took the stage to reveal the recipient of the prestigious Larry Thorne Award, recognizing service of excellence within Special Forces. Each year, the Larry Thorne Award is bestowed upon the best ODA within the Tenth Special Forces Group. Major Larry Thorne was a former Finnish soldier declared missing in action in Vietnam who is remembered for his remarkable military career. He was a recipient of the Knight of the Mannerheim Cross, a recognition equivalent to the Medal of Honor. After his remains were identified in Vietnam in 2003, he was interred at Arlington National Cemetery.

To our surprise, ODA 043 emerged as the unequivocal winner of the Larry Thorne Award, recognized for exceptional contributions during combat operations in support of Operation Iraqi Freedom from January to August of 2006.

I was humbled when Colonel Ken Tovo read the following: "Our Thorne Award for the best operational unit goes to an ODA that unmistakably proved themselves as the best of the best during combat operations in support of Operation Iraqi Freedom (IV) (OIF) from January 2006 to August 2006. This year's ODA earned recognition from the highest levels of command in Baghdad. ODA 043 served as an advanced Special Operations team located at a remote area in eastern Baghdad. This ODA was directly responsible for operations that resulted in the successful capture of several high-level enemy personalities and numerous direct-fire engagements with the enemy. Due to heroic actions, ODA 043 was awarded three Bronze Star Medals with valor and three Army Commendation Medals with valor. ODA 043 is an outstanding group of men and truly represents the highest standards and warrior ethos established by Larry Thorne. ODA 043's unique spirit and successful approach to prosecuting the War on Terrorism exemplifies the true nature of the unconventional warrior. This detachment, ODA 043, is representative of what it is to be Special Forces."[4]

---

[4] Ken Tovo, "2006 Thorne Award Presentation Narrative for Operational Detachment-Alpha 043" (speech), 2006.

It took a while for those words to sink in. I felt honored, humbled, and grateful for the excellent team of warriors that I had the honor of serving alongside.

Later, my mentor and brother, Chief Steve Dayspring, shared his thoughts on the Larry Thorne Award:

"This is an incredibly difficult competition, one that is very prestigious. During the annual ball, the team is recognized amongst all their peers with a plaque, and their names are put down in a bit of a memorial. It looks at a variety of aspects, such as the team's reputation within the command, their demonstrated fiscal capabilities, their demonstrated tactical proficiency, and sometimes things are just happenstance—right place, right time participation in historical events where obviously they rose to the occasion and did amazing things. You're going to make a better case for a team to be a recipient of the award than a team that didn't deploy that year. That's just the way it works. It's an incredibly prestigious honor within the original Special Forces group, especially in a time like 2006 in Iraq when every team is out there killing bad guys and doing amazing things and Green Beret-ing their asses off. To make the case that what your team did was above and beyond everybody else—that you employed creativity, ingenuity, and innovation and used the tools available to you to accomplish the objectives that were far above and beyond what was expected—those were the circumstances that ODA 043 was putting their hat in the ring for and ultimately recognized for following that rotation. Every single team was deployed, in direct combat, and executing acts of valor that will never be recorded in history appropriately. For ODA 043 to make the case and to rightly be recognized during that period as being the best of the best is significant."

The commendation recognized our team's unwavering commitment and embodiment of the highest standards and warrior ethos set by Larry Thorne. Out of over fifty Special Forces teams in the Tenth Group, ODA 043 was distinguished as the pinnacle. The experience resonated with me deeply to my core and left an indelible mark on all who were part of it. The acknowledgment of being singled out as the best was truly surreal and remains a poignant memory etched in my mind and heart for a lifetime.

Not long after winning the Larry Thorne Award, we took a few weeks leave to rest and recharge. Upon my return to the company, I found a tie and a plaque on my desk. The plaque bore my name and was from the First Special Service Force Association. The Frederick Award for Military Excellence, it said in bold letters across the top.

I couldn't help but wonder if this was a prank. Our guys were known for their sense of humor. But this felt different—it was too nice, too legitimate seeming. *Could this Frederick Award for Military Excellence really be the real deal?* I thought to myself as I turned it over.

I soon discovered that the award was named after Major General Robert T. Frederick, who commanded the First Special Service Force during the Italian campaigns until July 1944. He was then reassigned to lead the First Airborne Task Force that parachuted into southern France as part of Operation Dragoon. The Frederick Award for Military Excellence is a dual award presented to a US Special Forces soldier and a Canadian Special Operations Forces soldier each year. The criteria involved each component service unit selecting a Special Forces non-commissioned officer whose duty performance had a significant impact on the Special Forces community during the past year.

I found out that I had been nominated, even though I had no prior knowledge of it, and was chosen as the new United States Army Special Forces Command recipient of the Frederick Award for Military Excellence. This award held an incredible level of prestige; it left me speechless. Among the five active-duty Special Forces groups and two National Guard Special Forces groups, there was only one US Special Forces recipient. I felt humbled to be the chosen one. I was honored and immensely proud.

Of course, the team guys wasted no time in giving me a hard time and cracking jokes about it. Team room humor—you can't beat it. No one is immune or above the fray. Everybody is eligible to be humbled, even those in leadership positions. It's the nature of the business.

Just when things couldn't get any better, in early November 2006, Vice President Dick Cheney paid a visit to Fort Carson and delivered an address to the troops, and I stood along with the rest and listened to his speech.

"Today we take special pride in recognizing some of our best, including fine units that have just recently returned from Iraq," he began. "We're grateful to the Tenth Special Forces group. The Green Berets know what it means to undertake missions that are difficult, dangerous, urgent, and secret. You've engaged the enemy in Iraq with the toughness, precision, and effectiveness that we expect of you, and we are grateful. Ladies and gentlemen, everywhere I go in this country, I am struck by the depth of gratitude and admiration that the American people have for our military. In this challenging time for our country, we have learned the stories of so many Americans who have faced the enemy and who have lost their lives or who suffered serious injury."

To my surprise and great humility, Vice President Cheney mentioned my name in his speech alongside several other deserving service members.

"With us today are Sergeant Brian Gray, Specialist Marcella Neiswonger, Specialist Kevin Spangler, Specialist Jeffrey Enlow, Sergeant Gabrielle Rivera, Master Sergeant Darrell Utt, Chief Warrant Officer 2 Bill McKenna, and Captain Sarah Piro—recipients of the Purple Heart, the Bronze Star, the Air Medal, and other military distinctions, and fellow citizens of ours who have paid the price for this nation's freedom. Soldiers, it's a high honor to be in your presence. You make all of us proud to be Americans.

More than that, ladies and gentlemen, the people of this country admire your character. You've taken an oath to serve. You live by a code of honor. No words could fully express just how much you mean to this country. In a new generation, we're seeing once again that the American soldier in battle places the mission first, never accepts defeat, never quits, and never leaves a fallen comrade. The spirit of the American soldier is to be honorable and just, and, even amid the cruelties of battle, to be decent and humane. By their courage, members of our military are taking the fight to the enemy, and they are winning the war on terror."

As I walked away from the speech that day, I was struck by a single thought: success is never a solitary path. In every step of my journey, I've been acutely mindful of the dedicated men and women whose unwavering commitment, time, skills, and sacrifices formed the bedrock of my accomplishments. The success I've experienced is a direct reflection of our collective hard work, trust, and steadfast support in one another.

The resonance of this truth loudly echoes on the team of men I was privileged to lead and serve with in 2006. Their valor, readiness to confront our enemies, and risk-taking even in the face of danger served as the propellant behind our victories. Any recognition or awards attributed to me are inherently intertwined with the tireless efforts of the entire team. This also includes the courageous interpreters and local allies who stood shoulder-to-shoulder with us throughout all our trials and tribulations.

As the curtains drew on the 2006 tour, I felt honored, humbled, and deeply grateful. Honored to have served alongside some of our nation's finest warriors, humbled to be recognized for our innovation and courage on the battlefield, and deeply grateful that the entire group of ODA 043 that took off from American soil landed back safely again.

But we were far from done. Before long, the destination for our 2007 mission would be revealed. Shortly after, the Bush administration would authorize the US military to implement a kill/capture directive targeting any member of Iran's Revolutionary Guard Corps, including its intelligence operatives within Iraq. This strategic move aimed to diminish Iran's influence in Iraq and pressure the government to halt its nuclear program. The goal was clear: defeat IRGC-QF and its proxies to disrupt malign Iranian influence.

In the early months of 2007, Baghdad would begin witnessing two to three thousand deaths per month, many of them due to sectarian violence. In response, a new strategy unfolded, intensifying US Special Forces combat operations in and around Baghdad.

And ODA 043 was going to be at the tip of the spear.

CHAPTER 14
THE GRIT CODE

It's now been seventeen years since my last combat mission and seven years since I officially retired from active duty. In total, my military service spans 26.5 years. Following my transition from the military, I pursued various roles in the corporate sector. My most recent position was chief of operations for the National Medal of Honor Museum Foundation in Arlington, Texas, a role I held for two and a half years. Looking ahead, I'm eager to expand my involvement in speaking engagements and share my expertise with a broader audience.

The time I spent serving in the military and as a Green Beret taught me leadership, hard work, sacrifice, mental strength, and much more. While there's nothing innately unique about these words or concepts, the *context* in which I learned them certainly was. I learned about leadership in situations where every decision I made was a matter of living or dying. I learned about hard work when I realized that the only way to become great at anything is through grueling repetition, dedicated practice, and an unwavering commitment to your craft. I learned about sacrifice when I was faced with choices that tested whether I was willing to risk my life to save someone else. I learned about mental strength when my body said it couldn't go on, when I wanted to quit, when I was on the brink of failure, yet I kept going anyway.

The time I've spent in the corporate world also taught me about leadership, hard work, sacrifice, and mental strength, only in very different ways. These two contexts in which I learned, improved, and applied these principles could not be more different. And yet I find that, at the core, the principles remain unchanged. They are cornerstones of a life well lived—from the theater of war to the corporate boardroom and every facet of life in between. I learned many lessons through victories. I learned even more through failures. Both are great teachers if you let them be.

As a result of this, I identified eight foundational elements of what I like to call the Grit Code. These core principles form a blueprint for navigating challenges and achieving success with resilience, tenacity, and an unwavering commitment to excellence.

The Grit Code:

1. Control What You Can Control
2. Eradicate Arrogance
3. Possess an Extreme Work Ethic
4. Adopt a No-Surrender Mindset
5. Embrace Innovation
6. Calm Breeds Calm
7. Relentlessly Execute
8. Courage Is Contagious

What I'm about to share over the next several pages is not just a collection of nice anecdotes. These are deeply personal, hard-earned life lessons that I have gathered throughout my journey. The Grit Code, like me, is straight up and no-frills. But first I want to give you a warning—if you decide to put the Grit Code into action, the entire trajectory of your life will change. It will change the dynamics of your family, career, and personal life. It will change the kind of leader you are both on and off the battlefield and in or out of the boardroom. Some people will cheer you on, some will hate you, some will admire you, and some will envy you. You will see major shifts take place in your life. Some of them will feel fantastic as you unleash your true potential and feel the glory of it all. Other shifts will be fucking *hard* as you push through challenges and rely on pure determination to get you through. But I can guarantee you this: You'll achieve beyond your wildest dreams, and you'll turn once-unattainable feats into tangible realities. The Grit Code is not meant to be read; it's meant to be acted upon. So don't just read these pages—put them into practice *immediately*. And then brace yourself.

Because it's about to be one hell of a ride.

1. Control What You Can Control

One of the greatest lessons my military service taught me is this: control what you can control. In life, it's far too easy to spend energy on the things you *can't* control and neglect to spend it on what you *can*. This leaves you worn out, exhausted, and frustrated while simultaneously stuck in a holding pattern without growth. The *Control What You Can Control* mentality revolves around being proactive, taking charge, directing your energy where you can make a difference, and refusing to worry about the rest. This is a simple yet powerful concept made up of two essential facets.

First, *Control What You Can Control* emphasizes the importance of taking initiative in every single area where you want to grow or make positive changes. Instead of waiting for others to act, it pushes you to assess your life, identify what's within *your* control, and then be proactive in making decisions and taking decisive action without hesitation.

On the flip side, *Control What You Can Control* also encourages you to recognize when something is genuinely beyond your control. Once you've made every effort that is within your control, you gotta let go of the rest. Don't waste your precious time, energy, and mental focus on things beyond your control. By letting go of the uncontrollable, you free yourself from unnecessary stress and frustration.

There are a hundred examples I could give from my military career that exemplify this lesson in real life. Countless times I found myself in a high-stakes situation that was out of control, but I made decisive, calculated moves to do the one or two things that *were* within my control and refused to waste energy worrying about the rest. Many of the stories in this book are full of such examples.

In this chapter, I want to share with you how this mentality made a very real impact on my personal life after retiring. It's not easy for me to open up and share what I'm about to, but it's incredibly important for anyone from the military community, law enforcement, first responders, service members, or federal government who is reading this to understand what I'm about to say. All of us who chose to serve our country in any of the capacities mentioned above know that the job comes with many challenges. We know the difficulties, hurdles, and obstacles contained within the nature of our work. But there is another set of challenges that come *after* we transition out of the service. This is a subject that is being talked about more often now than it used to be, but still not enough.

There are challenges that all military service members face, especially combat veterans and special operators upon returning to civilian life. This reality is starkly apparent within the veteran community, as evidenced by multiple undeniable indicators, especially concerning mental health. We are only just scratching the surface in understanding the impact of the intense experiences endured by combat veterans and operators on the human body and mind. I sure don't have the answers to these complex questions. But what I do know is that many of my brothers and sisters from the service community are struggling with depression, anxiety, addiction, failed relationships, physical discomfort and sickness, and many other struggles.

I had to face my own set of challenges when I returned to civilian life and still, to this day, proactively fight with my demons. I'm very much a work in progress. I do not possess the credentials nor the eloquence to diagnose, heal, or speak with authority on these complex subjects, but I will share with you a few simple truths that have made a significant difference in my life. My hope is that by sharing my experiences and injuries, I will be able to point you in a positive direction if you find yourself struggling or feeling lost.

When I first transitioned out of the military, one of the greatest challenges I had was with the stark difference between the man I was on the battlefield and the one I was expected to be when I returned home. Out on the battlefield, everything was black and white. Yes, no. Right, wrong. Success, failure. Life, death. My world was filled with high stimulation, high stakes, high pressure, and high stress. The instinctual drive for survival is a powerful, powerful mechanism. When you learn how to flip on that switch and live in that frame of mind and body, it becomes addictive. When you learn how to surpass the mental and physical barriers created by your own instinctual fear of death, you unlock an entirely new perspective on life. You feel invincible; you feel courageous; you feel free.

Many of you know exactly what I'm talking about. We learned to thrive within chaotic scenarios, to thrive in survival mode, and to surpass our own fear of death. We lived for the adrenaline, the hunt, the fight, and the struggle. Even pain became both a catalyst for growth and a badge of honor that we pressed into without reservation.

And then we came home.

One plane ride and we find ourselves waking up in an alternate reality. We *want* to appreciate the fact that we are safe, loved by our families, and living a life of convenience. We *want* to be happy. But if most of us are honest, we miss it. We miss the adrenaline; we miss the raw animal within us that came out when we were faced with the need to survive. We miss the action. We miss the pressure. We miss the high stakes. We miss the person we became in those situations, the greatness that emerged when the chips were down, and that primal desire to *fight to live* and *fight to kill* rose up and unleashed itself with a mighty roar. And as time passes in civilian life, we slowly begin to realize that we might never get to feel that feeling again. We struggle to find a sense of passion, meaning, purpose, drive, and motivation within the stimulus of ordinary life because we have become so desensitized by the extreme nature of the things we lived.

Additionally, many of us struggle with the aftereffects of physical symptoms left by injuries we incurred in active duty, both seen and unseen. Sometimes these injuries are obvious, such as the loss of an arm or leg or a visible scar on the body. Other times, these injuries are much harder to recognize and diagnose, which has the potential to affect the body and mind for years.

At first, I was resistant to even consider the fact that the nature of my military career might affect my mental and physical state after retirement. Most of us learned to ignore pain, hide injuries, and downplay any type of physical or mental struggle. We were taught that ignoring the pain and suffering of our bodies was a sign of resilience and strength. Success belonged to those who figured out how to compartmentalize and disconnect from the suffering of the physical body to complete the mission. We also figured out very quickly that reporting an injury often resulted in being labeled unfit to do the mission we'd all trained so hard for. Nobody wants to be benched right before the game starts. So we learned to hide it. We learned not to tell anyone when we're in pain, especially not medical professionals or anyone in authority unless we wanted to face the possibility of missing out on the action.

Case in point: Ryan Land began the 2006 rotation with a broken collarbone. We all knew it, and we all helped him keep it quiet because we knew that he'd rather have a slightly off-center collarbone for the rest of his life than miss out on the action we'd all been preparing a lifetime for. We also had another significant injury that took place within the leadership of our team that was never reported. There was an unspoken code that we all understood. Nobody wants to be labeled as weak, injured, or unfit. Nobody wants to be benched. So, we suck it up, ignore it, and suppress it. This is even more true with invisible injuries incurred by trauma. No one wants to be labeled the guy or gal who needs a shrink, is mentally unstable, or weak-minded.

This is the environment that we all lived and operated within for many years. When we return home, the habits don't die easily. Nine times out of ten, veterans suppress, compartmentalize, ignore, deny, downplay, and hide their suffering, both mentally and physically. I think we're all still afraid of being labeled. We're afraid of being benched in life. We're afraid that if we admit that we're struggling, it automatically means that we're a lost cause, crazy, or weak.

I was very afraid of this. It took me years to be able to even admit that I was struggling or acknowledge the mental and physical symptoms I was dealing with. If I'm honest, just having the courage to admit it was the hardest part. Once I finally did, I discovered how much wasted energy I had expended trying to suppress and avoid the challenges I was confronting. I came to understand that there were straightforward and actionable solutions for many of the issues I silently endured.

This isn't easy for me to say, but since 2017, I've been 100 percent totally and permanently disabled due to service-connected disabilities. When I first found this out, I was walking on a treadmill inside a Marriott hotel in Denver, Colorado. Tears started streaming down my face. I was forty-five years old and 100 percent disabled.

D-A-M-N.

Gut punch.

The conditions that contributed to my 100 percent disability were post-traumatic headache, obstructive sleep apnea, post-traumatic stress disorder (PTSD), and traumatic brain injury (TBI) with both a visual spatial orientation facet and subjective symptoms facet. Out of all these conditions, TBI is the one that I spend a lot of time talking about. I'm passionate about sharing my experiences with this condition because I think it goes unrecognized by far too many people. When most people think of TBI, they think of a concussive impact or blunt force trauma to the head. But what a lot of people fail to consider is that TBI is also caused by blast-wave exposure. It was a revelation when I came to understand that there was a whole set of symptoms that I was dealing with post-combat that were all related to TBI, and yet, because I hadn't suffered from a concussive impact, I didn't know to look for it. Here's the thing about TBI—the effects can be hard to identify, *and* they can last for many years after the initial event. It can result in low mood, insomnia, irritability, low motivation, low energy, poor concentration, low testosterone, and severe hormone disruption, just to name a few.

One of the leading professionals to shine a light on TBI is Dr. B. Christopher Frueh, PhD, whom I met after an introduction by Ryan Land. Ryan happens to be very good friends with Dr. Frueh and benefited greatly from his work. Dr. Frueh is a clinical psychologist and professor of psychology at the University of Hawaii at Hilo with extensive experience in working with military veterans and active-duty personnel. With over three decades in the field, he has conducted clinical trials, epidemiological studies, historical research, and neuroscience investigations, resulting in over three hundred scientific publications. Dr. Frueh's work also extends to several organizations, including the SEAL Future Foundation (where he chairs the medical advisory board), Boulder Crest Foundation (where he serves on the scientific advisory panel), Military Special Operations Family Collaborative, The Mission Within, VETS, Inc., and the Quick Reaction Foundation. His work has been recognized at the national level. He has testified before the US Congress and worked as a paid contractor for government agencies such as the Department of Defense, Veterans Affairs, US State Department, and the National Board of Medical Examiners. Additionally, he has contributed commentaries to various publications, including the *National Review, Huffington Post, The New York Times, TIME, Men's Journal*, and the *Special Operation Association of America*. Dr. Frueh's insights have been cited in prominent media outlets like the *Wall Street Journal, The Economist, The Washington Post*, and *Scientific American*, among others.

So yeah, he's a badass. And if you won't listen to your ol' pal D about this stuff, you can't ignore a guy with a resume like that.

Dr. Frueh is not only a leader in the conversation around TBI and veterans but has also identified a distinct set of healthcare difficulties within the Special Operations community, which he and others have termed Operator Syndrome. This designation is used due to the unique and common pattern of interrelated medical, psychological, and quality-of-life impairments experienced by this group. These impairments include a range of issues that impact the overall health and well-being of Special Forces operators.

Dr. Frueh's work has also shed light on the issue of TBI within the veteran community and its long-term effects. An area of particular concern is the impact of blast exposure, a topic that is often not discussed enough. Many operators receive extensive training in demolitions and breaching involving prolonged exposure to explosions and the overpressure caused by blast waves. Furthermore, their training includes the use of various weapons systems, such as Carl Gustaf rifles that fire rockets, resulting in significant blast exposures. Even the act of firing a rifle or a handgun involves micro-blast exposures. These exposures accumulate over time, just like concussions and impact force blows affect the head. Now it is estimated that a significant portion of operators, more than 85 percent, may sustain a traumatic brain injury from training alone, even before they are deployed to an operational theater. The cumulative dose of blast wave exposure throughout an operator's career is often several orders of magnitude greater than that experienced by soldiers in conventional forces. This underlines the importance of addressing TBI and its consequences within the veteran and special operations communities.

Research has already pointed to the heightened challenges faced by veterans with comorbid symptoms, as well as the increased risk of developing additional combat-related disorders if one is already present. This phenomenon is known as "cumulative disadvantage," representing the accumulating burden of adversity over time. Dr. Frueh's extensive work with the Special Operations community has highlighted the profound impact on the health and quality of life of experienced operators.

I'm passionate about blast exposure and TBI because I know from my own experience that it can have long-lasting effects on various aspects of health. One of the most profound aspects of this is endocrine dysfunction. TBI has a pronounced dysregulating impact on the endocrine system. According to Dr. Frueh, this is due to the overactivity of the hypothalamic-pituitary-adrenal axis, which results from acute or chronic stress. This overactivity disrupts hormonal interactions between the brain region and the adrenal gland, including those involving gonadal and thyroid axes. Consequently, there is an increased secretion of cortisol and norepinephrine, leading to issues like insomnia and disrupted sleep patterns. His research also shows that TBI is closely associated with hypogonadism. Certain hormonal imbalances, such as low testosterone, can contribute to symptoms resembling depression, including low mood, fatigue, irritability, and impaired concentration, and may even lead to gynecomastia.

Now let's be clear, I'm not even 100 percent sure how to pronounce gynecomastia. I am not a medical professional or qualified to speak with authority on this stuff. But I *can* tell you that I was surprised to discover how many of the symptoms I was facing were related to TBI and endocrine dysregulation induced by blast exposure. What's more, I found that I matched many of the characteristics of Operator Syndrome as laid out by Dr. Frueh's work. This helped me put the pieces together and see the big picture a lot better.

Dr. Frueh recently released a book titled *Operator Syndrome,* which goes into far more detail than I will here, but I'd like to give you a very condensed list of injuries associated with Operator Syndrome taken from a research paper written by Dr. Frueh.[5] In doing so, I hope that some of you can put some puzzle pieces together and see the picture of your own life a little more clearly.

Injuries Associated with Operator Syndrome:

1. Traumatic brain injury (TBI)
2. Endocrine dysfunction
3. Sleep disturbance
4. Obstructive sleep apnea

---

[5] B Christopher Frueh et al., "'Operator Syndrome': A unique constellation of medical and behavioral health-care needs of military special operation forces," *The International Journal of Psychiatry in Medicine* 55, no. 4 (February 2020): 281–295, https://doi.org/10.1177/0091217420906659.

5. Chronic joint/back pain, orthopedic problems, and headaches
6. Substance abuse
7. Depression and suicide
8. Post-traumatic stress disorder (PTSD)
9. Anger
10. Worry, rumination, and stress reactivity
11. Marital, family, and community dysfunction
12. Problems with sexual health and intimacy
13. Being "on guard" or hypervigilant
14. Memory, concentration, and cognitive impairments
15. Vestibular and vision impairments
16. Challenges of transition to civilian life
17. Existential issues common to operators
18. Collective pattern of challenges

If any of these symptoms or characteristics ring a bell for you, you can learn more in Dr. Frueh's book, *Operator Syndrome*, which dives into the subject in much greater detail. And please, do not hesitate to reach out and get some help. Nobody wins by you suffering in silence.

But let's get back to the heading of this section: control what you can control. Don't worry, we're still coming back to the main point here; we're just taking the scenic route to do so. You're probably thinking that talking about Operator Syndrome and TBI has nothing to do with the *Control What You Can Control* mentality, but it does, and I'm going to tell you exactly why.

For any of us who have dedicated our lives to military service, we understand that our experiences bring a unique set of challenges. This rings especially true for those who have operated in active combat zones. Many of us grapple with a wide range of mental and physical symptoms resulting from both visible and invisible injuries. The magnitude of these challenges can be overwhelming, leaving us feeling powerless and unsure of how to cope. But I'm a practical person, and that's why I appreciate practical solutions.

Here's what has helped me the most when I find myself struggling: adopting a *Control What You Can Control* mentality. I've come to accept that certain injuries may never fully heal, some habits will always be an ongoing challenge to break, and specific issues related to my military career will be a part of my daily life. Nevertheless, there are aspects absolutely within my control that significantly impact my quality of life and my ability to cope with these challenges.

The Three Main Things I Can Control:

1. My Choice to Prioritize or Neglect My Mental and Physical Health

Many people tend to overlook the basics, and let me tell you, it's a real game-changer. There are so many big improvements you will see by taking care of the simple stuff. Exercise. Eat right. If you're going to drink, drink in moderation, not in excess. It's important to be mindful of the use of pain medication to avoid potential risks. Consider getting a sleep study to ensure you're catching those Zs effectively. And here's a big one—check your hormones. Shockingly, hormonal imbalances often slip under the radar because some healthcare providers skip crucial blood tests. Make it a routine to go for those comprehensive blood lab tests. That's how you catch and tackle those imbalances head-on. If you're carrying unseen struggles or grappling with mental health, don't tough it out solo. Talk to a licensed therapist or counselor.

Let me be crystal clear: you've got control of your own mental and physical health. Take radical responsibility for every choice you make. No whining, no victim mentality. If you're not doing the fundamentals, don't expect the results. You've got this!

2. My Choice to Negatively or Positively Impact the People Around Me

Our actions and attitudes don't just affect us; they have a ripple effect on those around us. It's within our control to choose whether we want to contribute positively or negatively to the lives of our loved ones, friends, and colleagues. Being aware of the impact we have on others and striving to be a source of support, empathy, and positivity can lead to stronger connections and a much more fulfilling life.

It's also within our control to choose who we allow into our circle. Being selective about the tribe in which you run can pull you toward greatness or mediocrity. Just as we have a choice about how we influence others, we have a choice about the people we allow to influence us.

3. My Perspective and Outlook on Life

How we view the world and our circumstances plays a pivotal role in our overall health. While we can't always control what happens to us, we can control how we respond and the perspective we adopt as a result. Cultivating a resilient and optimistic outlook can make a world of difference in how we navigate life's challenges. It's about finding meaning in adversity, focusing on personal growth, and embracing a mindset of continuous improvement.

That brings us to the final point of this section. If you are honestly and truly doing *everything* within your power to control what you can control consistently over a long period of time, I am willing to bet good money that you will see a significant improvement in your quality of life. And the rest? Let it go. If it's not within your control, if it belongs to the past, if it's something that you cannot change—*let it go.*

Control what you can control.

2. Eradicate Arrogance

One of the greatest lessons I learned as a Special Forces operator is that arrogance of any kind must be eradicated. Arrogance shouldn't be confused with confidence. Confidence is a tremendous asset. It is the driving force behind you that says, "I can do this. I am built for this. I can and I will succeed." Confidence is an absolute necessity if you have big dreams and goals. But when confidence mutates into arrogance, it will blind you to your own flaws, and it will always kill progress. This is a lesson I've learned time and time again.

People often perceive Special Forces operators as, well, *special* individuals. But I can tell you that while Special Forces operators may possess some natural talents and skills, the elite level of their abilities is achieved through extreme hard work, repetition, and the ability to utilize criticism as a catalyst for improvement. That means that good is not good enough. You need to be better. When you aim for excellence, you automatically agree to face every part of yourself that requires improvement.

My journey from a West Virginia boy to a Green Beret didn't come easily. It took a lot of hard work, humility, and a willingness to continuously strive for improvement. Throughout my journey, particularly in the Special Forces, I learned that arrogance had no place in achieving success. From the intense challenges of Special Forces Assessment and Selection (SFAS) to the grueling Special Forces Qualification Course (SFQC), I faced numerous obstacles that absolutely demanded perseverance and a humble mindset.

That's the thing about becoming a Special Forces operator—there are countless specific skills that you have to acquire and hone to operate at the highest level. I quickly realized that every accomplishment I made was just a qualifier to enter an even more demanding phase. My previous achievements were just stepping stones to becoming a beginner in a higher-stakes game. This continuous cycle taught me the importance of putting my ego aside and focusing on the task at hand.

By embracing humility and the determination to improve, I conquered the challenges in front of me. Rather than letting arrogance hinder my progress, I chose to work hard, push my limits, and strive to be better every day. This mindset became a driving force in my journey toward becoming a successful Special Forces operator. The truth is, if you don't learn to eradicate arrogance from your mindset, you'll struggle to keep up and eventually fail because you are not benefiting from constructive feedback.

As I spoke about in Chapter 9, after every mission was completed, we conducted what we called the after-action review (AAR). These sessions were anything but gentle or sugar-coated. There were no congratulations or words of encouragement. Instead, we got straight down to business. We pointed out what could have been done better and where mistakes, no matter how small, were made. Some might have seen our AAR process as brutal or harsh, but they were all about efficiency and progress. These sessions were solely focused on making improvements for future operations.

Sure, it wasn't always easy to hear our shortcomings exposed and dissected in such a direct manner. It required us to set aside our egos and be open to criticism. But that was the only way we could grow and become better as a team. We understood that each mission was an opportunity to learn, adapt, and refine our skills. With an environment free from arrogance, we embraced the lessons learned from our mistakes, making us more effective, efficient, and capable operators.

In the battlefield or in any arena of life, the eradication of arrogance is crucial. It will allow you to accept and appreciate constructive criticism, no matter how harsh it may seem at first. By doing so, you will be able to identify areas that need improvement and work relentlessly to enhance your performance.

Throughout my life, I've been honored to take on a variety of leadership roles, and I've upheld a simple but powerful principle in each: arrogance has no place on my team. It's just not tolerated. Confidence is welcomed, provided that it is rooted in humility. I uphold this value in both my personal and professional life. Remember this: Arrogance always needs to advertise. Confidence speaks for itself.

Spotting arrogance in ourselves and our team members is crucial for personal and professional growth.

Here are four signs to look out for that indicate that there is arrogance that needs to be eradicated.

1. Resenting Constructive Criticism from Authority Figures
If you find yourself complaining or feeling angry after receiving feedback from a teacher, coach, boss, mentor, or commanding officer, it might be time to take a closer look in the mirror. Arrogance often blinds us to the valuable insights that authority figures can provide for our growth. I remember feeling very uncomfortable the first time I got called out by Coach Thornburg on the field in high school. At first, I felt angry and hurt, but then I realized that all of his feedback was aimed at helping me improve. His criticism meant that he saw value in me. That's when everything changed.

2. Avoiding Situations Where You Won't Be the Best Right Away
Arrogant people shy away from scenarios where they might not immediately excel. They constantly seek to be recognized as the best, which limits their potential growth. Embracing being a beginner and stepping out of your comfort zone is essential for personal and professional development.

3. Considering Yourself the Smartest Person in the Room
If you constantly view yourself as superior to everyone else, it may be a sign of arrogance. In every phase of life, there is always an opportunity to learn from others who possess more knowledge or experience. Expanding your circle and humbly seeking wisdom from those ahead of you can lead to valuable personal growth.

4. Making Frequent Excuses
Excuses often stem from an arrogant mindset. Rather than taking responsibility for shortcomings or failures, arrogant people tend to place blame elsewhere. Being accountable and owning up to our mistakes is an important aspect of personal growth and development.

Arrogant people often disregard the opinions and perspectives of those around them. They believe that their viewpoint is the only valid one. Openness to different perspectives and a willingness to listen and learn from others are essential for personal and collaborative growth.

Don't forget that when you make that bold decision to pursue greatness in any area of your life—relationships, business, or even your military career—you need to brace yourself for feeling like a total beginner at first. It's normal. It's natural. If you give up at the first sight of your own imperfections, you're depriving yourself of the chance to truly excel at anything. Greatness doesn't come easily. It requires grit, resilience, and a commitment to keep going even when things get tough.

In the pursuit of excellence, embracing humility becomes crucial. Humility allows you to set your ego aside and welcome criticism with open arms. It empowers you to seek guidance from those who have walked the path before you, those who can share their wisdom and experiences. By humbling yourself, you acknowledge that you don't have all the answers and that there's always room for improvement.

Eradicate arrogance.

3. Possess an Extreme Work Ethic

My interest in joining the Special Forces community stemmed from a desire to serve alongside the best. The Green Berets' reputation for taking on a wide variety of missions at the highest level caught my attention, and I couldn't quench a burning desire to be a part of it all.

The Green Berets, as well as other members of the special operations community, were my superheroes as a young man. They were the guys out there handling all sorts of complex missions while the rest of us looked at them in awe. They were renowned for extensive training, adaptability, and ability to work in small teams, even in the most challenging and complex environments across the globe.

That intense desire to join the ranks of those I had revered and respected throughout my early career was the fuel that drove me to pursue the path of becoming a Green Beret. There was an element of mystery to it all that intrigued me, and I wanted to discover what separated this elite fighting force from the rest.

But one of the things I quickly realized through SFAS and the SFQC is that possessing exceptional skills wasn't the only thing that set members of the Special Forces apart. It didn't take long for me to uncover the secret behind those seemingly superhuman abilities possessed by Special Forces operators, and it's not the glamorous answer most people hope for. It's something much simpler yet incredibly powerful.

What sets apart the Special Forces community is an extreme work ethic and the ability to execute a variety of tasks with absolute precision. Special Forces operators didn't just stumble upon greatness one day. They weren't born into this world with some magical talent. Sure, some of them had natural abilities, but that's not what sets them apart—it is the unyielding dedication that drives them to spend countless hours of sweat, practice, and repetition to hone their skills to absolute perfection. While you might expect a grand explanation for what makes Special Forces operators so exceptional, the truth is simple: they acquire a wide array of skills, master the fundamentals, and execute them with unparalleled precision. They know that true greatness isn't found in flashy shortcuts but in the day-to-day grind of putting in the work until those fundamental skills become second nature.

When I made the life-changing decision to follow the path of becoming a Green Beret, it wasn't about adventure-seeking or garnering admiration. It was something much deeper. It was about joining a community that embodied grit, resilience, and an extreme work ethic. Becoming a part of the Special Forces for me was not about simply the Green Beret or earning a title; it was about embodying a mindset and a way of life that values hard work and discipline.

But here's the thing: I wasn't blessed with the kind of physical genetics that gave me a leg up. Everything I've achieved—from completing SFAS to conquering the demanding SFQC, sniper school, ranger training, airborne operations, advanced International Morse Code (AIMC), and various other courses—required me to outwork everyone around me. Looking back, I realize the incredible sacrifice, discipline, and drive it took to accomplish what I did. I never backed away from putting in the hard work and consistently pushed myself to achieve my goals, even if it meant facing challenges head-on. The journey was tough, both physically and mentally, but I wouldn't change a thing because it's what shaped me into who I am today.

Transitioning from my military service to the corporate world, I've come to realize that most success, whether on the battlefield or in business, boils down to having grit and a strong work ethic. And you know what? There's a certain beauty in the fact that an extreme work ethic is the great equalizer. It doesn't matter where you come from, what your background is, or what resources you have at your disposal. Your ability to rise above the rest ultimately comes down to the lengths you're willing to go and the effort you're willing to invest into your dreams and goals.

While natural talent may give some an initial advantage, it's the burning desire to continuously improve, to push the envelope, and to stretch beyond your limits that truly propels you towards greatness.

Growing up in West Virginia taught me a thing or two about the value of hard work and determination. My story is proof that success isn't just for the lucky few. It is for anyone, including me, who has a fire inside to keep improving and dreaming big.

Hard work beats talent when talent doesn't work hard. I'm living proof of that.

More often than not, what separates extraordinary people from the average simply comes down to an extreme work ethic. Sure, certain goals may demand a touch of natural talent. No matter how hard I work, I have to admit that I won't be dazzling audiences as a Dallas Cowboys cheerleader anytime soon—let's keep it real here. But apart from a handful of those rare, born-with-it skills, the vast majority of extraordinary accomplishments can be realized through the power of an extreme work ethic, along with a commitment to expanding your skillset and mastering the fundamentals flawlessly.

If you gain one valuable lesson from my story, it's this: Elite success is not reserved for a select few. It's open to anyone willing to put in the work and strive for greatness. Take inspiration from those who have gone before you, but don't be intimidated by them. The lie that there is some extraordinary "X factor" that separates the good from the great will hold you back if you're not careful.

Here are a few game-changers when it comes to possessing an extreme work ethic.

Get Clear on Exactly What You're Working Toward
An extreme work ethic means nothing if you don't know what you're working toward. Without a clear vision, you risk burning out or drifting aimlessly. It's important to be brave enough to declare what you want and *then* create the steps to get there.

Far too often, people fear failure, so they avoid clarifying what they're striving for. But if you don't have the bravery to get clear on what you're working toward and declare it, you'll never get where you want to go. Set your goals. Be detailed and specific about what you want to achieve. Paint a vivid picture of your vision. Identify the actions required to reach your goals and break them down into manageable steps. This not only gives you a clear direction but also empowers you to take control of your path toward success. By getting clear on your objectives, you will be able to create a roadmap that gets you where you want to go.

Others may doubt you or discourage you, saying you don't have what it takes or that your dreams are too big to achieve. Don't let that criticism deter you. Instead, let those doubts fuel your fucking fire! Use their skepticism as motivation to work even harder and prove them wrong. Don't be afraid to own your dreams, no matter how audacious they may seem. Take all the time you need to discover and define your goals in life with precision, visualize your desired outcome, outline the steps needed to make your dreams a reality, and then PUT THE FUCKING WORK IN!

Love the Results
Hard work isn't a walk in the park. There will be moments when you face grueling tasks, setbacks that knock you down, or mundane assignments

that make you question your sanity. That's why it's so important to appreciate and embrace the results that your efforts bring forth. If you don't love the results of your hard work and celebrate them, you'll eventually burn out. Those results could be acquiring a new skill, conquering a project, achieving a personal milestone, or making a tangible, positive impact on your team.

Loving the results also means embracing the journey itself. Cultivate habits around celebrating small victories, learning from failures, and embracing personal growth amidst hardships. Each hurdle you overcome and every ounce of determination you pour into your work contributes to the results you achieve.

Go the Extra Mile
This is what separates ordinary people from high achievers—the willingness to go the extra mile. Having the mental fortitude to go the extra mile is the only way I achieved what I have in my life. I had to grind and hustle for every single win.

Going the extra mile means showing up day in and day out, no matter how tough things get. It means pushing yourself beyond what you thought was possible, shattering your own preconceived notions of what you're capable of. It's about giving it your all even when the odds are stacked against you.

Take a minute and think about a goal that you want to achieve. With that in mind, I want you to list everything you are doing to get there. Count up the time, money, and effort you're currently investing into achieving that goal and write it down. Got it? Okay. Take a hard look at your list. You're staring at the mile you've already agreed to go. Now let me ask you an important question. Can you double it? Can you triple it? Take a look at your list again and at least sign up to do more than you did yesterday. Refuse to settle for mediocrity, push through the pain, and give it everything you've got.

Having the grit and resilience to achieve greatness isn't reserved for the chosen few. It's within all of us. Find that burning desire within to achieve something great, embrace the challenges, embrace the grind, and watch yourself come out on top!

Take Time to Forge New Capacities
I want you to take a minute and picture someone you admire and think about where they started. I want to remind you that their ability didn't magically appear overnight. They forged it through years of consistent building, steadily pushing their limits and gradually expanding their capabilities. So, be patient with yourself. Embrace the fact that developing new capacities takes time. Success requires incremental progress and continuous growth. It's okay to start small and work your way up. Celebrate the small victories along the way and don't let setbacks discourage you. Success is a journey, and it takes time to develop the skills and capacities needed to overcome challenges and achieve greatness.

If my story proves anything, it's that in the end, what separates successful people from the rest is a dedication to mastering the fundamentals with surgical precision and possessing an extreme work ethic.

4. Adopt a No-Surrender Mindset
One of the most powerful lessons I have learned through my life experiences, from combat boots to business suits and everything in between, is the power of a no-surrender mindset. There is something to be said for being the one person in the room who just won't quit.

Every Special Forces operator has a story that takes them back to a moment in time when they faced a daunting challenge, some instance that demanded them to dig deep and rely on nothing but pure determination. Typically, these stories revolve around enduring a freezing night in the pouring rain, pushing through mile after mile of heavy rucking, or plunging into freezing water and battling against the icy waves. These are the epic moments that movies are made of, the tough situations that test even the finest warrior's physical and mental limits.

But the moment that pushed me to my limits wasn't a freezing night in the rain or a long grueling run. Mine was dots and dashes. *Fucking dots and dashes.*

Back in 1997, all of us 18Es had to learn and pass Advanced International Morse Code (AIMC), and let me tell you, it was a real ballbuster. For eight long weeks, we were immersed in the world of Morse code. We were required to master the intricacies of International Morse code and prove our skills by passing a verification test that included sending and receiving a certain number of word groups per minute. No exceptions.

By the second day, my brain felt like mush. Doubts crept in, and I found myself on the verge of having an *oh-shit* moment. After everything I had accomplished during my Special Forces training, I started to worry that I wouldn't be able to meet the standards to pass the verification test. The doubt grew stronger, and on the third day, I just wanted it to be over.

But then, something inside me shifted. I remembered all the challenges I had overcome in the past.

Fuck you, Morse code. You're not about to break me. I will not surrender.

No matter what, I was not going to quit. Day after day, I pushed myself to decipher those dots and dashes. I practiced tirelessly. I dreamed in Morse code. I tapped it out on my leg while eating and even while driving. I teetered on the brink of Morse Code–induced insanity. And then, slowly but surely, my confidence grew. And when the day of the verification test finally arrived, I faced it head-on.

No surrender. I passed the test, and my triumph was not just over Morse code itself but also my own self-doubt.

But that wasn't the only time life presented me with tough challenges that tested my limits and caused me to dig deep. Another one of the greatest lessons I learned on the importance of having a no-surrender mindset was when I attended Robin Sage, a four-week training course that is the culminating event of the Special Forces pipeline. Named after OSS operative Colonel Jerry Michael Sage, who escaped from Nazi captivity after numerous attempts, Robin Sage is a rigorous test that must be passed before earning the prestigious Green Beret. Throughout

Robin Sage, we were tested on our proficiency in all the skills that we'd been taught during the Special Forces Qualification Course, more commonly known as the Q course. The Q course had pushed our physical and mental limits beyond what we thought we could handle. By the end of it, we felt invincible. Robin Sage was there to keep us humble.

Situated in an area spanning approximately fifty thousand square miles of North Carolina's wilderness, Robin Sage provided all of us young candidates with our first real immersion into the world of Special Forces. Robin Sage is designed to test all the skills that Green Berets are known for: training foreign forces; conducting counterterrorism operations and reconnaissance missions; carrying out small-scale raids and ambushes; operating in twelve-man detachments; and actively collaborating with partner forces. Robin Sage was the first time we got to experience the multifaceted nature of Special Forces operations.

Robin Sage presented all of us with numerous lifelike scenarios where we had to collaborate with a guerrilla force (typically led by retired Green Berets) to overthrow a fictitious illegitimate government. This exercise mirrored the concept of proxy warfare prevailing in contemporary conflict zones. We had to forge relationships with the guerrilla force, provide training, and conduct combat operations against a superior occupying enemy force. We learned to work by, with, and through our partner forces.

All the challenges presented during Robin Sage were designed to test our knowledge, skills, and adaptability. We would instruct our partner forces in small-unit tactics, deliver medical care, establish outposts, and set up crucial lines of communication with headquarters. We conducted reconnaissance missions and executed raids and ambushes, all while facing a variety of complex scenarios that demanded strategic decision-making. Some scenarios even put us in tough ethical dilemmas, where we had to navigate delicate situations without compromising the trust and support of our allies or violating the laws of war. In these critical moments, we saw just how important the dynamic human element was in determining the success or failure on the battlefield. But Robin Sage isn't just about testing knowledge and skills. It's also designed to push you to the brink of your mental fortitude and test your ability to stay strong under extreme circumstances.

There was one ruck in particular that still sticks out in my mind to this day. It taught me a hard lesson in refusing to surrender over the course of about eight hours. The task seemed simple enough: a long ruck over a rugged landscape with our rucksacks strapped to our backs, each weighing more than a hundred pounds. Keep in mind that I participated in Robin Sage as an 18E (communications sergeant), which meant that I was responsible for carrying a particularly heavy rucksack filled with more than just the usual gear and essentials. I was packing radios, batteries, and necessary odds and ends that could make a pack mule break a sweat. The terrain varied from steep hills to dense forests, challenging our every step. Robin Sage doesn't play. Anyone who fell behind or couldn't keep up was automatically cut. It was a total dog-eat-dog situation—everyone was fighting for their spot. There was intense anxiety pumping through all of us if it was even perceived we were weaker or falling behind. None of us wanted to be the one to get left in the dust.

My body screamed at me to slow down, but quitting was never an option. It was a brutal battle, both physically and mentally. But I was dead set on proving to myself that I had what it takes to overcome any obstacle. I would not surrender, no matter what. One foot in front of the other. *Stay in the fight. Just get it done.*

Rucking is all a mental game. There is no room for hesitation or half-hearted effort. Every part of the challenge is designed to test your resolve—the weight on your back, the distance ahead, and the exhaustion that slowly creeps in and doesn't relent. It is in those moments that you understand whether or not you have what it takes to execute. In those moments, you cannot afford to give in to self-doubt or fatigue; instead, you have to push through and get the victory through pure grit and determination.

That ruck taught me a lot of invaluable life lessons. It taught me that if you want something, you've got to have the grit to chase that goal with wild obsession. Nobody is going to do it for you. You have to know what you want and then aggressively grab hold of it. That ruck also showed me that I could adapt and overcome any obstacle that came my way. I discovered the depth of my own capabilities and realized that I possessed the strength and resilience to triumph over adversity as long as I stayed the course and refused to surrender.

It also expanded the boundaries of my mind. When I thought I had reached the edge of my mental capacity, I learned that I could break through those limits and create even more space to grow, learn, and improve. Pushing myself beyond what I thought was possible opened up new potential and unleashed a sense of inner strength I never knew I had. It taught me to challenge my own self-imposed restrictions and embrace discomfort as a catalyst for personal growth. It taught me that having grit means possessing the determination and perseverance to overcome challenges. It means putting in consistent, intense effort, pushing your limits, and doing whatever it takes.

Maybe you're reading this and nodding along but inwardly thinking, "Okay, D, this is a cool story. I don't have any plans of attending Robin Sage or going for an eight-hour ruck anytime soon." And maybe you're right. But I want to give you a little wake-up call: if you are in the world of business right now and want to achieve something big, you're in a Robin Sage of your own. In the professional world, if you fall behind, you're out. It's a dog-eat-dog world. I don't care what industry or position you're in; it's a highly competitive environment out there. Even if you operate in one of these super friendly, we-support-each-other work environments, trust me—it's still a fierce competition. If you allow complacency to set in, you're going to wake up one day and suddenly realize that *you* are the teammate who got left in the dust because you slacked off. If you have a big dream or goal, you've gotta have that dawg in you and that no-surrender mindset.

The no-surrender mindset applies across all areas of life. Let's explore a few major ones.

Fighting for Those You Love with a No-Surrender Mindset
Having a no-surrender mindset isn't just for the battlefield. It also applies to those you love. Let's face it, raising children and nurturing family relationships isn't easy. For many of us, it's even harder than the stuff we faced out on the field. There are moments when you want to throw in the towel, times when you're lost and clueless, and occasions when you doubt your abilities as a parent or partner. In the face of challenges, you have to show up with a no-surrender mindset. You have to refuse to let anything or anyone tear your family apart. You have to show up with a love that is fierce, relentless, and unconditional.

A no-surrender mindset means fiercely believing that the ones you love are worth fighting for, no matter what. This demands resilience, patience, and an unshakeable conviction. There will be days when you're exhausted, overwhelmed, and questioning your choices. Take a breath and keep showing up. Embrace the challenges, the setbacks, and the messy imperfections of life. Learn from them, grow from them, and become an even stronger warrior for those who mean the most to you. In a war for those you love, there's no room for surrender. Take on the battles that life throws at you and refuse to let go.

Fighting for Yourself with a No-Surrender Mindset
In the military, we are often taught the values of self-sacrifice and putting the needs of others before our own. A sense of duty to serve is deeply engrained in our identity. This is an admirable quality. However, because this mindset runs so deep, we as veterans often struggle to prioritize ourselves. While we are busy fighting for our country, our family, and those we love, we end up losing the battle when it comes to fighting for ourselves. That's why it's vital to understand that caring for yourself is not a selfish act.

First of all, taking care of yourself allows you to be in the best position to show up for those who rely on you. Taking the time to prioritize your own goals, health, and well-being is not only beneficial for you, but it also enables you to continue making a positive impact on the lives of those around you. Taking care of yourself doesn't mean neglecting others.

Secondly, if you don't fight for yourself, who will? If you throw in the towel and surrender the ground of your own health, career, or mental well-being because you're so busy prioritizing everyone else, everything will crumble.

In case you need to hear it: you deserve to be strong, healthy, and happy. If you've given up ground and feel like there are parts of yourself slowly slipping away, it's time to get your head right and get back in the game. Don't you dare surrender on yourself.

There are several important aspects of fighting for yourself with a no-surrender mindset. First is your mental and physical health. This is at the center of everything. Think of all the time you spent investing in your mind and body to prepare it for the challenges of combat. In the same way, you have to invest time and effort into your mind and body to prepare it for the challenges of life. If your physical health is struggling, don't sit back and surrender. Stand up and take action. Get the professional help and treatments you need if you are suffering from a serious health concern. If you find yourself exhausted and lethargic all the time because you're not eating right and exercising, stop listening to your own BS excuses and do the work. Challenge the voice that tells you that you're too old, too broken, or too busy. If you can, surround yourself with a supportive community of like-minded individuals who understand the unique struggles you are facing. If not, show up for yourself and be that positive person for someone else: remind them of their strengths and push through any doubt or self-limiting beliefs. Incorporate regular exercise into your routine, adopt nutritious eating habits, and actively seek ways to manage stress. Commit to practices that improve your physical, mental, and emotional health. By committing to show up for yourself, you can also set a positive example for others.

On this note, it is important to remember that the no-surrender mindset in health and fitness doesn't always mean constantly pushing your body to the extremes. While it's important to challenge yourself, the true essence of the no-surrender mindset lies in consistently showing up and refusing to quit, not going through cycles of extreme action followed by burnout. If you have physical challenges you're dealing with, don't give up. Find a way to take consistent action and fight for yourself. Believe me, I know firsthand how tough is can be. I've had to work through many physical setbacks, which I shared at the beginning of this chapter. But the same resilience and adaptability that served me on the battlefield have helped me overcome hurdles in my own health. It will for you too.

Just as important, if not more so, is your mental health. Many of us know all too well that the battle in our minds is often the hardest of all to face. That's why I want you to listen up to what I'm about to say. If you find yourself struggling to win the battle that's happening inside your mind, it's okay to call in some support. If you were pinned down in a firefight, you wouldn't think twice about radioing in a call for support, would you? You wouldn't just keep going at it alone when there are resources available to give you the backup you need to gain the upper hand. The same is true in life. The problem is that for most of us, it's much harder to pick up the phone and call for help when we are struggling mentally than it was to pick up a radio and call for help in the middle of a firefight. I get it. But you have faced far greater challenges, and you can conquer this, too.

Stay in the fight. Do whatever it takes to win the fight. Call in some backup when you need it and get the support you need. Most importantly, *do not surrender on yourself.*

Here are a few key aspects of adopting a no-surrender mindset.

Know Your "Why"

Understanding your purpose and the motivation behind your actions is crucial for personal and professional growth. It gives you a clear direction and provides the fuel to stay motivated during challenging times. Knowing why you are pursuing a particular goal or dream allows you to tap into a deeper level of determination and resilience.

Remember That 99 Percent of Success Is Built on Failure

Failure is not the opposite of success; it is an essential part of the journey toward success. Every failure is a valuable learning opportunity that helps you grow stronger and wiser.

Opportunities Are Often Disguised as Challenges and Hard Times
When faced with adversity, it's easy to get discouraged and give up. However, it's important to recognize that challenges and difficult periods in life are often the catalysts for growth and transformation. In disguise, they present opportunities for self-improvement, resilience building, and gaining valuable experience. Embrace these moments as chances to push yourself beyond your comfort zone and unlock your true potential.

Do Not Surrender to a Setback
Setbacks and failures are inevitable, but surrendering to them only prolongs your journey to success. Instead, view setbacks as temporary roadblocks and use them as opportunities to reassess your strategies, learn from your mistakes, and adjust your approach. Remember that even the most successful people have faced numerous failures before achieving their goals.

Keep Your Internal Voice Positive
Remind yourself of your own tenacity and keep your inner dialogue positive with thoughts like "I will not surrender" and "I will not quit." This conviction will help you push through obstacles and stay focused on your journey to success. When you feel discouraged or drained, remind yourself of your commitment and find the inner strength to keep going.

Convince Yourself That You're Doing It
Self-belief is a powerful motivator. Convince yourself that you are capable of achieving your goals and that you have what it takes to succeed.

Convince Yourself That You're Built Different
Embrace your unique qualities and strengths. Recognize that you have a distinct set of skills, experiences, and perspectives that set you apart from others. This mindset allows you to approach challenges with a

sense of confidence, knowing that you have what it takes to overcome them. Embrace your individuality and use it as your competitive advantage on the path to success.

The most important thing is to apply the same grit and determination to every aspect of life as you did to overcome your greatest challenges in life. Fight for those you love with a no-surrender mindset. Fight for your goals and dreams with a no-surrender mindset. Most importantly, fight for yourself with a no-surrender mindset.

5. Embrace Innovation

In recent years, "innovation" has become something of a buzzword. But the meaning behind it isn't just a passing trend. It holds profound meaning and incredible potential to revolutionize the way we strategize, plan, and execute in any area of life. Embracing innovation is not just about accepting change; it's about actively seeking out new ideas and solutions in a constantly changing environment. It is about recognizing that stagnation and complacency are the enemies of progress. Innovation requires us to challenge the status quo, break free from traditional thinking, and open ourselves up to new possibilities.

Case in point: During my 2003 rotation in Iraq, the threat of IEDs was nearly non-existent. By my 2006 deployment, the scenario had drastically changed. The insurgency had evolved, and by necessity, so did our approach to fight it. The unarmored vehicles we initially used had to be replaced with up-armored gun trucks, and speed became our ally to outmaneuver remote detonations. We began to integrate civilian vehicles to reduce our visibility. The ever-shifting dynamic forced us to stay one step ahead and required us to embrace innovation as an imperative, not a luxury.

But here's the thing: when you have all the time and resources in the world to play around with and nothing is riding on the outcome, innovation is easy to embrace. Introducing new methods and making a bold, unpredictable move isn't so scary when the stakes are low. On the flip side, when the stakes are high, it's easy for all of us to cling to what we know and have always done. The familiarity of routine can provide a sense of security in high-stress environments.

But there are pivotal moments in various aspects of life, be it in business or even in battle, where innovation becomes absolutely necessary. Whether we're talking counterinsurgency, rapidly evolving market landscapes, shifting customer preferences, warfare, or unexpected challenges, there are times when clinging to the way things have always been done just isn't going to cut it. That's why it's important to learn how to innovate under pressure.

When we ran into those roadblocks on April 17, 2006, we were faced with a situation that demanded us to do just that. I had to rely on my instincts and act swiftly in a situation that demanded immediate action. I knew that staying put in the truck wouldn't get us anywhere. The only way to overcome this obstacle was to take control of the situation, push past the tangled barbed wire, and clear a new path forward.

The ability to think quickly and make tough decisions sets exceptional leaders apart from the rest. This is a principle that's just as relevant in the business world as it is in battle.

The 2006 rotation drilled this lesson into me over and over again. We lured Omar out with sexy phone calls; we confiscated an entire car lot to gain leverage with a known insurgent; hell, we even called in a mind reader to get intel. If we hadn't learned to innovate and pivot when the stakes are high, we wouldn't have been successful in any of those cases. I've also seen this ring true in my professional world as well. The most successful people in the world understand how to innovate under pressure. While it may be more tempting to reject change when stakes are high and stress levels increase, holding onto the way things have always been done limits the potential for growth. Organizations that recognize the importance of innovation, even in challenging circumstances, will be better positioned to grab hold of opportunities, overcome obstacles, and thrive in an evolving world.

But it's easier said than done. Why?

First and foremost, when you embrace innovation, you step outside of the expected and venture into uncharted territory. In simpler terms, innovation means sticking your neck out there with your ass on the line for it. The fear of failing and being exposed holds many people back. It's comfortable to cling to convention, expectation, and tradition even if they no longer serve a purpose because even if you fail, you'll fail *quietly* underneath the shadow of the status quo. But when you stand up and try something *different,* when you embrace innovation in high-stakes scenarios, that spotlight shifts directly to *you*.

It's easy to tell you stories of how we used innovative tactics and methods as a team during the 2006 rotation because I know how the stories end. Any tech pioneer or executive can stand up in front of a whiteboard and give a PowerPoint about it after they damn well know that their innovative idea led to a successful outcome. It's easy to talk about after it's worked. But I'll be the first to tell you that it wasn't easy or comfortable to stick my neck out there over and over again with outside-of-the-box ideas on the battlefield. Change and innovation rarely come without resistance or criticism. As a leader, you have to have thick skin, weather these challenges, face judgment, and learn to be okay with it. You have to stay laser-focused on winning the battle and achieving the goal, not playing it safe or playing it to be liked. This is one of the most fundamental aspects of being a good leader, but few people talk about how uncomfortable it is while you're in the midst of it. However, the uncomfortable nature of embracing innovation under pressure is precisely what separates those who make a lasting impact from those who stay stagnant.

Here are a few important lessons I learned about innovating under pressure.

Intelligence in Action: Leveraging Information to Your Advantage
I want to make this abundantly clear—innovation should not be confused with impulsive actions or unplanned reactions in high-pressure situations. True innovation requires strategic planning, gathering

quality information, and acting on a solid foundation of knowledge. When you're faced with a tough decision in high-stakes and stressful scenarios, the most crucial step is to gather as much quality information as possible before you make a move.

In this book, I've shared numerous stories that showcase the action-oriented aspects of decisions because that's the shit that's fun to read. But behind the scenes, there were hours of intelligence gathering and meticulous planning that formed the backbone of those strategic plans that we acted upon. None of our missions happened by accident.

If you want to innovate effectively under pressure, you have to invest time in gathering quality information before making any moves. Rushing into decisions without a solid understanding of the situation can be catastrophic. In high-stakes situations, the pressure to act quickly can be overwhelming. But when you take the time to gather information, you equip yourself and your team with the insights needed to make informed and effective decisions. This allows you to assess the risks, analyze potential outcomes, and develop a clear roadmap for implementing new ideas or approaches. Without this groundwork, innovation is just a gamble and you're betting your ass on luck rather than calculated strategies.

This is as true on the battlefield as it is in the boardroom. Before you innovate, gather insights, information, and intelligence. Use them to inform your strategies, stay ahead of the competition, and dominate the market. And don't be afraid to get creative when it comes to getting the information you need. Be bold.

Team Unity and Cohesion

As you lead a team in pursuing innovation, unity and cohesion become incredibly important. You can have a great concept or theoretical idea, but if you don't have team unity, you'll never pull it off. It's easier to maintain cohesion when you're following the status quo or doing what's expected. But when you decide to tackle a problem with an unconventional approach, you also have to make sure that every single person on the team is clear on the vision and prepared for the execution. Innovative ideas and solutions are only valuable if you can implement them properly. This is crucial in both the military and the business world.

In the business world, people often talk about team building exercises, team unity, and team synergy. But the business world offers certain safety nets when it comes to actually relying on your team. You don't have to trust Karen from HR or Steve from accounting to cover for you while bullets are raining over your head. And that's probably a good thing. In the world of Special Forces, the idea of teamwork isn't just a topic for a nice keynote speech at a business conference—it's a matter of life or death. To accomplish any mission, you are forced to rely on your team members. You have to trust them to have your back and vice versa. The pressure of being responsible for the members of your team is extreme. You don't get to have off days or *oopsies*. You have to bring your absolute best to the table *every fucking day*.

War has been described as an unforgiving business. I can tell you beyond a doubt that it's true. It demands discipline, cohesion, and a shared commitment to a common vision. You can't afford to check out or half-ass anything. One mistake and the whole team suffers the consequences.

When it comes to life beyond the military, I'm not saying that everyone should live under the pressure of every decision being a matter of life and death. What I am saying is that if you want to lead a team successfully, you've got to instill a sense of radical responsibility in every single member. You, as a leader, have to help your team understand that their choices affect the entire group positively or negatively.

You also have to ensure that there is effective communication happening at every level. Most people don't fully realize the importance of communication in active combat scenarios. In these types of situations, communication is not just a nice-to-have skill but an absolute necessity. That's why we prioritize communication training and establish protocols for every possible scenario—so that when chaos erupts, our team remains unified.

In the business world, the importance of communication is just as vital as it is in the military. A good leader should implement high standards of team communication in mundane operations so that the team is prepared when chaos erupts. A good leader should *especially* enforce good communication in high-stress scenarios when the team is innovating and performing under pressure. Unfortunately, when stress levels rise, there is a natural tendency in the business world for team members to communicate poorly or withdraw altogether. Everyone is worried about taking the blame if something doesn't go well or too shy to face confrontation head-on if improvements need to be made. But that's precisely the time when effective communication becomes even more critical. As leaders, it is our responsibility to create a culture that values and encourages communication, no matter the circumstances. In high-pressure situations, communication is not just about relaying information; it's also about building a foundation of trust and collaboration that can withstand the harshest of conditions.

The lessons I learned during my military experience have stayed with me throughout my journey. Effective communication, especially during moments of intense stress, requires a willingness to put your team's needs ahead of your own and to foster an atmosphere where communication flows freely and honestly. If you want to lead a team through the process of innovating under pressure, you've got to ensure that your team stays well-informed, unified, and cohesive.

Embracing an Element of Unpredictability

In any high-pressure situation, maintaining an edge of unpredictability will give you the upper hand. This principle holds true whether it's on the battlefield, where lives are on the line, or in the cutthroat world of business, where competition is fierce. Sun Tzu's quote from *The Art of War* perfectly sums it up: "Do not repeat the tactics which have gained you one victory, but let your methods be regulated by the infinite variety of circumstances."[6]

---

[6] Sun Tzu. *The Art of War*. Translated by Lionel Giles. Fall River Press, 2015.

An experienced operator in an active combat environment knows the dangers of repeatedly using the same tactics that initially led to victory. They understand that the enemy will soon catch on, adapt, and gain an advantage. In contrast, successful operators thrive on unpredictability by consistently changing their tactics, keeping the enemy on their toes, and maintaining the upper hand.

Similarly, in the business world, strict adherence to a single strategy can result in stagnation and weakness. Companies that grow complacent and depend solely on past achievements will quickly be surpassed by more agile and creative competitors. Think of Kodak, Blockbuster, and Toys"R"Us. Embracing unpredictability involves recognizing the constantly evolving nature of the business environment and being ready to adapt, innovate, and surprise the competition. By incorporating an element of unpredictability, you not only position yourself to outpace the competition but also to capitalize on opportunities as they arise.

Unpredictability is not synonymous with recklessness; it is a calculated and strategic move. Just as you adapt on the battlefield to ensure you stay one step ahead of the enemy, successful businesses must also continually seek new ways to adapt their products, approach, and marketing strategies to match the evolving needs of the customer. By doing so, they gain a competitive edge and outmaneuver the competition.

If you're stuck in a rut or facing a challenge, try injecting a little unpredictability into your actions to gain the upper hand. Embrace the element of surprise and take an unexpected approach. Open yourself up to new possibilities and create opportunities for advancement. Don't be afraid to embrace innovation.

6. Calm Breeds Calm

In the fall of 2003, my team deployed to Kosovo and was tasked by our commander, Special Forces Major Gary Bloomberg, to track down and capture persons indicted for war crimes (PIFWCs, pronounced PIFF-wicks—fun to say, right?). Gary was an outstanding commander and was all about rolling up the bad guys, which played well with the team.

On one particular mission, we were tasked with taking down a notorious PIFWC named AJ. His reputation preceded him as one of the biggest, baddest motherfuckers in the region, and we prepared ourselves for a fight as we surrounded his location and prepared to take him down. But when we moved in, AJ was so consumed by fear that he did the unthinkable: the guy *actually* shit his pants. No lie. And yes, you bet your ass we still wear that story like a badge of honor. It's another level of badass when your enemy is so afraid of you that he actually shits himself.

But here's the main point: I've seen guys with larger-than-life reputations as tough guys crumble under pressure more times than I can count. It still cracks me up that for the long rap sheet that ol' AJ the PIFWIC had, he's remembered most by us not as a formidable adversary but as the scaredy cat that shit his pants. That's a punishment in and of itself.

Having grit means possessing the ability to stay calm under pressure. And you know what I've noticed? The more panicked you are, the more panicked you feel. The calmer you are, the calmer you feel. *Calm breeds calm.*

This isn't just a phrase; it's a mindset that has carried me through countless tough situations in my life. When you stay calm under pressure and don't let chaos get the better of you, you'll find that it gets easier to maintain your composure over time. Staying calm breeds more of a sense of calm in your mind. If you are a leader, whether in a professional setting or within your family and community, your demeanor and response to chaos will have a ripple effect. As a leader, you set the emotional climate for those around you, and your response has the power to influence the mindset of an entire team or organization. When you stay calm amidst the storm, your team is likely to follow suit. On the flip side, the moment you let chaos get the better of you, shit's gonna hit the fan.

Let me take you back to April 17, 2006, a.k.a. Alive Day. When we pulled up to assist the Iraqi force who'd been pinned down for hours by insurgents, I could see that their faces were filled with panic. I knew that sprinting towards them with panic would only escalate the fear and chaos. That's why I decided to stay calm and composed and walk steadily toward the Iraqi Army command post. My goal? To instill confidence and spread a sense of calmness throughout the team. It was a strategic choice; I firmly believed that steady hands and collected minds were always better equipped to handle high-stress situations. Giving into panic wasn't an option. Panic breeds panic and then panic creates chaos.

But the *calm breeds calm* principle goes beyond the battlefield. Your reaction as a leader in any scenario sets the tone for your entire team. Your reaction as a parent or spouse sets the tone for your family. Panic infects and breeds chaos, but remaining calm stabilizes emotions and paves the way for rational decision-making.

A calm leader has a powerful psychological effect on their team. First and foremost, it builds trust. When the team sees a leader staying composed and collected in the face of adversity, they start to believe in their ability to handle any situation. They trust the leader's judgment and decision-making because they exude a sense of confidence and calm. This trust helps foster a strong bond between the leader and the team. A calm leader also has the incredible ability to reduce stress levels within the team. When chaos or uncertainty hits, it's natural for stress levels to skyrocket. A calm and composed leader helps to diffuse tension and anxiety so the team can think more clearly, problem-solve effectively, and perform at their best.

Strategies for Cultivating a Calm Mind in High-Stakes Scenarios
Prepare for (But Don't Indulge In) Hypotheticals
As a leader, you need to prepare your team for a variety of worst-case scenarios. You need to equip your team with a contingency plan in case things go south. Having said that, it's important to resist the temptation to indulge in wasting mental and emotional energy by obsessing on hypothetical worst-case scenarios that drain your energy. Any of us who had to prepare for entering into an active combat zone knows just how important this mental discipline is.

As I assumed the role of team sergeant for the 2006 rotation, I understood that I couldn't allow myself to constantly obsess over the possibility of not returning home or the potential implications that would have on my children. While I prepared for the very real possibility of such outcomes, I knew that I could not indulge in these hypotheticals and waste valuable emotional and mental energy on these scenarios. This wasn't just a personal coping mechanism; it was an absolute necessity for the job at hand. Why? Simple: the lives of my teammates depended on my ability to think clearly and operate with strategic excellence. If I allowed myself to take an emotional detour by indulging in hypotheticals, my judgment would be clouded and I would put every member of the team at risk. As a leader, I had to develop the mental discipline necessary to stay focused and composed, just as I would develop any other skill.

Leaders need to prepare for the worst, be aware of potential risks, and plan accordingly. But there is a fine line between preparation and hopping on an internal emotional rollercoaster that can impair decision-making processes and jeopardize the success of the entire team. Indulging in hypothetical scenarios and allowing emotions to dictate your thoughts leads to unclear judgment and hasty actions. When faced with high-pressure situations, the team looks to the leader for guidance and reassurance. If the leader spends their mental and emotional capacity indulging in fantasies of the worst-case scenario, the team will inevitably suffer.

Maintaining mental discipline means consciously refusing to allow yourself to become paralyzed by what-ifs and worst-case possibilities. It means acknowledging those potential outcomes but remaining focused on the present moment and the challenges that arise in real time. This disciplined approach will allow you, as a leader, to think critically, make rational decisions, and effectively strategize without being hindered by unnecessary emotional fluctuations.

Look at the Facts, Make Objective Decisions, and Act Accordingly

Another important aspect of staying calm under pressure is relying on data and facts rather than reacting emotionally or getting caught in indecision. Several of my mentors taught me this, and those lessons proved to be valuable to my team's success throughout the 2006 rotation. It is human nature to let emotions take the wheel in high-pressure situations, but that will inevitably lead to impulsive decision-making. A calm leader understands the value of looking at data, gathering information, and objectively evaluating the situation before making any conclusions or choices. By taking a step back and analyzing the relevant facts, you can prevent emotional biases from clouding your judgment. But analyzing on its own isn't enough. What sets good leaders apart is the ability to make objective decisions with concrete data in front of them and act accordingly.

When you demonstrate the ability to fairly weigh out the pros and cons and make objective decisions under pressure, your team will instantly feel a sense of relief. They know that you have their backs and will make well-thought-out choices even in the most intense situations. In high-pressure scenarios, a leader's ability to make calm, objective decisions is what will keep a tough situation from spinning out of control. When your team watches you take the time to thoroughly assess the situation, consider different perspectives, and take decisive action, it will give them a sense of calm. They will rest easy knowing that your decisions are not swayed by panic or emotions but grounded in rational thinking.

On the flip side, if you let the pressure overwhelm you and make impulsive decisions without considering all the information, your team will feel the impact. Panic and uncertainty will ripple through the team, and everyone's performance will suffer as a result. And it won't stop there. The next time a stressful situation occurs, your team will struggle to trust your decision-making process because they know your track record. That's why it's vital to look at the facts, make objective decisions, and act accordingly.

Control What You Can Control

I'm going to revert to the very first Grit Code point we started with because it ties in here. If you want to cultivate a sense of calm under pressure, you have to focus on controlling what you can control. By narrowing your focus to a few key areas that are within your sphere of influence, you can direct your energy and effort effectively. Instead of wasting emotional energy on things outside your control, concentrate on the tasks and responsibilities that have a direct impact on your objectives. Prioritize them based on their importance and urgency. The first step is always to simply *breathe*. By refusing to waste emotional energy on things beyond your reach, you maintain a composed mindset that is calm and collected.

But if all hell breaks loose and you forget everything I just said, at least remember this: don't be the guy who shits his pants when things get crazy or it's all you'll ever be known for.

7. Relentlessly Execute

Countless people have stood right on the brink of success with big concepts and detailed strategies, only to fail because they couldn't execute effectively. Well-crafted plans will *always* fall short without relentless execution. This is what divides the average and the legendary. Legends aren't defined by their ideas; they're known for their ability to execute those ideas. Nobody makes history by having a good plan; they make history by turning that plan into action.

A great example of this is a story I told in an earlier chapter, which took place on April 17, 2006. In the middle of an intense firefight, the engine block of my gun truck was shot out and stopped working.

Our trail vehicle radioed, "ROWDY 7, you are leaking fluids from the engine block." That's never a good thing to hear. Before I could relay the message, my driver said, "I have no power, it's dead." The engine was shot out in the middle of the biggest firefight we had ever been in, which lasted over two hours. Spoiler alert: there is no AAA Roadside Assistance in Iraq.

Fortunately, we were prepared and reacted appropriately. We trained for this scenario and executed a self-recovery of the shot-up vehicle. We towed it back to camp, switched it out with another vehicle, and returned to the fight. That's relentless execution.

Here are several things I've learned about relentless execution.

You Can't Fake Preparation

I can't stress this enough: you can't fake preparation. Preparation involves deliberate practice, constant learning, and pushing yourself to improve. It means setting goals, developing a plan, and consistently putting in the necessary effort and dedication. It's the foundation of success. It's not enough to simply have talent or rely on luck; you have to put in the work to prepare yourself for the challenging road to success. This includes physical preparation, mental training, and acquiring the skills and knowledge necessary to achieve the task at hand. Success only comes to those who have invested time and effort into honing their craft and are ready to seize opportunities when they arise.

You Don't Rise to the Occasion; You Rise to Your Level of Training

As a marathon runner, you'd never show up to a race and hope that a positive mindset and a handful of motivational quotes will get you to the finish line. Hell no. You'd work your ass off to train, practice, and prepare. The same goes with professional athletes. They don't rely on luck or hope to perform at their best when game day comes. Instead, they spend countless hours on practice, grueling workouts, and meticulous attention to technique, which become the building blocks of their performance. The strength, agility, and mental fortitude they develop through training allow them to succeed when pressure is at its peak.

The same is true for any area of life. You can only rise to the level of your training. If you have big dreams or goals but have failed to achieve them, it's time to take a hard look in the mirror and see if you've put in the work to prepare yourself to rise to the level of success you desire. In the professional world, that might mean taking courses or workshops to acquire new knowledge and skills, seeking out mentorship from experienced individuals in your field, or dedicating yourself to consistent practice and improvement. By actively investing in your training, you are preparing yourself to be ready when the time comes. Don't wait for opportunities to fall into your lap; create them yourself. Do whatever it takes to reach out and seize the moment. When you know you have trained well and are prepared for the challenges ahead, you'll find that it's much easier to aggressively grab hold of opportunities when they come.

I still vividly recall the intense period leading up to our deployment in 2006. We were the youngest and least experienced team, and we were about to be faced with navigating the dangerous and violent streets of Baghdad. Every decision we made had the potential to be a matter of life and death. We needed to arrive on the scene as a strong and cohesive team, capable of handling any challenge that lay ahead. You can't fake preparation, so we pushed ourselves to train around the clock, put in the extra hours, and outwork everyone around us.

I carried the weight of responsibility as the team sergeant, knowing that the lives of my men depended on my leadership. I vowed to them, their families, and myself that I would do everything in my power to ensure their safety and success. I would not allow complacency or lack of preparation to be the reason for any loss. And guess what? Our hard work paid off. Despite being the underdogs compared to more seasoned teams, my Special Forces team received the humbling designation as the best team in the entire Tenth Special Forces group. Our relentless dedication may have gone unnoticed initially, but the results spoke for themselves.

If you have a professional or personal goal, you can apply the same formula. Identify the skillset or ability you need to acquire or improve to take your game to the next level. Set specific, measurable goals, and then go ALL IN. Put in the extra hours and stay driven and hungry when others become complacent.

Know What You're Doing

The more you invest in your training, the stronger your foundation becomes, which allows you to proceed with confidence because you know what you're doing. When challenges arise, you'll be able to draw on the depth of your training knowing that you have invested the time and effort to be well-prepared. There's nothing that brings a sense of calm more than knowing exactly what you're doing. How? Simple.

- **Do it repeatedly:** Mastery comes from repetition. Continuously practicing and refining your skills is essential for success. Each repetition will allow you to fine-tune your technique, improve your efficiency, and develop a deeper understanding of your craft. Practice deliberately, focus on specific areas of improvement, and actively seek out opportunities to refine your skills.

- **Do it consistently:** Consistency is a major key to achieving your goals. Small, consistent actions compound over time and lead to significant results. Make a commitment to consistently show up and put in the work, even when you don't feel motivated or when obstacles arise. By maintaining a consistent approach, you develop discipline, build momentum, and increase the likelihood of achieving long-term success.

- **Do it with laser-sharp focus:** Distractions will always hinder your progress and dilute your efforts. To achieve that level of relentless execution, cultivate a laser-sharp focus on the task at hand. Eliminate unnecessary distractions, set clear priorities, and direct your energy towards actions that align with your goals. By staying focused, you maximize your productivity and make the most of your time and resources.

- **Do it with mental strength:** The journey toward success is often filled with obstacles, setbacks, and challenges. To endure and overcome these trials, you need mental strength and resilience.

Cultivate a mindset that embraces difficulties as opportunities for growth and views setbacks as learning experiences. Stay committed to your mission even when faced with short-term discomfort, and draw upon your mental fortitude to stay on course.

Remember, Rookies Only Have Ideas
What separates the rookie and the pro? The ability to execute. That's it. Both rookies and pros have passion, enthusiasm, and great ideas. The only difference? Pros have great execution. Ideas and passion alone are not enough to achieve success. Relentless execution is the driving force that transforms aspirations into accomplishments. That means taking action, following through on plans, and making consistent progress towards your goals. Implementing your ideas with discipline, determination, and precision is what turns them into reality.

Learn How to Pace Yourself
Let's face it, we've all been there—caught up in a big moment of motivation and determined to conquer the world, we set lofty goals and push ourselves to the limit, convinced that our extreme path will lead us to greatness. But here's the reality check we often forget—sustainable success isn't built on one intense burst of productivity, but rather on a consistent pace over time.

Relentless execution does NOT mean going to extremes and then burning out. While there are situations that call for pushing ourselves to the breaking point, steady action wins the race most of the time. Consistently delivering high-quality, efficient work over a long period yields better results than sporadic, intense bursts of action. Think of it this way: running a marathon at your fastest one-mile sprint time is simply impossible. Sure, you might be able to knock out a few adrenaline-fueled speedy miles, but how long can you sustain it?

That's why pacing yourself is crucial. Understanding when to push and when to pull back, when to sprint, and when to steadily march is a skill that will take you far in achieving your goals. Success rarely comes easily or overnight. It requires sacrifice, discipline, and an unyielding drive to continuously improve.

Don't Let Setbacks Discourage You

In life, setbacks are inevitable. Setbacks are not the end of the road; they are just bumps, potholes, and detours on the path to success. But if you're not careful, they have the power to shake your confidence, test your resilience, and even make you question your goals. It's important to stay focused and determined and refuse to let setbacks discourage you from pursuing your goals.

When faced with setbacks, it's crucial to keep a resilient mindset. It's normal to feel down or frustrated, but it's even more important to see setbacks as chances to grow and learn. Take a moment to evaluate the situation, figure out what lessons you can take from it, and adjust your approach accordingly.

If you are set on relentlessly executing your goals, you will find a way to turn challenges into opportunities and overcome any obstacle on your path to success. Setbacks are not permanent roadblocks unless we allow them to be.

8. Courage Is Contagious

Courage is a quality that is often attributed to military warriors, and it's easy to understand why. Military warriors embody bravery and sacrifice as they stand on the front lines to defend our freedoms. Their extraordinary courage is evident as they willingly face the unknown, step into dangerous situations, and navigate through hostile environments. It takes a lot of courage to push forward in the face of fear.

But courage is not just an attribute of those in uniform.

Courage is an important quality both in the military and on the battlefield of life. And it's something we need a lot more of, especially these days. There is a long line of courageous men and women who inspired me and prompted me to stand up and do whatever it takes to fulfill my purpose in life. I could fill pages with these names.

Colonel James Nicholas "Nick" Rowe stands out to me for his resilience and unwavering commitment to duty and country, even during his harrowing years of captivity in Vietnam. His ability to maintain mental and physical strength under extreme conditions serves as a powerful reminder of the sacrifices made in service of a cause larger than oneself.

In a different setting but no less significant, the selflessness displayed by Master Sergeant Gary Gordon and Sergeant First Class Randy Shughart during the Battle of Mogadishu leaves a lasting impact. Their courageous actions in defending their fellow soldiers epitomize valor and brotherhood. Learning about their ultimate sacrifice and unwavering resolve reinforces the values of loyalty, courage, and devotion to duty that resonate deeply with me, shaping my own perspectives on service and sacrifice.

I think of Coach Thornburg, who inspired me, taught me resilience, and showed me what it means to be a warrior in any context of life. I can say beyond a shadow of a doubt that if it weren't for him, there would never have been a Green Beret on my head.

Also, the heroic deeds of Master Sergeant Raul Perez "Roy" Benavidez and the leadership lessons gleaned from Colonel David Haskell Hackworth have left profound impressions on me. Benavidez's unwavering determination to rescue his comrades despite severe injuries reflects selflessness and dedication beyond measure. Through Hackworth's insights chronicled in *About Face*, I learned valuable lessons in leadership, strategy, and dedication to your team. Their stories inspired me to lead by example, advocate for those under my command, and uphold the values of courage, sacrifice, and unwavering dedication in all aspects of life. Their stories continue to inspire me to strive for excellence and uphold the values of courage, sacrifice, and steadfast dedication in all aspects of life.

Officer Paul J. Harmon of the Huntington, West Virginia police department was tragically killed on December 14, 1981, near my house on Jefferson Avenue. He was killed by two men who were burglarizing a service station. I was nine years old and I didn't understand why anyone would want to hurt or kill a cop. What I did understand was his courage and heroism. He sacrificed his life to keep his fellow citizens and community safe.

Donna Norris was my fifth-grade teacher at Westmoreland Middle School in Huntington. Despite me being a less-than-ideal student, Mrs. Norris advocated for me and encouraged my critical thinking and growth. She embodied resilience, integrity, and empathy. She empowered me to navigate challenges and pursue my dreams fearlessly.

Each of these remarkable individuals comes from a different background. Each has a different story. But all of these people exemplify what it means to be a courageous leader on the front lines.

That "front line" looked different in every case, as it should. The important thing is that they each took a stand in their respective fields and fought for what they believed in. Each of these people led by example. In challenging situations, they stepped forward and took charge. They embodied the qualities of fearlessness and audacity, unafraid to confront situations head-on. They didn't shy away from challenges or shrink from the unknown. Instead, they approached difficult circumstances with a clear mind, relying on their training, experience, and instincts to navigate through uncertainty. They acted, even amidst criticism or backlash. They demonstrated dedication to the greater good and a willingness to take responsibility for necessary decisions. They combined bravery, calculated risk-taking, and skilled decision-making. I've always found inspiration in those who exhibit courage in the face of adversity, going beyond the ordinary to uphold their principles and serve a greater purpose.

And here's the thing I've noticed. When one person possesses courage and acts upon it, others follow suit. I'm walking proof of that. Courage has a way of inspiring and motivating those around us, showing them what is possible and encouraging us to step outside of our comfort zones. When we witness someone displaying courage, it challenges us to confront our own fears and act with conviction. When we see someone taking risks and pursuing their dreams, it sparks a fire within us to do the same. Seeing someone else's courage gives us the confidence and belief that we *can* do the same. It serves as a reminder that we, too, are capable of facing challenges and overcoming obstacles. Courage has the capacity to spread from one person to another, igniting a chain reaction of bravery as we begin to realize that fear is not an insurmountable barrier; it's just a stepping stone toward growth. By embracing courage and demonstrating it in our own lives, we not only open doors for ourselves but also create an environment that encourages and supports others to stand up.

Webster's Dictionary defines courage as "(the) mental or moral strength to venture, persevere, and withstand danger, fear, or difficulty."[7] Courage enables us to break free from the limitations that hold us back. Courage allows us to overcome doubts and insecurities and to take bold steps toward the future we want. Courage is the willingness to confront challenges head-on, to persevere in the face of adversity, and to take calculated risks when necessary. Courage is not about being fearless; it is about acknowledging our fears and still finding the strength to act. Without courage, we will find ourselves stuck in a cycle of mediocrity, constantly settling for less than we deserve.

As we bring this book to a close, I hope that one thing is abundantly clear to you through my journey from a boy in small-town West Virginia to a Green Beret: Heroes aren't born special. They're made that way from layer after layer of courage, sacrifice, hard work, determination and grit.

So here is my question to you. What are you facing that is dangerous or difficult right now? What is your big audacious dream or goal that scares the shit out of you? Maybe it's becoming a Special Forces operator. Maybe it's starting your own small business. Maybe it's fixing a broken relationship by asking someone for forgiveness. Maybe it's sharing your

---

[7] Merriam-Webster, s.v. "courage (*n*.)," accessed May 23, 2024, https://www.merriam-webster.com/dictionary/courage.

creative work with the world. Maybe it's heading out on an adventure of a lifetime. Maybe it's making changes in your community, country, or the world. Maybe it's fighting for justice. Maybe it's fighting to be a better version of yourself. No matter what, your goals and dreams will involve putting yourselves out there, taking risks, and challenging the limits you've set for yourself. They will require taking a deep dive into your core values, having faith in your abilities, and being willing to step into the discomfort of the unknown.

Whatever your goal may be, it's going to take courage to achieve it. No matter what path you choose, whether it's pursuing professional aspirations, personal goals, or fighting for a cause that is close to your heart, you are bound to encounter obstacles and uncertainties. We need courage to stand up for what we believe in, to speak up, and to do what's right.

Courage is not a quality reserved for the fortunate or the brave in uniform. In a world that often seeks to tame our wild ambitions and quiet the inner warrior inside us, it is our responsibility to rise above the noise and stand strong on the front lines of our own lives, our communities, and our country. We need more individuals who dare to dream big, who refuse to settle for mediocrity, and who dare to shatter the limitations they have set for themselves. We need more people who are willing to stand with courage because it will inevitably inspire others to do the same.

Because ***courage is contagious.***

CLOSING

As we come to the end of this story, I hope that some part of my journey has resonated with you. I hope this book encourages you to think, *If he did it, I can too.* I hope it inspires you to grab hold of your goals and dreams with determination and refuse to give up. More than anything, I hope it instills in you the belief that greatness isn't just for a chosen few; it's within you too, waiting to be unleashed.

Many people wonder what makes those in the Green Beret community stand out. They ask the same question my son did: "What makes the Green Berets so special?"

This book is an answer to that question. It demonstrates that Green Berets and anyone else who has achieved great things aren't any different from the rest. They weren't predetermined for glory. They weren't born special. These legends were made that way through layers of courage, sacrifice, hard work, determination, and sheer grit.

And you know what that means? It means that you can do it too. *Grit to glory.*

PART 2
SNEAK PEEK

Get ready for another action-packed journey through the streets of Baghdad as the team reunites to face a new wave of ruthless insurgents in 2007, making the 2006 rotation look like child's play. Join me and my team of dedicated operators as we navigate the rampant violence of war-torn Iraq and transform our human intelligence network into a lethal kill/capture machine. Part 2 of this series unveils the bold strategies, deviant methods, and divergent tactics used in pursuit of victory by the seasoned warriors of ODA 043.

If you are interested in reading Part 2 of a story of courage, camaraderie, and unwavering determination in the face of adversity, or if you have feedback on *Grit to Glory*, please reach out to Darrell Utt at rowdy7_dutt@outlook.com.

ACKNOWLEDGMENTS

One thing I've learned over the past year is that writing a book is incredibly hard work. It's challenging, mentally draining, and exhausting—more so than I anticipated.

Fortunately, I found an exceptional partner who just happened to be a bestselling author: Lauren Ungeldi. From our very first phone call, I knew Lauren was the right author for me. She turned out to be much more than just an author; she was a confidant, mentor, partner, therapist, counselor, buddy, and friend. Throughout the process, she challenged me, pushed me when needed, encouraged me, and helped me unearth details and stories I had compartmentalized for nearly twenty years ("Morgue Day"). I couldn't have done these stories justice without her. Lauren, you created a masterpiece, and I'll always be indebted to you. Thank you.

The person who stood by my side and weathered the ups and downs with me throughout this journey was my wife, Misti—my rock. None of this would've been possible without her unwavering support. From reading the very first draft of the manuscript to advising on the cover, handling the finances, and giving me the space to write and reflect, she was as crucial to this book's completion as I was. Thank you so much, love!

To my son, D, and my daughter, Britney, I hope I've made you proud. My most important legacy has always been, and will remain, you! I love you both unconditionally.

To my fellow warrior brothers, thank you for volunteering your time and sharing and re-sharing stories from almost twenty years ago. A big shout-out to Matt Girard, Ryan Land, Jody Thrasher, Brian Rainwater, Russ Hiatt, and a few others who can't be named. I'm extremely grateful.

Once you have a great story, finding a great publishing company is essential, and Ballast Books was that company. Their team—Lauren Green, Kayleigh Rucinski, Journey Mathewson, and Andy Symonds—exceeded expectations daily. They put the finishing touches on a great product and made it exceptional. Thank you for everything.

Thanks to my good buddy Luke Peelgrane and his company, Clandestine Media Group, for the early assist with the cover design. Thanks also to Matt Lingo for enhancing the cover design image. Exceptional work.

To all those who wrote testimonials, I was humbled after reading each one. For many, I was left speechless. I'm deeply grateful and will never forget what you did for me. Thank you.

To all my early mentors, thanks for showing a poor kid from West Virginia the way. For everyone who provided mentorship throughout my military journey, I'm extremely grateful. My corporate mentors, I appreciate you!

And to the men of ODA 043, my brothers and fellow warriors, it was one of the greatest privileges of my life to lead you in combat. I hope this book makes you proud of what we accomplished together.

To all those who served, who continue to serve, and who will raise their right hand to serve in the future, you have my deepest respect.

It's difficult to thank everyone, and I'm sure I've missed someone. If I did, I'm very sorry. Next time I see you, the beer is on me.

IN MEMORIAM

David B. Roten Jr.
3/21/1980 – 11/27/2014

In memoriam of Staff Sergeant David "Dave" B. Roten Jr., who served in the United States Army as a decorated Special Forces weapons sergeant in the Tenth Special Forces Group (Airborne) while a member of ODA 043. After his honorable discharge in 2010, Dave supported the US government in austere environments and was killed in action on November 27, 2014, in Afghanistan.

Dave, also known as "Achilles" and "Hooch," was the very best of us. He lived and served with unwavering commitment, passion, and courage, always pushing himself to be the very best in how he both lived and died. Dave inspired others to greatness and continues to do so to this day.

I want to convey my heartfelt gratitude for Dave's selfless service and offer my deepest sympathies to his family. You carry the greatest weight of this loss.

PAY IT FORWARD

I'm pleased to announce that a portion of the proceeds from the sale of *Grit to Glory: A Green Beret's Journey from West Virginia to the Streets of Baghdad* will be donated to support the following non-profit organizations:

#1. **Green Beret Foundation (GBF)**. The GBF serves the Army's Special Forces, our nation's most elite soldiers. The GBF believes Green Berets are our nation's greatest assets. Every day, GBF honors their commitment to Green Berets past and present, as well as their families, by connecting them with the right resources to prosper and thrive.

https://greenberetfoundation.org/

#2. **The Woody Williams Foundation**. The Woody Williams Foundation is a charitable 501c(3) organization that pursues specific endeavors and goals through the vision of Medal of Honor Recipient Hershel "Woody" Williams. With the assistance of the American public and community leaders, the foundation works on establishing permanent Gold Star families memorial monuments in communities throughout the United States, conducting Gold Star family outreach across the country, and providing Living Legacy scholarships to eligible Gold Star family members.

https://www.woodywilliams.org/

#3. **We Fight Monsters (WFM)**. WFM is dedicated to transforming lives through strategic interventions across various fronts. From revitalizing communities to empowering the vulnerable, each project that WFM undertakes is a step toward a brighter, safer future.

https://wefightmonsters.org/

> Your purchase helps make a difference.
> Thank you for your support!
> —Darrell Utt

ABOUT THE AUTHORS

Master Sergeant (Ret.) Darrell Utt has displayed a commitment to excellence and extraordinary service throughout his decorated military career, consistently exemplifying the qualities of a dedicated and exemplary leader. Raised in Huntington, West Virginia, Utt joined the elite Green Berets and led high-stakes missions in hostile environments worldwide. Known for his tactical acumen and strategic thinking, Utt's leadership combines humility, discipline, and dedication, inspiring his team and fostering unity. He also mentors aspiring soldiers and Green Berets, sharing his knowledge and instilling values of courage, selfless service, duty, and loyalty.

Utt's awards include five Bronze Star Medals, one with valor for heroism in Baghdad (2006), and the Larry Thorne Award for best operational detachment in the tenth Special Forces Group (Airborne). He also received the Robert T. Frederick Award for military excellence in 2007. Utt retired from the US Army in January 2017 and now resides with his wife in Denton County, Texas.

Lauren Ungeldi, a celebrated bestselling author and international speaker, is widely recognized for her collaborations with prominent world leaders, business tycoons, politicians, spies, war veterans, and media personalities. Her powerful storytelling has produced numerous acclaimed and bestselling nonfiction books that captivate audiences worldwide. With a wealth of global travel experiences shaping her unique perspective on current events, Lauren enjoys exploring diverse food cultures, engaging in adventure sports, and embarking on new travel adventures during her leisure time.

www.ingramcontent.com/pod-product-compliance
Lightning Source LLC
Chambersburg PA
CBHW030243010526
44107CB00030B/1313/J